D1164787

ALSO BY ALFREDO VIAZZI

Alfredo Viazzi's Italian Cooking

Alfredo Viazzi's
Cucina
e Nostalgia

Alfredo Viazzi's

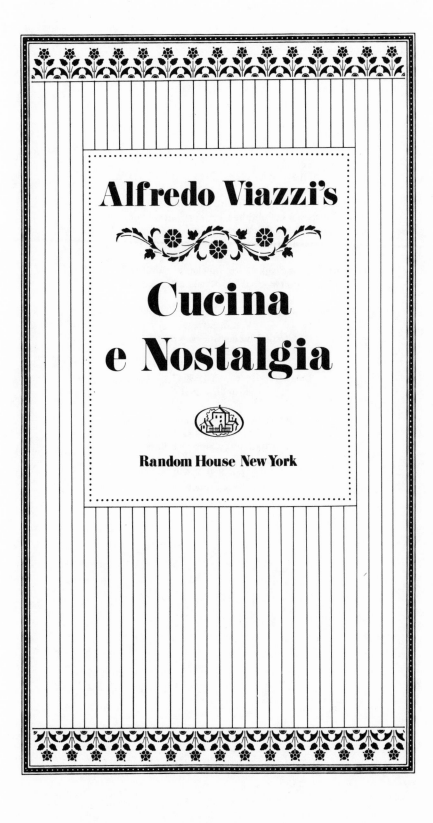

Cucina
e Nostalgia

Random House New York

Copyright © 1979, 1983 by Alfredo Viazzi

All rights reserved under International and Pan-American Copyright Conventions. Published in the United States by Random House, Inc., New York, and simultaneously in Canada by Random House of Canada Limited, Toronto.

Portions of this work were previously published in *Alfredo Viazzi's Italian Cooking*, Random House, Inc. 1979.

Library of Congress Cataloging in Publication Data
Viazzi, Alfredo.
Alfredo Viazzi's Cucina e nostalgia.
Includes index.
1. Cookery, Italian.   I. Title.
TX723.v528   1983   641.5945   82-42795
ISBN 0-394-52841-7

Manufactured in the United States of America
Typography and Binding Design by J. K. Lambert
Illustrations by Stan Skardinski

2 4 6 8 9 7 5 3
First Edition

For my sisters Ginetta and Iolanda,
who still wonder what I am all about

Remembering with deep affection
and gratitude Signora Pina, Donna Concetta,
Celestina, Titina, and all the wonderful women I have
met in my life—and Chef Gino Ratti.

My heartfelt and deepest thanks to Jane,
who still patiently corrects my horrendous spelling
To James A. Beard, who generously answers
my phone calls whenever I cry for help
To Ruth Richards, for her typing and jokes
And especially to Jason Epstein

Contents

Nostalgia Menus and Recipes

Introduction

People often ask me: Where did you learn to cook, what attracted you to food in the first place, what eminent culinary school have you attended? Up to now, I've given answers more or less accurate, more or less amusing. This time, however, in this book, the sequel to *Alfredo Viazzi's Italian Cooking*, I thought that really I should tell you more, for, after all, I've learned more, about Italian food and myself, about the way I learned how to cook—or, I should say, the way cooking "happened" to me. Food has played such an important role in my life that it became the protagonist and I the bit player.

I come from a country where food is the topic of all conversation; while seated at lunch we seriously discuss what we will eat at dinner that night. *"Una bella mangiata, il giornale, un'espresso, sigarette, una discussione politica, una bella donna accanto."**
That is an old Italian philosophical saying that still holds after many centuries of change.

In this book I deal with the food that is cooked and served in Italy in *trattorie*, restaurants, homes, the food that often brings

---

* "A wonderful dinner, the newspaper, an espresso, cigarettes, a political discussion, the company of a beautiful woman."

to mind places you've been and places you long to revisit. It is the type of food generous friends have fed me and taught me how to prepare.

I have divided this book into chapters, each being an event in my life. My memories of these events are very close and precious to me, for they forecast my future and my good fortune and, above all, provided me with immeasurable pleasure in my days in the kitchen, at the table, and in my relationships. These memories will also account for the culinary schools I never attended, my passion and love for food.

I compiled the recipes in this book in the form of menus rather than in the conventional categories. I have included a list of ingredients, since so many exceptionally good ingredients—imported and domestic—are now available in our markets.

I have supplied a wine list, mostly my favored ones and what is available in wine shops, and I have also put together a list of favorite restaurants, since friends and patrons about to leave on vacation very often ask me where they should eat.

The recipes are conjured up out of the sweet and bitter memories of my youth, some of them accurate to the last sprinkle of salt, others reconstructed later—years later—with the help of further exposure to the food of my country. In any event, they are true recipes of the Italian kitchen, whether my own creations, improvisations, or simply my nostalgia for the food that perhaps I was never offered or served but wish I had been. That's what makes up this book.

Those of you who have enjoyed, used, and still use my first cookbook know my unorthodox style of cooking. I am my food. I only hope that my sharing more of my menus and recipes with you will bring pleasure into your own kitchen and onto your table. In any event, I urge you to try your own variations as you see fit; let yourself be inspired by tempting ingredients, substitute for what the recipe calls for. When herbs and spices ask you, urgently, to be used instead of those I have suggested—do it!

The Race

That afternoon Via Poggi was more crowded than usual with vociferous groups of children. They lined both sides of the street, mostly boys clad in pleated black school smocks, their blue cravats knotted into flamboyant bows, excitedly waiting for the soapbox derby to start. I had organized the race myself but had been able to muster only six racers to compete in it, including myself. The average age of the drivers? Eight years old.

My sister Iolanda had a dozen or so of her school chums lined up at the bottom of Via Poggi, ten meters from the finishing line. There they stood, those eleven-year-old girls in their dark blue school uniforms and white stockings, divided into two groups, one on each side of the street, just as Iolanda had planned it. I knew that they had been instructed to screech and carry on insanely at the magical moment when I would dash by, down the steep incline, driving my car at "breathtaking" speed. The street was then—and is today, after so many years—a steep, somnolent street flanked by small, rust-colored, semipatrician villas occupied mostly by doctors, dentists, and lawyers; bougainvillea and ivy hang from walls and iron gates. At that time, no automobiles ventured up Via Poggi—and, for that matter, one would encounter few pedestrians on the street, aside from the afternoons when a long, brown string of Cappuccini friars made its way up to the convent located behind the pencil-thin cypress trees at the top.

I began to feel the tingling excitement of imminent victory. And at that moment I also noticed a group of Cappuccini reluctantly making their way uphill, smiling, children themselves among us children. Then, suddenly, from the convent came the peals of tinny bells, as if to hurry the slow-moving brothers toward home or to reprimand them gently for indulging a little in the event about to begin. I felt even surer of a victory now. How could I possibly fail with God and his workers on my side, too? What an omen! How totally Italian.

Our racing cars stood at the ready, waiting for Michele to shout the starting signal. We had constructed and rigged our own cars with some help from parents or older brothers. Mine had been put together with the considerable help and advice of my brother-in-law Achille, who happened to be one of the best carpenters in town. Oh, what an Italian wouldn't do for a racing car! I even remember that on that afternoon I wore a white jumpsuit with a Gomme Pirelli sticker on my left breast and a white pilot's helmet, handsewn by my older sister Ginetta. My sister Iolanda had insisted that I wear about my neck a pale blue, pure silk (mind you) scarf that belonged to my mother. In sum, I cut a most elegant sporting figure, one whose destiny could only and inevitably be victory. *Mio Dio!* It happened fifty-four years ago.

So, the race began. Down the hill we came, at what seemed like vertiginous speed, cheered on loudly by our friends and some adult passers-by (Italians young and old get quickly transported by a car race, no matter what its size). Down, down we raced, the ends of my pale blue scarf streaming behind me like banners at the Palio in Siena. What could go wrong? Absolutely nothing!

Down raced the first four cars, past the taciturn faces of Iolanda's chums. Down drove I, in fifth position in a race of six, and came to a dead stop almost at the point of my sister's shoes. Ah, the ignominy! The shame! The unspeakable disgrace! The scarf hung limply about my neck. I saw tears in my sister's eyes. Dramatically I yanked off pilot's helmet and scarf and kicked my racing car. Defeated! Totally, absolutely defeated! Armando

Celli, the winner, laughed, scratched, blabbed loudly among his fans just a few paces away from me. Eight years old and ten feet tall.

Soon after, Via Poggi, the street of my unbearable shame, returned to its normal self. We walked hurriedly toward home—myself, my sister, and a cortege of half a dozen loyal though disappointed friends of hers. The boys from my own school had made fun of me and had even given me the old stiff finger.

That evening at dinner I couldn't bring myself to eat anything, oppressed as I felt by the weight of my unconscionable defeat.

It took me a good many years to live down the experience of the race. Even now, after my share of defeats and successes, that old memory comes to the surface now and again to remind me that it takes more than "dressing up" to make a winner—or, for that matter, to make a chef.

The Sign on
Our Door

We lived with that sign on our door for three years, during the last two of which my father defiantly had it framed under glass. It represented an ignominious accusation, not unlike what the yellow star was supposed to mean for the Jews. The darkness in some men's hearts was the blackest of black in those days of Fascism. The sign that hung on our well-polished door, the entrance to our apartment, said in grim words:

"Here lives a family whose son is a traitor to his Country and the Fascist Party."

My brother Beppin had chosen to join the International Brigade to fight for the Republic of Spain against Franco. That's what the sign on our door was about. It was taken down three years later when Beppin was killed, when he no longer presented a threat to the Fascists.

At first, no one among the families living in our building paid much mind to the sign, ignoring it by not looking at it. Later, for fear of being observed by the Caposcala—the Party-appointed ferret, one in every apartment building, who informed the Fascist authority on the activities of the tenants—they refrained from greeting us whenever we met on the stairways or even in the streets nearby.

Soon we were almost totally isolated in our neighborhood. The postman no longer rang our bell to deliver our mail, but dropped it on the floor a few feet away from our door, sometimes even sequestering pieces of mail that looked suspicious to him. The parish priest would greet us with only the slightest nod of the head when he ran into one of us in the street.

My sister Iolanda and I had to leave the school in our neighborhood and walk an hour and twenty minutes each way every day to attend classes in Albisola Mare, outside the city limits. And soon we had to endure the embarrassing and infuriating attitude of the local merchants and shopkeepers, who would ignore us whenever we entered their premises, making us suddenly invisible right in front of their eyes. We usually left quietly, except when my sister Ginetta chose to call a few selected curses down on them. We started purchasing our daily food in Zinola, at the market near the cemetery, which meant a two-hour trip coming and going on the rickety white trolley car. It also meant a great deal of lugging and carrying, mostly on my mother's part. However, freethinking French lady that she was, she would respond to the merchants' contempt, dictated by their fear, with arrogant hauteur. Never would she accept lesser-quality products, which often enough they tried to push on her, without an eloquent argument.

My father, for his part, never bowed to the alternative offered him by the local Fascist authority: to repudiate his son Beppin's right to fight for what he believed.

"We will all starve inside this apartment before I'll show my face in that filthy office," he'd say whenever the subject was brought up by some of the few remaining friends who were sympathetic to our struggle.

That is why, or one of the reasons why, during those three years we very often had our meals at the Trattoria del Porto, an inexpensive place on one of the grimy, poorly lit streets along the waterfront. The other reason—perhaps the main one—was that my mother was a terrible cook.

The Trattoria del Porto had always been one of my favorites among the places we frequented. As I still vaguely recall, out of memories long gone, the food was truly excellent. A rough, fun-loving Corsican owned the place, as I remember. Pencil-written, grease-spotted sheets of paper served as menus, but the ambience was noisily festive on all occasions.

The recipes that follow are of course largely reconstructed—perhaps even improved upon—from the actual ones dimly recalled from my youth. Even so, I still associate them with those early childhood days.

❊ ❊ ❊

SARDINE IMBOTTITE E FRITTE
(Fried Stuffed Sardines)

ZUPPA DI ZUCCHINE CON CARNE E RISO
(Zucchini Soup with Meat and Rice)

PETTI DI POLLO VALDOSTANA
(Breasts of Chicken Valdostana)

BIETOLE STRASCICATE
(Sautéed Swiss Chard)

MELE E AMARETTI DI SARONNO
(Apples and Amaretti)

CAFFE
(Coffee)

Wine: A white Orvieto Secco will do well.

SARDINE IMBOTTITE E FRITTE
(Fried Stuffed Sardines)

SERVES 6

12–14 fresh sardines, if obtainable, or the equivalent frozen
2 cups coarsely chunked Italian bread, with crusts
1 cup heavy cream
¼ cup freshly grated Parmesan cheese

1½   teaspoons finely chopped Italian parsley
      Sprinkle of freshly grated nutmeg
1   egg
      Salt and freshly ground black pepper to taste
2   tablespoons all-purpose flour
½   cup olive oil
2   whole cloves garlic, peeled

Wash sardines well under cold water. If using frozen sardines, defrost under cold water; *do not use hot.* Chop off heads, leave on tails, slit on belly side, remove entrails. Open fish completely without separating them in two. Carefully remove spines, flattening fish gently to avoid breaking them.

Break up bread into chunks and soak in the heavy cream 10 to 15 minutes. Make of it a mushy mixture; if too wet, drain off some of the cream. Add cheese, parsley, and nutmeg. Beat egg separately, then add to mixture. Mix well with your hands. Taste; add pepper, and salt if necessary. Proceed to stuff sardines evenly and firmly until all the stuffing is used up, keeping sardines flat and open. Dust lightly with flour.

Heat olive oil in frying pan until hot and brown garlic without burning. Remove and discard garlic. Place sardines in hot oil, backs down, and fry 1 minute or less. Turn fish to stuffed side, carefully, so stuffing will not fall off. Fry until golden brown. Turn; fry until golden brown on second side. Remove sardines from oil, placing on paper toweling to absorb excess oil. Serve 2 sardines per portion. You may serve them either hot or cold.

ZUPPA DI ZUCCHINE CON CARNE E RISO
(Zucchini Soup with Meat and Rice)

SERVES 8

1   pound boneless chuck
1   tomato, cut in half
2   stalks celery, washed and scraped

½   medium onion, peeled and cut in half again
Salt and freshly ground black pepper to taste
Shells of 2 eggs (keep eggs for other use)
½   tablespoon tomato paste
5   medium zucchini, washed and trimmed
½   cup vegetable oil
½   cup rice, preferably Arborio rice
Freshly grated Parmesan cheese

Place meat, tomato, celery, onion, salt, pepper, and egg shells in a 2-quart soup pot. Fill pot with cold water to within 2 inches of brim. Set over medium flame, then cook, uncovered, for 1½ hours, or until beef is very well done. Remove meat and set aside to cool. Strain consommé; discard egg shells. Mash vegetables through a fine wire strainer over soup pot. Return mashed vegetables to consommé, add tomato paste, mix well, and set over low flame to simmer. When beef has cooled, cut into small chunks and set aside.

Cut zucchini into rounds ½ inch thick, then pat dry with paper toweling. Heat vegetable oil over medium heat. Fry zucchini slowly until golden on both sides. Drain zucchini on paper toweling.

Bring consommé to a boil. Cook rice in it until *very* al dente, no longer than 8 minutes. At this point, add beef chunks and fried zucchini. Cook over low flame until rice is done. Serve with grated Parmesan on the side and freshly ground black pepper. Leftover soup may be kept refrigerated for at least 4 days.

PETTI DI POLLO VALDOSTANA
(Breasts of Chicken Valdostana)

SERVES 6

3   large whole plump chicken breasts, skinned and boned
⅓   cup all-purpose flour
2   eggs
1½   tablespoons heavy cream
2½   tablespoons freshly grated Parmesan cheese
1   teaspoon chopped Italian parsley
    Salt and freshly ground black pepper to taste
½   cup vegetable oil
8–9   large fresh mushrooms
½   pound lightly salted butter
6   pieces imported dried porcini, presoaked in lukewarm
      water at least 1½ hours in advance, drained
    Sprinkle of ground ginger
    Sprinkle of freshly grated nutmeg
1   cup dry white wine
6   slices giambone or boiled ham
6   slices Fontina cheese, preferably, or mozzarella

Divide each breast in two and pound each half between two pieces of aluminum foil, making sure not to tear meat. Do not pound too thin. The half breasts should now look like cutlets. Dust cutlets in flour and set aside.

Prepare batter by mixing together eggs, heavy cream, Parmesan, parsley, salt, and pepper; blend well. Soak chicken cutlets thoroughly by leaving in batter while you heat vegetable oil in a large skillet. When oil is rippling, remove cutlets from batter, letting excess batter drip off. Sauté chicken cutlets in oil until golden brown. Place cutlets on paper toweling.

Preheat oven to 400°F.

Wash fresh mushrooms, then slice, not too thinly, through caps and stems. Over medium flame, melt butter in a baking pan. Sauté fresh mushrooms and porcini in melted butter for 5 minutes. Add ginger and nutmeg. Add wine and let it reduce approximately

10 minutes. Add salt and pepper to taste. Lay a slice of ham over each chicken cutlet and a slice of Fontina over the ham. Arrange cutlets in baking pan and bake, uncovered, 10 minutes. Remove pan from oven and place under broiler for about 1 minute or until cheese is glazed.

Serve hot, one-half breast per person, spooning the mushroom sauce next to the chicken on the plate.

BIETOLE STRASCICATE
(Sautéed Swiss Chard)

SERVES 6

2 pounds green and tender Swiss chard or fresh leaf spinach
½ lemon
  Salt
¼ cup olive oil
2 whole cloves garlic, peeled
3 anchovy fillets, drained
  Freshly ground black pepper

Wash chard very well under cold water. Cut leaves in half and discard hard spines. Bring 1 quart salted water to boil in large saucepan. Immerse chard in water, then squeeze in juice of ½ lemon. Boil, uncovered, 5 minutes. Drain chard very well by squeezing all the water out of it.

Heat oil in sauté pan until rippling, then add garlic and anchovy fillets and sauté, stirring, 6 minutes. Remove garlic and discard. Sauté chard in oil 2 minutes. Serve with freshly ground black pepper on the side.

MELE E AMARETTI DI SARONNO
(Apples and Amaretti)

Some good and crunchy apples such as Granny Smith or Golden Delicious and 3 or 4 Amaretti di Saronno per person makes a wonderfully light dessert.

2

The Fig Tree

The fig tree must always have stood in the front yard. It was already there when my family moved into the dilapidated four-story apartment building. When I was five years old, the tree resembled the foreleg of a very large elephant—the same color and texture and so tall that I couldn't climb it.

It seemed less tall when I turned seven and succeeded in climbing it to half its height. By the time I was ten, the fig tree reached above our apartment, beyond the second floor of the house, but I—skinny, lively, and curious—could climb all the way to the top! Not that it bore figs that ever ripened enough to pick. My father said that was because the sun never hit the right spot in the yard where the tree stood. Nevertheless, all the tenants of the house loved the fig tree, including the cats and dogs and the pet birds. And it gave many pleasant surprises.

In summer I would hide among its leafy branches to daydream, or to pelt the unwary cats, dogs, and children below with unripe figs tough as golf balls. From the upper branches strong enough to support my weight I could also look directly into the kitchen of Signora Pina, a widow who lived above us on the second floor and one of my mother's best friends. What a thrill that turned out to be, to lie hidden and unsuspected, watching.

At age ten I thought Signora Pina was the most beautiful, most gracious, and most perfumed woman I had ever met. I would see her often in our apartment, visiting with my mother at around four in the afternoon, when they would sip coffee together. Later I was to discover that it wasn't coffee at all but dark sherry, which enlivened the latest gossip of the neighborhood. Signora Pina aroused me when I looked at her, crossing and uncrossing her well-turned, black-stockinged legs. And she knew it. She always wore black satin smocks around the house—the traditional costume of mourning in my country. But every one of hers fit her like the skin on a zucchini, and the longest one ended eight inches above her smooth kneecaps. Her skin was ivory-colored, like Belgian endive.

So, I began to spy into her kitchen from my leafy perch starting in late spring, through the hot summer, right up to the autumn and the last leaf on the fig tree. If she knew I was there she never acknowledged it for at least a full year, which brought me to age eleven. I would roost there, mesmerized, in my camouflage of leaves, unmindful of the fruit flies and occasional belligerent wasps. I would watch her every movement, lost in the most delicious confusion. It's a wonder I never fell out of the fig tree. I would marvel at the prodigious dexterity of her hands, chopping and dicing, mixing and stirring, balancing pots and pans while preparing her meals. Sometimes she also sang, in a shaking soprano, the most romantic arias from opera. And the smells that emanated from that window were sublime, balsamic, wickedly tantalizing; the aromas of the food that must, I thought, be served in Paradise to well-behaved souls.

Finally, one early September afternoon, Signora Pina paused at her window and, clapping both plump hands to her rosy cheeks, sang out in fake fright and surprise: "Oh, my God! What are you doing up there, my little *tesoro*? But—you might fall. Be careful."

I must have blushed to watermelon red, but finally I said, "I'm watching you cook." I smiled. No matter what age, the Italian male knows the edge he's got over the ladies. She laughed, amused. Her beauty and her laughter almost knocked me off my perch. She then asked me to get down from that dangerous position and go ask my mother if she would consent to let me have dinner in her apartment. I came down in a flash. My mother agreed after calling to Signora Pina from our window to make sure I hadn't shamefully begged for the food. She delayed my going until I washed my hands and knees well enough. At eleven I still wore short pants.

Signora Pina's apartment was full of her perfume and the aroma of her cooking, mixed with the smell of furniture polish. She embraced me so warmly and tightly, my nose pinched between her generous breasts, that for a moment I thought I'd never breathe again. She laughed, amused, when I confessed to having watched her for a year. She hugged me again and kissed me on the cheeks. Then we sat down to dinner.

We became very close friends until my mother discovered us. Then they became enemies for well over a year, or until my mother—good, logical French lady that she was—understood and, I believe, somehow approved. The fig tree became obsolete after that first dinner.

As you may well question the accuracy of my eleven-year-old's memory, the fact is that these recipes are truly from the *cucina* of Liguria. However, the style of cooking them is solely Signora Pina's.

Years later, when I was again privileged to taste Signora Pina's food, I was able to establish the accuracy of these recipes. By then, alas, Signora Pina was no longer the young, attractive widow.

※ ※ ※

MENU ONE

PASTA DELLA DOMENICA
(Pasta for a Sunday)

Wine: Signora Pina always served one or two glasses of wine with her meals. For this menu and the two that follow, I would like to suggest a full-bodied Chianti Classico of the likes of Castello di Uzzano or Riecine, if you can find them in the wine shops. Or a Cabernet Sauvignon like Clos du Val from California.

PASTA DELLA DOMENICA
(Pasta for a Sunday)

SERVES 6–8

1 flank steak (about 2 pounds when trimmed of all fat)
½ cup olive oil
1 small onion, peeled and cut in quarters
2 small carrots washed and scraped, cut into strips
  Sprinkle of dried oregano
  Sprinkle of dried rosemary
3 bay leaves
  Salt and freshly ground black pepper to taste
1 tablespoon lightly salted butter
1½ teaspoons chopped Italian parsley
½ teaspoon chopped garlic
1 tablespoon tomato paste
½ cup chicken consommé (see page 207)
3 cups canned peeled tomatoes
½ cup robust red wine
1½ pounds imported dried pasta (rigatoni, mostaccioli, occhi di lupo, or any short pasta you prefer)
¼ cup freshly grated Parmesan cheese

Preheat oven to 400°F.

Pour oil into a roasting pan and roll flank steak in it so it will be well basted. Add onion, carrots, oregano, rosemary, and bay leaves to pan, then sprinkle some salt and pepper over all. Roast 30 minutes.

Remove flank steak from roasting pan and set aside to cool. Strain oil from roasting pan through fine wire strainer. Save cooked onion and carrots; chop very fine. Set a saucepan over a medium flame and pour strained olive oil into it; add the butter and heat. Add parsley and garlic to oil and sauté 1 minute. Add chopped onion and carrots and sauté 5 minutes. Add tomato paste diluted in the consommé. Cook 5 minutes. Add tomatoes and cook down for 30 minutes. Add salt and pepper to taste. Add wine and cook until it evaporates (approximately 10 minutes).

Cut flank steak into chunks 1½ inches long. Strain sauce through food mill. Pour sauce into clean saucepan and add chunks of beef. Cook 15 minutes. Set aside over very low flame.

Cook your pasta in a large pot of salted boiling water. (Cooking time for short macaroni is approximately 12 minutes.) Drain pasta well. Put pasta in a sauté pan, ladle the sauce over it, and mix well until pasta is completely coated with sauce. This should take 1 minute over a low flame.

Serve, making sure to distribute chunks of beef evenly. Serve the freshly grated Parmesan over the pasta.

❊ ❊ ❊

MENU TWO

CIMA ALLA GENOVESE
(Stuffed Breast of Veal)

ZUCCHINE ALL'OLIO E LIMONE
(Zucchini with Oil and Lemon)

FRITTELLE DI CORLEONE
(Fritters Corleone Style)

CIMA ALLA GENOVESE
(Stuffed Breast of Veal)

SERVES 8

1	lean breast of veal (4 to 5 pounds)
½	pound fresh calves' brains
½	pound boiled ham
½	pound prosciutto
¾	pound lean chopped beef

1　tablespoon pignoli (pine nuts)
1　tablespoon pistachio nuts
1½　pounds fresh spinach
¾　cup fresh or frozen peas, if frozen defrosted, dry (using
　　　no water), at room temperature
8　pieces imported dried porcini, presoaked in lukewarm
　　　water at least 1½ hours in advance, drained
½　teaspoon chopped garlic
　　Good sprinkle of dried marjoram
　　Sprinkle of freshly grated nutmeg
6　eggs
¾　cup freshly grated Parmesan cheese
　　Salt and freshly ground black pepper to taste
1　fresh ripe tomato, halved
½　medium onion, peeled
2　stalks celery, washed and scraped
2　carrots, washed and scraped

Have your butcher prepare the breast of veal for you, boning it and cutting a pocket into it so that the meat is ready to be stuffed.

Blanch brains in boiling water 1½ minutes. Drain and set aside to cool. When cool, remove membranes. Chop ham, prosciutto, and brains into small pieces. Place in large mixing bowl along with chopped beef. Add pignoli and pistachio nuts. Wash spinach extremely well under cold water, then drain very well. Chop roughly and add raw to mixing bowl. Add peas. Drain presoaked porcini, wash under cold water, chop coarsely, add to bowl. Add garlic, marjoram, nutmeg. Mix all the ingredients well, with your hands.

Beat eggs in separate bowl (keep aside shells from 2 of the eggs). Add Parmesan cheese and amalgamate well, then pour into the bowl with the other ingredients. Mix again. Add salt and pepper to taste while mixing.

Stuff the breast of veal with this mixture. Close up pocket mouth by sewing it with a heavy needle and strong thread. Lightly puncture veal with fine-pointed fork. Wrap veal in a double layer of cheesecloth. Secure ends of cheesecloth with twine.

Place veal in a large pot of hot (not boiling) water and add some salt. Set pot over medium flame. Add tomato, onion, celery, carrots, and egg shells. Simmer 2 hours, uncovered. Remove veal; drain in a deep pan by pressing down on it with a flat heavy object. Strain broth, discarding vegetables and egg shells. Keep broth for future use. Unwrap veal and slice into ½-inch-thick slices. It is excellent served at room temperature. It can be served with a light sauce such as vinaigrette or green sauce (see page 216) or with hot parsley and butter sauce spiked with fresh horseradish.

ZUCCHINE ALL'OLIO E LIMONE
(Zucchini with Oil and Lemon)

SERVES 6

4–5 medium zucchini, washed and trimmed
  3 tablespoons virgin olive oil
    Salt and freshly ground black pepper to taste
    Strained juice of 1 lemon

Cook zucchini in a large pot of salted boiling water 4 to 5 minutes. Drain and set aside to cool. Cut cooled zucchini in strips lengthwise, the width of a finger.

Heat oil in skillet until hot and sauté zucchini for 2 to 3 minutes. Add salt and pepper to taste. Arrange zucchini strips on serving dish and douse with lemon juice. Serve.

FRITTELLE DI CORLEONE
(Fritters Corleone Style)

SERVES 6 (12–15 FRITTERS)

1   cup sifted all-purpose flour
1   cup Marsala wine or sweet sherry
1   cup milk
2   egg yolks
     Pinch of salt
¼   cup golden raisins
1   cup vegetable oil
1   tablespoon confectioners' sugar

Blend well flour, wine, milk, egg yolks, and salt to make a dense, creamy batter. Stir in raisins. Let sit for 30 minutes. Heat oil in a deep frying pan until rippling. Spoon batter into hot oil 2½ tablespoons at a time, to make fritters the size of a demitasse saucer or even a bit smaller. Fry fritters to golden brown. Remove from oil and let drain on paper toweling. Sprinkle with sugar and serve.

❋ ❋ ❋

MENU THREE

RISOTTO PASTICCIATO
("Messy" Risotto)

INSALATA DI RADICCHIO
(Radicchio Salad)

RISOTTO PASTICCIATO
("Messy" Risotto)

SERVES 6–8

½ pound fresh sweetbreads
2 cups rice, preferably Arborio rice
½ pound lean veal, cleaned of all sinews
½ pound chicken livers, cleaned
1 small chicken breast, skinned and boned
4 tablespoons lightly salted butter
   Sprinkle of freshly grated nutmeg
   Sprinkle of ground ginger
   Freshly ground black pepper to taste
2 tablespoons dry white wine
2 cups meat sauce (see page 212), keep hot
1 cup chicken consommé (see page 207), keep hot
½ cup freshly grated Parmesan cheese

Soak sweetbreads in ice water for at least 30 minutes. Drain and remove all membranes. Set aside.

Boil rice, uncovered, in 2 quarts of salted boiling water for approximately 8 minutes; drain. At the same time, cut veal, chicken livers, chicken breast, and sweetbreads into bite-size pieces.

Melt butter over a medium flame in large skillet, to which add all the meats. Sprinkle with nutmeg and ginger and shower with black pepper, then sauté, stirring, for about 15 minutes. Add wine, then lower flame and let cook another 8 minutes. Keep warm over very low flame.

Pour drained rice into a sauté pan and ladle meat sauce over it. Cook rice slowly in meat sauce over a low flame, stirring continuously with a wooden spoon. It should take approximately another 6 minutes for rice to finish cooking. Now you have a risotto.

While cooking the rice, if it should become too dry, add hot consommé, 1 tablespoon at a time. Finally, just before risotto is ready, sprinkle the Parmesan cheese over it and blend well.

Spoon sautéed veal, livers, chicken, and sweetbreads into serving platter and cover with hot risotto. Serve.

INSALATA DI RADICCHIO
(Radicchio Salad)

SERVES 6

3   medium heads radicchio, brownish leaves discarded
3   tablespoons virgin olive oil
1½   tablespoons balsamic vinegar
     Salt and freshly ground black pepper to taste
3   slivers of fresh garlic

Open up leaves of radicchio, wash thoroughly under cold water, and drain well. Tear leaves into smaller pieces with your hands and put into a salad bowl. Mix all other ingredients together. Taste, then pour dressing over salad leaves. Toss well. Serve.

3

Borgo
San Frediano

In 1935 I was fourteen years old and seriously determined to be the greatest Italian painter of our time. Therefore, I needed an earnest start. I left home one morning in June of that year, buying a third-class one-way ticket on the 9:30 A.M. train to Florence. I carried with me a small pressed-cardboard suitcase containing a few belongings and three books on art. My older sister Nuccia had made me a clandestine loan of 200 lire—at that time the equivalent of $40—to be repaid eventually. Only a handful of close friends knew of my move. My parents were completely in the dark.

I spent my first three hours in Florence in total awe, observing, moving slowly, whispering to myself. I started at the Ponte Vecchio, went on to Piazza della Signoria and the Loggia dei Lanzi and ended up, of all places, in the Borgo San Frediano.

San Frediano is a working-class quarter of Florence on the Lungarno Soderini, most of its inhabitants employed in the raffia and straw industry. I walked about hurriedly, not knowing where I was, disturbed by the squalid surroundings. I stopped, attracted by a storefront shop, the façade of which was covered with an abstract masterpiece of wide brush strokes and colors I'd never dared to imagine. I stood there, my suitcase leaning against my right ankle, trying to explain to myself that orgy of brilliant color. Suddenly I felt a gentle hand rest on my head, and a kind voice behind me said:

"It's just a bit of folly."

I turned to face a short, powerfully built middle-aged man wearing working clothes spotted with paint. I smiled.

"What are you doing here?" he asked, eying my suitcase. I shook my head. I did not know. We both smiled.

His name was Pietro Luccardini, he lived in back of his shop and was a house painter of renown. There had been times, I learned later, when he had even been summoned to do restoration work in some of the famous churches of the city.

He invited me into his shop, full of fascinating disorder and of the smells of paints and benzine. After some small talk, I confessed to him why I happened to be in Florence and what my ambitions were.

He laughed warmly and remarked without irony, "You couldn't have come to a better place. But, how about your family?"

I lied, reassuring him that they knew where I was. He shook his large head, accepting my lie, and invited me to stay the night at his place, since I hadn't the foggiest idea as to where to go.

The following day, Pietro Luccardini extended the invitation to share his place until I knew what I was going to do. As it turned out, I started working as his helper in painting apartments, stores, and whatever else needed a coat of paint.

On his free days and mine he showed me that stupendous city, its art, architecture, its light at different hours of day and evening. He explained to me the masterpieces and the treasures of Florence, with the patience and simplicity of a truly accomplished teacher. We walked for hours and hours: the Baptistery, Palazzo Medici-Riccardi, the Uffizi Gallery, Piazza della Signoria, Palazzo Pitti, the Bargello. We'd stop to eat a sandwich on Piazzale Michelangelo, then on to Santa Maria del Fiore, San Miniato al Monte, and Santa Maria Novella. And on, and on, and on.

He also began to teach me how to paint, which showed me that I would never become the greatest Italian painter of our time. Months went by in unblemished happiness regardless. I must confess in shame that never a thought about my family occupied my mind. Certainly my parents must have known that

I was in Florence by now, because my sister Nuccia couldn't possibly, nor in all humanity, have kept that secret in the face of their anguish. But where in Florence? The *carabinieri* were at work, and soon I was to be found out.

In those months, however, Pietro Luccardini introduced me to the cooking of Tuscany. Almost every evening we had our meals at the Trattoria del Pozzo in Vicolo dell'Orto in Borgo San Frediano. It was Pietro's favorite place, and very reasonably priced.

The Trattoria del Pozzo's clientele was a loud, boisterous amalgam of local shopkeepers, house painters, restorers—from the "fakes" to the real "artisans"—prostitutes, and on-the-way-to-be-famous painters. Horse-and-buggy drivers and occasional "signori" in search of good food came there, too. Pietro Luccardini had frequented the Trattoria del Pozzo for over twenty years and so was a privileged and respected patron, liked and listened to by the other patrons, especially for his outspoken criticism of Mussolini's invasion of Abyssinia.

The menu at the Trattoria del Pozzo changed every day. Although it was a *prezzo-fisso* and *scelta-unica* menu—that is to say, fixed-price and one-choice only—the fare was excellent and imaginative. I thought so at fourteen and I still think so today after so many years, so many meals of all caliber and price, and so much cooking of my own.

However, before I share those menus and recipes with you, let me tell you that the *carabinieri* finally tracked me down in San Frediano and returned me to my family. Reluctantly, I went back.

Here are seven menus from the Trattoria del Pozzo; almost all of the following recipes were "checked out" and confirmed years later when I went back to Trattoria del Pozzo and various other *trattorie* in Florence.

❊ ❊ ❊

LUNEDI
(Monday)

ZUPPA DI LATTUGHE RIPIENE
(Stuffed Lettuce Soup)

MANZO UBRIACO
(Drunken Beef)

FUNGHI, AGLIO E BASILICO
(Mushrooms with Garlic and Basil)

PERE E CACCIOTTA DI SIENA
(Pears and Cacciotta Cheese from Siena)

Wine: This meal calls for a good Chianti wine, such as Melini or Antinori. At Trattoria del Pozzo it was served with an excellent house wine.

ZUPPA DI LATTUGHE RIPIENE
(Stuffed Lettuce Soup)

SERVES 6–8

1   large head iceberg lettuce
3   tablespoons lightly salted butter
½   pound lean beef, cut into small cubes the size of a salad crouton
½   small onion, peeled and thinly sliced
1   stalk celery, washed and scraped, finely chopped

    2 small carrots, washed and scraped, finely chopped
    1 tablespoon chopped Italian parsley
      Salt and freshly ground black pepper to taste
      Sprinkle of freshly grated nutmeg
  1½ quarts chicken consommé (see page 207)
    1 cup "insides" of Italian bread or white bread soaked
        in a few tablespoons of consommé
    8 slices Italian bread
    1 clove garlic, peeled and cut in half
    2 eggs
   ¾ cup freshly grated Parmesan cheese

Separate the lettuce leaves, making sure not to damage them; you should have approximately 16 to 18 leaves. Cook in lightly salted boiling water 1 to 2 minutes. Drain carefully, run cold water over the leaves, drain again, and set aside.

Melt butter in sauté pan and sauté diced beef 10 minutes. Add onion, celery, carrots, parsley, salt, pepper, and nutmeg; sauté, stirring occasionally, over a low flame 20 minutes. Add a few tablespoons of the consommé, if necessary. Add soaked insides of bread and cook 2 minutes, mixing with all other ingredients. Remove from fire and let cool briefly.

Rub each slice of Italian bread with a cut garlic half, then toast and set aside.

Whip together eggs and ¼ cup of the cheese. Add meat and vegetable mixture to bowl; blend well with eggs. Using about 1½ tablespoons of stuffing per leaf, proceed to stuff lettuce leaves by folding in the fashion of little packages, or roll as for stuffed cabbage. Fasten with toothpick and set aside.

Bring consommé to boil. Gently drop stuffed lettuces into consommé and cook 2 minutes.

Arrange slices of toasted bread in soup plates, one slice per portion. Serve 2 stuffed lettuce leaves per person. Ladle hot consommé over them. Serve the remaining ½ cup Parmesan cheese on the side.

MANZO UBRIACO
(Drunken Beef)

SERVES 6

6   tablespoons lightly salted butter
¼   pound pork fat or prosciutto fat, finely chopped
1   medium onion, not too thinly sliced
2   stalks celery, washed and scraped, coarsely chopped
1   small bunch Italian parsley, washed well in cold water;
        do not chop
3   pounds brisket of beef, in one piece, extra fat cut off
5   whole cloves
     Salt and freshly ground black pepper to taste
3   ounces anisette liqueur
1   cup dry white wine
1   cup beef or chicken consommé (see page 207)
¾   cup tomato sauce (see page 211)

Melt butter in Dutch oven, add pork fat or prosciutto fat; cook 5 minutes. Add onion, celery, parsley, beef, cloves, salt, and pepper. Cook, uncovered, over low flame until meat is well browned on all sides. Add anisette, and cook, uncovered, 15 minutes. Add wine; cook, still uncovered, 20 minutes. Add consommé so that beef does not dry out, a tablespoon at a time. Add tomato sauce. Cover pan, then cook over low fire until beef is tender and flaky. Take beef out of pan, cut into thick slices, arrange on serving platter, and pour sauce over it (discard parsley but do not strain sauce). Serve.

FUNGHI, AGLIO E BASILICO
(Mushrooms with Garlic and Basil)

Serves 6

2 pounds fresh mushrooms
¼ cup olive oil
2 tablespoons lightly salted butter
1½ teaspoons chopped garlic
12 fresh basil leaves, washed, left whole
    Salt and freshly ground black pepper to taste

Wash mushrooms well under cold water, then drain. Slice thin through caps and stems; let dry on paper toweling.

Heat oil in sauté pan. Add butter and garlic and sauté 2 minutes. Add mushrooms; sauté, stirring, 6 to 7 minutes. Add basil leaves, salt, and pepper. Sauté 3 minutes longer. Serve hot, with beef.

PERE E CACCIOTTA DI SIENA
(Pears and Cacciotta Cheese from Siena)

Cacciotta di Siena is a rather dry, semihard cheese that can be delicious with crunchy fruits because of its faint smoky taste and its pleasing texture. Cacciotta is made all over Tuscany, and it naturally takes on the name of the location in which it is made. It is a favored cheese with the hunters in Maremma, who carry it, along with a good bread, for snacks during the hunt. Serve Cacciotta di Siena with ripe Comice or Bartlett pears.

MARTEDI
(Tuesday)

Tuesday in Borgo San Frediano was *Giorno di Mercato*, or Market Day. Stalls would be set up in a little square, offering all sorts of fare: food, shoes, bolts of material, kitchen implements, tools, balsamic cure-it-all liniments, old and new books, hats, bags, canes, secondhand crutches, et cetera. Therefore, all the *trattorie*, *osterie*, and restaurants in the vicinity of the Mercato would feature a larger menu because of the influx of people. Trattoria del Pozzo followed the rule.

✻ ✻ ✻

FINOCCHIONA, OLIVE AMARE
E BURRO DI CAMPAGNA
(Finocchiona, Bitter Olives, and Country Butter)

MAFALDE ALLA PISANA
(Mafalde Pisa Style)

POLLO ARLECCHINA
(Chicken Harlequin)

LUMACHE IN UMIDO
(Snail Stew)

PURE DI FAGIOLI ALLA SALVIA
(Purée of Beans with Sage)

SEDANO FRITTO
(Fried Celery)

FRITTELLE DI MELE
(Apple Fritters)

Wine: A good Vino Nobile di Montepulciano is in order, or Barbera Sebastiani from California.

FINOCCHIONA, OLIVE AMARE E BURRO DI CAMPAGNA
(Finocchiona, Bitter Olives, and Country Butter)

Finocchiona is a Tuscan salami that is not easy to find in stores in the United States. However, substitutes can be used, such as a good Oldani Genova or Citterio Milanese salami. *Olive amare*, or bitter olives, are obtainable. They are small black olives picked before they become completely ripe, then preserved in olive oil, garlic, and bay leaves. They are delicious! *Burro di campagna* is a type of whipped butter, very yellow in color and very creamy, rich in taste.

The three ingredients make up a most delightful appetizer or antipasto, served with crusty bread and a dry Orvieto wine.

MAFALDE ALLA PISANA
(Mafalde Pisa Style)

SERVES 6–8

- 2 tablespoons olive oil
- 2 whole cloves garlic, peeled
- 1 pound completely lean veal, cut into small cubes
- ¼ pound pancetta or bacon, coarsely chopped
- 8 tablespoons lightly salted butter
- 4 anchovy fillets
- 1 tablespoon chopped Italian parsley
  Sprinkle of dried marjoram
  Sprinkle of freshly grated nutmeg
- 6 leaves fresh basil, finely chopped, or ½ teaspoon dried basil
  Freshly ground black pepper to taste
  Salt (optional)

1   cup fresh or frozen peas, if frozen defrosted, dry (using
     no water), at room temperature
½   cup tomato sauce (see page 211)
1½   pounds imported mafalde, or any long dried pasta,
     such as fettuccine or fettuccelle; or make your
     own (see page 223)
½   cup freshly grated pecorino cheese

Heat olive oil in skillet and sauté garlic until brown; discard garlic. Sauté veal and pancetta or bacon in garlic-flavored oil for 15 minutes. Set aside.

Melt 4 tablespoons butter in a saucepan and sauté anchovy fillets 3 minutes. Add parsley, marjoram, nutmeg, basil, and pepper; taste to see if salt is needed (because of the anchovies). Add veal, pancetta or bacon, including the oil, cook 10 minutes. Blend well. Set aside. If using fresh peas, blanch for 2 minutes in boiling water. Drain and add to all other ingredients. Or add the now-defrosted peas, but do not blanch. Return pan to very low flame, add tomato sauce, and heat through, stirring to mix well.

Cook pasta the usual way: 10 to 12 minutes for mafalde. Drain.

Melt remaining 4 tablespoons butter in large sauté pan. Add pasta and sauté well, stirring, 1 minute. Pour sauce over, mix well, and sauté 1 minute. Serve with the grated pecorino cheese.

POLLO ARLECCHINA
(Chicken Harlequin)

SERVES 6

3   large whole plump chicken breasts, skinned and boned
¼   cup all-purpose flour
2   eggs
1   tablespoon heavy cream
2½   tablespoons freshly grated Parmesan cheese

  Sprinkle of freshly grated nutmeg
  Sprinkle of dried marjoram
  Salt and freshly ground black pepper to taste
2 slices white bread, crusts removed
¼ pound boiled ham, in one piece
½ pound Fontina cheese
3 pieces roasted red pepper
1 cup fresh or frozen peas; if frozen, defrosted, dry
   (using no water), at room temperature
½ cup vegetable oil
1½ tablespoons olive oil
½ pound lightly salted butter
½ cup dry white wine

Divide each breast in two. Pound each half breast lightly between two pieces of aluminum foil, making sure not to tear meat. Dust cutlets lightly with flour and set aside.

Prepare batter by whisking together eggs, heavy cream, 1 tablespoon of the Parmesan cheese, the nutmeg, marjoram, and salt and pepper to taste; blend well. Set aside.

Cut bread slices into ¼-inch cubes. Cut ham and Fontina the same way. Julienne roasted peppers. Set aside. If using fresh peas, parboil 1½ minutes in boiling water, drain, and set aside; or have now-defrosted frozen peas, if using, ready; do not parboil.

Preheat oven to 400°F.

Heat vegetable oil in large skillet until rippling. Soak chicken cutlets thoroughly in batter. Fry chicken until golden brown on both sides. Place on paper toweling to drain.

Heat olive oil in second skillet. Sauté bread cubes, mixing in remaining 1½ tablespoons Parmesan cheese. Cook until crisp and dry. In clean skillet, melt 4 tablespoons butter and sauté ham and peas for 2 minutes. Mix together bread croutons, ham, peas, and julienned peppers. Set aside.

Melt remaining butter in a flameproof baking pan. Arrange chicken cutlets in baking pan and pour white wine over them. Bake 15 minutes. Sprinkle with ham, bread croutons, peas, and peppers. Add salt and pepper, if necessary. Bake 5 more minutes. Sprinkle Fontina cubes over top of chicken and place baking pan under broiler for 1½ minutes, or until Fontina begins to melt.

Serve one chicken cutlet per person. Spoon sauce from the pan over each portion.

LUMACHE IN UMIDO
(Snail Stew)

SERVES 6

4   tablespoons lightly salted butter
¾   teaspoon chopped garlic
½   medium onion, peeled and finely chopped
1   tablespoon chopped Italian parsley
    Sprig of fresh rosemary or 1 teaspoon dried rosemary
1   can (8 dozen) snails, preferably French, washed under
        cold water and drained
10 pieces imported dried porcini, presoaked in lukewarm
        water at least 1 hour in advance, drained, and
        coarsely chopped
1   cup robust red wine
1   cup brown sauce (see page 209)
    Salt and freshly ground black pepper to taste
6   slices whole-wheat bread
¼   cup freshly grated Parmesan cheese

Melt butter in large skillet. Add garlic, onion, parsley, and rose-mary and sauté 2 minutes. Add snails and sauté, stirring, 5 min-utes. Add porcini and sauté 2 minutes. Add wine and cook, until wine evaporates (about 10 minutes). Add brown sauce and cook, 5 minutes. Add salt and pepper to taste.

When snails are ready, toast the bread. Sprinkle cheese over each slice, then place one slice of bread in each plate. Spoon snails and sauce over, making sure to give each person 16 snails, more or less.

PURE DI FAGIOLI ALLA SALVIA
(Purée of Beans with Sage)

SERVES 6

1 pound dried cannellini beans or 1½ cans (16 ounces each) cannellini, drained
4 tablespoons lightly salted butter
½ teaspoon chopped garlic
4–5 fresh sage leaves, finely chopped, or ¼ teaspoon dried sage
Salt and freshly ground black pepper to taste

If using dried beans, soak overnight in cold water. Drain, then cook in unsalted fresh water for 1½ hours, or until tender. Drain again.

Purée beans in food processor. Melt butter in a large saucepan. Add garlic and sauté 1 minute, then add beans and mix well. Add sage and cook 5 minutes. Add salt and pepper to taste.

SEDANO FRITTO
(Fried Celery)

SERVES 6

3 bunches celery, outer stalks removed and leaves cut off
2 eggs
1 tablespoon heavy cream
2 tablespoons freshly grated Parmesan cheese
½ cup fine unflavored bread crumbs
¼ cup olive oil
3 tablespoons lightly salted butter

Cut larger celery stalks in half lengthwise, then cut all into 2-inch-long strips. Wash very well in cold water, then parboil in salted water for 8 minutes. Celery should remain crisp. Drain, run cold water over celery, and drain again.

Make a batter by beating together eggs, cream, and cheese until well blended. Dip celery strips in batter; let soak well. Roll celery in bread crumbs and coat well. Heat oil in skillet and add butter. When butter has melted and mixture is very hot, fry celery strips, turning as necessary, until golden. Serve immediately with one of main dishes.

FRITTELLE DI MELE
(Apple Fritters)

SERVES 6

4–5   cooking apples, peeled, cored, and sliced into ¼-inch-
         thick rounds
½   cup rum
1   cup all-purpose flour
     Pinch of salt
½   cup dry white wine
½   cup vegetable oil
2   tablespoons confectioners' sugar

Soak apple rounds in rum for 2 hours. Make a batter by beating flour, salt, and white wine until well blended. Batter should be creamy but not too thick.

Drain apple slices; dip in batter, using tongs. (Remaining rum can be kept for another use or made into a cocktail, if you so wish.) Heat oil in skillet; when very hot, spoon apple rounds into it, making sure that each round is well covered with batter. Fry to a puffy golden brown on both sides. Drain while hot on paper toweling; sprinkle sugar over them. Serve immediately.

❊ ❊ ❊

MERCOLEDI
(Wednesday)

FETTUCCELLE DEL POZZO
(Fettuccelle Pozzo Style)

VITELLO SAN FREDIANO
(Veal San Frediano Style)

PATATE, CAROTE E SEDANI AL FORNO
(Oven-Baked Potatoes, Carrots, and Celery)

FRUTTA FRESCA ASSORTITA
(Assorted Fresh Fruits)

Wine: The wines suggested here are dictated by my taste. A good California Cabernet Sauvignon such as Clos du Val. Or a good Merlot from the Friuli region. Or a cold "Eye of the Ram" Carneros Creek Rosé from California.

FETTUCCELLE DEL POZZO
(Fettuccelle Pozzo Style)

SERVES 6–8

Fresh pasta, white or green (see pages 223 or 226), or imported dry fettuccelle or any pasta of your choice

2 small heads Savoy cabbage

1½ pounds Italian sweet pork sausage, removed from casings

2 eggs
1 tablespoon heavy cream
5 tablespoons grated cacciotta cheese
  Sprinkle of freshly grated nutmeg
  Freshly ground black pepper to taste
¼ cup all-purpose flour
½ cup vegetable oil
½ cup virgin olive oil
3 whole cloves garlic, peeled
4 anchovy fillets
1 tablespoon chopped Italian parsley
  Sprinkle of dried marjoram
  A few leaves of fresh basil, coarsely chopped, or ¼
    teaspoon dried basil
5 tablespoons lightly salted butter
3 tablespoons dry white vermouth
½ cup freshly grated Parmesan cheese
  Crushed red pepper

If using fresh pasta, roll out as thin as possible. Cut shells into strips slightly narrower than ¼ inch (fettuccelle). Sprinkle with flour, cover with a towel, and set aside.

Wash cabbage well under cold running water. Separate leaves, discarding tough outside leaves. Dry well, then roll into a bunch and cut into strips as if you were making sauerkraut. Set aside.

Using your hands, mix sausage meat with eggs, cream, cacciotta cheese, nutmeg, and black pepper until well amalgamated. Proceed to make small balls the size of marbles. Roll in flour, covering on all sides. Heat vegetable oil in a skillet. When hot, fry sausage balls until well browned on all sides. Set aside on paper toweling to drain.

Heat olive oil in clean skillet and sauté garlic until deep yellow. Discard garlic. Add anchovies and sauté 2 minutes; add parsley, marjoram, basil, and black pepper and sauté 2 minutes longer. Add cabbage strips and stir well to coat all over with oil. Stir in 3 tablespoons of the butter and cook, covered, over low flame 10 minutes. Add dry vermouth and cook an additional 3 minutes. Add sausage balls to cabbage, stir well to combine, and keep warm.

Meanwhile, cook your pasta the usual way—2 to 3 minutes for

fresh, 6 to 7 minutes for dried pasta. Drain. In a saucepan, melt remaining 2 tablespoons of butter and sauté pasta quickly in it, tossing to coat with the butter. Place pasta on serving platter. Pour cabbage and sausage-ball mixture over and toss well. Serve with grated Parmesan cheese and a few flecks of crushed red pepper.

VITELLO SAN FREDIANO
(Veal San Frediano Style)

SERVES 6

 12 veal scaloppine
 ¼   cup all-purpose flour
 ¼   cup vegetable oil
  8 slices pancetta or bacon, julienned
4–5 medium zucchini, washed and trimmed
 ½   pound lightly salted butter
     Salt and freshly ground black pepper to taste
1½   teaspoons chopped Italian parsley
     Sprinkle of dried thyme
     Sprinkle of freshly grated nutmeg
     Sprinkle of ground ginger
  1 cup Marsala wine or sweet sherry
 10 pieces imported dried porcini, presoaked in lukewarm
        water at least 1½ hours in advance, drained, and
        some of soaking water reserved

Have your butcher prepare the veal scallops for you or pound each piece of veal between two pieces of aluminum foil until very thin. Dust veal scaloppine lightly with flour. Heat vegetable oil in a large skillet and brown scaloppine quickly on both sides. Transfer carefully to a warm platter. In separate skillet, fry julienned pancetta or bacon until crisp yet still soft. Set aside.

Preheat oven to 400°F.

Cut zucchini into sticks 2 inches long by ½ inch thick. Dry on paper toweling. Melt 3 tablespoons of the butter in a flameproof baking pan over low flame. Arrange zucchini sticks in melted butter, making sure each stick is well coated with butter. Add salt and pepper, then place in oven, and bake 10 minutes.

Meanwhile, melt remaining butter in clean large skillet and sauté scaloppine on both sides briefly. Add all the herbs and spices, and salt and pepper if necessary. Add the wine and let it evaporate uncovered, approximately 10 minutes. Add porcini and 2 tablespoons of their water (strained). Add pancetta or bacon. Cook 6 to 7 minutes.

Arrange scaloppine on serving platter and surround with zucchini sticks. Pour porcini-pancetta sauce over veal and serve.

PATATE, CAROTE E SEDANI AL FORNO
(Oven-Baked Potatoes, Carrots, and Celery)

SERVES 6

5   medium potatoes, washed and peeled, and cut into chunks
6   medium carrots, washed and scraped, cut in halves lengthwise
8   stalks celery (inside stalks only), washed and scraped, cut into sticks 3 inches long by ½ inch wide
5   tablepoons lightly salted butter
    Salt and freshly ground black pepper to taste
4   ounces Gruyère or Parmesan cheese, or any other cheese of your choice, grated

Preheat oven to 400°F.

Parboil potatoes, carrots, and celery separately in lightly salted water. Drain when approximately equally cooked—about 10 to 15 minutes.

Melt butter in flameproof baking pan over low flame. Add potatoes, carrots, and celery to pan, stirring to coat with butter, being careful not to damage vegetables. Add salt and pepper to taste. Bake 5 minutes, then add cheese and bake 3 minutes longer. Place under broiler for 1½ minutes before serving.

FRUTTA FRESCA ASSORTITA
(Assorted Fresh Fruits)

Pears, apples, grapes, oranges, figs, etc. Or whatever is on the market according to the season.

❋ ❋ ❋

GIOVEDI
(Thursday)

ZUPPA DI CECI CON ERBE
(Chick-pea Soup with Herbs)

POLLO MONSIGNORE
(Chicken Monsignore Style)

PEPERONI SOTT'ACETO
(Peppers Marinated in Vinegar)

Wine: Spanna Vallana from Piemonte *è di rigore* with this meal.

ZUPPA DI CECI CON ERBE
(Chick-pea Soup with Herbs)

SERVES 6–8

1   pound dried chick-peas
    Salt
½   cup virgin olive oil
2   cloves garlic, peeled and finely chopped
15 pieces imported dried porcini, presoaked in lukewarm
        water at least 1 hour in advance, drained
2   leaves fresh or dried sage
2   tablespoons all-purpose flour
1   bunch Swiss chard, washed well under cold water,
        leaves cut in half
1   bunch escarole (center part only), washed well, cut
        into smaller sections
2   tablespoons lightly salted butter
10 whole slices stale Italian bread
    Freshly ground black pepper to taste

Soak chick-peas overnight in cold, lightly salted water. Drain and transfer to fresh, lightly salted water. Cook, uncovered, 1½ hours.

Meanwhile, heat oil in a saucepan. Add garlic and cook until golden, then add porcini and sage and cook 2 to 3 minutes. Add flour and blend well with wire whisk. Add salt to taste. When beans have cooked for 1½ hours, do not drain but add Swiss chard, escarole, and the mixture from saucepan, including the oil. Cook 20 minutes longer. Stir in butter, then add slices of stale bread and cook 1 minute. Serve with freshly ground black pepper.

POLLO MONSIGNORE
(Chicken Monsignore Style)

SERVES 6

3 large whole chicken breasts, skinned and boned
¼ cup all-purpose flour
2 eggs
1 tablespoon heavy cream
3 teaspoons chopped Italian parsley
5 tablespoons freshly grated Parmesan cheese
   Sprinkle of freshly grated nutmeg
   Salt and freshly ground black pepper to taste
½ cup vegetable oil
8 tablespoons lightly salted butter
¾ pound fresh chicken livers, well cleaned
1 hard-boiled egg, shelled
5 slices pancetta or bacon
3 tablespoons sweet vermouth
6 thin slices Fontina cheese
¼ cup brown sauce (see page 209)
¼ cup dry white wine

Divide each breast in two. Pound each half breast between 2 sheets of aluminum foil until fairly thin, being careful not to tear meat. Dust cutlets lightly with flour, set aside.

Prepare batter by whisking together the eggs, cream, 1½ teaspoons parsley, 1 tablespoon of the grated Parmesan, nutmeg, and salt and pepper to taste; blend well. Immerse chicken in batter, coating well on all sides. Let stand in batter while you heat the vegetable oil in a large skillet. When the oil is hot, fry chicken, in batches if necessary, until golden brown on both sides. Let drain on paper toweling. Set aside.

Melt 4 tablespoons of the butter in a clean skillet. Add chicken livers and sauté, stirring, 5 minutes. Add boiled egg, cut in half. Add pancetta or bacon, remaining 1½ teaspoons parsley, and remaining 4 tablespoons Parmesan cheese. Sauté 5 more minutes, stirring occasionally, then add vermouth and cook uncovered 10 minutes. Remove from fire and put through food processor to obtain a creamy yet not too soft pâté. (This may also be done by hand by chopping everything very fine. I prefer the "by hand" method; the texture of the pâté is better, in my opinion.) Taste for salt and pepper, then set aside.

Melt remaining butter in large ovenproof skillet. Arrange chicken breasts in it, spoon pâté over each piece and smooth out. (Leftover pâté can be served at another time over toast; keep refrigerated.) Cover each chicken breast with a slice of Fontina. Add brown sauce. Cook, covered, over medium flame 5 minutes. Add wine, and cook uncovered 10 minutes. Glaze under broiler for 1 minute. Serve, spooning sauce next to each portion of chicken.

PEPERONI SOTT'ACETO
(Peppers Marinated in Vinegar)

SERVES 6

4   large sweet bell peppers, either red or yellow
2   tablespoons olive oil
¼   cup balsamic vinegar
1   clove garlic, peeled and finely chopped
½   tablespoon chopped Italian parsley
    3 leaves fresh mint (if obtainable), coarsely chopped
    Salt and freshly ground black pepper to taste
    Generous sprinkle of dried oregano

Roast peppers under broiler, turning occasionally, until flimsy skin begins to blister and starts to turn black. Remove peppers from broiler and let stand a bit, then proceed to remove skin while peppers are still hot. Cut peppers into slices, discarding seeds and hard core; flatten slices in a deep dish and let cool to room temperature.

Mix oil, vinegar, garlic, parsley, mint, and salt and pepper; blend well. Pour over pepper slices and sprinkle with oregano. Let peppers sit in marinade for 1 hour before serving.

❋ ❋ ❋

VENERDI
(Friday)

SPAGHETTINI ALLA LIVORNESE
(Spaghettini Leghorn Style)

ANGUILLA D'ARNO MARINATA, ARROSTO
(Marinated and Roasted Eel from the Arno River)

INTINGOLO DI OLIVE E ACCIUGHE
(Mixture of Olives and Anchovies)

RUGHETTA E CIPOLLE IN INSALATA
(Arugula and Onion Salad)

BUDINO BIANCO
(White Pudding)

Wine: Antinori White Chianti or a cold Pomino or a California Sauvignon Blanc by Joseph Phelps.

SPAGHETTINI ALLA LIVORNESE
(Spaghettini Leghorn Style)

SERVES 6–8

15 fresh clams, washed, opened, removed from shells, juice reserved

15–20 fresh mussels, washed very well, steamed briefly until opened, removed from shells

10 medium shrimp, washed, peeled while raw and deveined

⅓   pound fresh bay scallops, washed well, drained
1   tablespoon coarsely chopped Italian parsley
1½ teaspoons chopped garlic
    Freshly ground black pepper to taste
    Sprinkle of freshly grated nutmeg
    Sprinkle of dried marjoram
½   cup olive oil
    Salt
1   can (16 ounces) imported Italian peeled tomatoes
2–3 fresh basil leaves, or sprinkle of dried basil
1½ pounds imported spaghettini
    Crushed red pepper or freshly grated pecorino cheese
       from Sardinia

Combine seafood, with clam juice, in bowl. Sprinkle parsley over seafood; add garlic, pepper, nutmeg, and marjoram. Add ¼ cup of the oil and mix well. Let seafood marinate for 30 minutes at room temperature.

Place seafood and juices in saucepan. Cook over low flame for 3 to 4 minutes. Stir; taste to see if salt is needed. Set aside.

Set salted water for spaghettini over the fire. During the time it takes water to come to a boil, cook peeled tomatoes in remaining ¼ cup olive oil over a medium flame, adding pepper, and salt if you think it needs it, and the basil. When pot of water comes to a boil, remove tomatoes from fire and blend with seafood. Keep warm. Cook spaghettini 5 to 6 minutes, then drain and place in a large bowl. Pour seafood sauce over pasta and toss well, like a salad. Serve with a sprinkle of crushed red pepper or, if you can find it, several tablespoons of grated pecorino cheese from Sardinia.

ANGUILLA D'ARNO MARINATA, ARROSTO
(Marinated and Roasted Eel from the Arno River)

SERVES 6

3 pounds large sea or river eels, heads and tails cut off,
   cleaned and thoroughly washed
½ cup olive oil
4 lemons, cut into slices ¼ inch thick
   Salt and freshly ground black pepper to taste
3 leaves fresh sage or a sprinkle of dried sage
   Sprinkle of dried rosemary
3 fresh basil leaves or ¼ teaspoon dried basil
2 tablespoons dry white wine

Cut eels into 2-inch pieces; let drain while you prepare marinade by blending well all the remaining ingredients. Soak the pieces of eel in marinade for ½ hour. Skewer pieces of eel, alternating with lemon slices. Roast over a lively fire, wetting eels with marinade while roasting. Roast 15 to 20 minutes. Heat up remaining marinade and spoon over platter of roasted eels. Serve.

INTINGOLO DI OLIVE E ACCIUGHE
(Mixture of Olives and Anchovies)

SERVES 6–8

1½ pounds assorted olives—Gaeta, Sicilian, Kalamata,
   green Spanish—pitted and cut up coarsely
1 tablespoon pignoli (pine nuts), mashed
4 anchovy fillets, drained, minced
   Sprinkle of crushed red pepper

  3   bay leaves
  ¼   cup virgin olive oil

Blend well all the ingredients; let stand for 30 minutes before serving.

RUGHETTA E CIPOLLE IN INSALATA
(Arugula and Onion Salad)

SERVES 6–8

  2   bunches arugula
  1   small onion, peeled and very thinly sliced
  1   clove garlic, peeled and cut in half
      Juice of 1½ lemons, strained
  5   tablespoons olive oil
      Salt and freshly ground black pepper to taste

Pick arugula with the smallest and greenest leaves. Cut off tough stems and wash leaves very well under cold water, then drain; refrigerate. Refrigerate sliced onion separately.

Rub salad bowl thoroughly with garlic halves. Discard garlic. Toss arugula and onion in the lemon and olive oil dressing, adding salt and pepper to taste.

BUDINO BIANCO
(White Pudding)

SERVES 6

  1   quart half-and-half
  4   ounces rice flour

5 tablespoons granulated sugar
4 eggs, separated and reserve whites
3 tablespoons Madeira wine or sweet sherry
3 drops orange extract
2 tablespoons Grand Marnier
Sprinkle of ground cinnamon
1 tablespoon lightly salted butter
8 amaretti, finely crushed
1 tablespoon confectioners' sugar

Combine half-and-half, rice flour, and granulated sugar in a copper pot. Cook over a medium flame for approximately 30 minutes, stirring constantly. Remove from fire.

Beat the egg whites until stiff; set aside. Beat yolks in separate bowl; fold into mixture in copper pot. Add Madeira or sherry, orange extract, Grand Marnier, and cinnamon. Return copper pot to fire and whip mixture with wire whisk, then cook another 20 minutes. Remove from fire and fold in beaten egg whites, blending well.

Melt butter and coat inside of 2-quart mold with it. Sprinkle buttered mold with crushed amaretti so that surface is completely covered. Pour pudding mixture into mold and let cool at room temperature for 10 minutes, then refrigerate for 45 minutes. Turn mold upside down onto serving platter. Remove mold. Sprinkle confectioners' sugar over the *budino*. Serve.

❊ ❊ ❊

SABATO
(Saturday)

GIARDINIERA
(Marinated Fresh Vegetables)

LASAGNETTE ALLA MODENESE
(Lasagnette Modena Style)

ANITRA DI MAREMMA
(Wild Duckling from Maremma)

RADICCHIO PROFUMATO
(Radicchio Salad)

FORMAGGI ASSORTITI
(Assorted Cheeses)

Wine: Sfursat from Valtellina (Nino Negri).

GIARDINIERA
(Marinated Fresh Vegetables)

SERVES 6–8

4 medium potatoes, washed and peeled, cut into cubes
2 handfuls fresh string beans, washed and trimmed, then
    cut into 2 or 3 pieces
2 medium zucchini, washed and trimmed, cut into cubes
1 red beet, washed, cooked, peeled, and sliced into ¼-
    inch rounds
3 stalks celery (inside stalks only), washed and scraped,
    cut into small pieces
4 small carrots, washed and scraped, julienned
2 leeks, white part only, washed well, julienned
½ cup fresh or frozen peas; if frozen, defrosted, dry
    (using no water), at room temperature
¼ cup olive oil
1 tablespoon white tarragon vinegar
    Salt and freshly ground black pepper to taste
1 cup garlic mayonnaise (see page 219)

In lightly salted water, cook vegetables separately until each is tender, being careful not to overcook. Do not cook frozen peas, if using. Drain all vegetables carefully, so as not to damage them.

Run cold water over them immediately, then let cool off completely. Toss cooled vegetables gently with olive oil, vinegar, and salt and pepper to taste. Set aside for 30 minutes.

Mix vegetables, including now defrosted frozen peas, with garlic mayonnaise, blending well. Smooth into an elegant shape. Serve as an antipasto.

LASAGNETTE ALLA MODENESE
(Lasagnette Modena Style)

SERVES 6–8

1   pound duck livers or chicken livers
3   tablespoons virgin olive oil
½   medium onion, peeled and thinly sliced
1   carrot, washed and scraped, grated
1   tablespoon chopped Italian parsley
4   ounces imported dried porcini, presoaked at least 1½
        hours in advance, drained
1   walnut, shelled and mashed very fine
2   bay leaves
     Salt and freshly ground black pepper to taste
6   tablespoons lightly salted butter
     Sprinkle of freshly grated nutmeg
¾   cup robust red wine
3   tablespoons brown sauce (see page 209)
1¼   cups tomato sauce (see page 211)
1½   pounds fresh lasagnette (see page 228) or imported
        dried lasagnette
¼   cup freshly grated Parmesan cheese

Use duck livers, if obtainable at your butcher; sauce will not taste the same with chicken livers, but nevertheless it will be excellent. Clean livers thoroughly; do not wash in water. Chop coarsely and set aside.

Heat oil in a skillet. Sauté onion until translucent, add carrot, parsley, porcini, walnut, and bay leaves. Add salt and pepper to taste. Cook 15 minutes over low flame, stirring frequently. Set aside. Melt butter in a separate skillet and sauté livers until lightly browned; add nutmeg and wine; cook, uncovered, until wine evaporates (10 to 15 minutes). Add brown sauce and cook 3 minutes. Add the onion-carrot mixture and blend well; cook 3 minutes. Add tomato sauce and cook 6 minutes. Stir everything well; keep warm while you cook the pasta.

Cook pasta the usual way. If using homemade lasagnette, cook 2 to 3 minutes; cook dried pasta 8 minutes. Drain. Place pasta on serving platter, cover with most of the sauce and toss gently; spoon extra sauce over each portion. Serve with Parmesan cheese.

ANITRA DI MAREMMA
(Wild Duckling from Maremma)

SERVES 6

 3 wild ducklings (2 pounds each), if obtainable, or
       domestic ducklings
 6 slices pancetta or bacon
 3 sprigs fresh rosemary or 1 tablespoon dried rosemary
 3 tablespoons olive oil
       Salt and freshly ground black pepper to taste
10 tablespoons lightly salted butter
 ¾ cup white wine
 1 tablespoon Dijon mustard
 1 packet saffron
       Sprinkle of freshly grated nutmeg
 1 cup Gaeta or Kalamata olives
1½ teaspoons chopped shallots

Chances are you will be able to purchase only frozen wild ducklings at specialty butcher shops, in which case defrost ducklings at room temperature overnight. If you should go out on a wild duck shoot, make sure to find someone to pluck the birds since the process is extremely difficult; clean birds, remove insides.

Preheat oven to 400°F.

Dress ducklings by inserting into each cavity 2 slices of pancetta or bacon and 1 sprig of rosemary. Combine oil and salt and pepper, then rub ducklings thoroughly on the outside with the mixture. Melt 2 tablespoons of the butter and use to coat roasting pan. Arrange ducklings in pan, breast side up, and place in oven to roast for 1 hour, draining off fat as necessary. When ducklings are well browned and crisp, drain off fat once more and set aside.

Blend together the wine, mustard, saffron, and nutmeg. Melt remaining 8 tablespoons butter in saucepan; add wine mixture. Cook, uncovered, over low flame until wine evaporates (approximately 10 minutes). Meanwhile, pit and crush half the olives. Add to saucepan along with shallots and cook 10 minutes. Add whole olives, then remove from flame and keep warm.

Cut ducklings in half lengthwise, removing backbones and breastbones. Arrange the 6 half ducklings in a large flameproof earthenware casserole. Pour sauce over them, cover, and place over a low flame; cook 15 minutes. Place ducklings on serving platter, arrange whole olives around them, pour hot sauce over, and serve.

RADICCHIO PROFUMATO
(Radicchio Salad)

SERVES 6

4 small heads radicchio
¼ cup balsamic vinegar
2 tablespoons virgin olive oil
  Crushed sea salt or kosher salt to taste
  Freshly ground black pepper to taste
1 tablespoon chopped fresh mint leaves

¼   teaspoon chopped garlic
3   leaves fresh basil
     Yolk of 1 hard-boiled egg, broken up with fork

Wash radicchio well under cold running water, then drain well; tear leaves with your hands into irregular pieces. Blend together remaining ingredients; toss radicchio in this dressing and serve.

FORMAGGI ASSORTITI
(Assorted Cheeses)

———— · ❁ · ————

Cacciotta   Grana-Parmigiano
Stracchino   Pecorino fresco

❊   ❊   ❊

DOMENICA
(Sunday)

TORTELLONI AL SUGO DI FUNGHI E TARTUFI
(Tortelloni with Mushroom Sauce and Truffles)

CONIGLIO AL FORNO AL SUGO DI CINGHIALE
(Roast Rabbit with Wild Boar Lard)

BRUSCHETTE

POLPETTONE DI PATATE
(Baked Mashed-Potato Loaf)

INSALATA DI ZUCCHINE,
POMODORI E CIPOLLINE
(Zucchini, Tomato, and Scallion Salad)

SPUMANTI DI AMARETTI
(Amaretti Delight)

Wine: A very dry white wine from San Gimignano and a Ghemme from Piemonte are perfect with this menu.

TORTELLONI AL SUGO DI FUNGHI E TARTUFI
(Tortelloni with Mushroom Sauce and Truffles)

SERVES 6–8

6	tablespoons lightly salted butter
1	whole clove garlic, peeled
4	ounces imported dried porcini, presoaked at least 1½ hours in advance, drained
6	fresh mushrooms, well washed and very thinly sliced through caps and stems
1	tablespoon chopped Italian parsley
	Salt and freshly ground black pepper to taste
	Sprinkle of freshly grated nutmeg
1	tablespoon good Cognac
120	tortelloni, homemade (see page 171) or purchased
1	small white truffle (optional)
¼	cup freshly grated Parmesan cheese

Melt butter in large skillet over low heat. Add garlic and sauté until golden brown, then discard garlic. Butter must not brown. Add porcini, fresh mushrooms, parsley, salt, and pepper. Sauté 6 minutes, mixing well. Add nutmeg and Cognac and sauté 2 minutes.

In the meantime, you should have set a large pot of salted water boiling for the tortelloni. Cook tortelloni no longer than 8 minutes. Drain carefully. Sauté tortelloni in sauce 1 to 2 minutes maximum. Transfer tortelloni to serving platter and slice truffle over. Serve with Parmesan cheese.

CONIGLIO AL FORNO AL SUGO DI CINGHIALE
(Roast Rabbit with Wild Boar Lard)

Many people seem to have what I call a sentimental aversion to eating rabbit. Who on earth would be so mean as to eat the Easter Bunny? Wrong! Get over your aversion. It is delicious—take my word for it.

SERVES 6–8

2 small fresh rabbits (approximately 3 pounds each); do not settle for frozen rabbits
   Red wine vinegar
   Cold beef consommé (see page 207)
6 tablespoons virgin olive oil
1 pound wild boar fat (cinghiale) or good fatback or prosciutto fat, cut into small chunks
4 whole cloves garlic, peeled
1 tablespoon chopped Italian parsley
5 bay leaves
2 sprigs fresh rosemary or 1½ teaspoons dried rosemary
4 leaves fresh sage or ½ teaspoon dried sage
3 leaves fresh tarragon or 3 leaves tarragon preserved in vinegar
   Sprinkle of freshly grated nutmeg
   Salt and freshly ground black pepper to taste
1 cup dry white wine
2 tablespoons Marsala wine or sweet sherry

This might seem like a lot of meat, but rabbits are very bony; have your butcher cut rabbits into smallish pieces. Wash each piece in red wine vinegar mixed with some cold beef consommé; pat pieces dry with paper toweling.

Preheat oven to 400°F.

Pour olive oil into roasting pan and roll each piece of rabbit in it. Add chunks of fat, arranging them around the rabbit pieces. Add all other ingredients except the wines, making sure you distribute herbs evenly around the rabbit. Place pan in oven, starting to baste rabbit as fat begins to melt. Add some consommé, spoonfuls at a time; add white wine. Wait 15 minutes, then add Marsala or sherry. Continue basting so that the meat will cook crisply without drying. Cook a total of 1 to 1½ hours. Arrange pieces of rabbit on serving platter and pour unstrained sauce over it. Serve, accompanied by *bruschette* (recipe follows).

BRUSCHETTE

SERVES 6–8

15   thick slices whole-wheat Italian peasant bread
    Melted sweet butter
    Freshly ground black pepper

Toast bread slices lightly under grill. Brush with melted sweet butter, then sprinkle generously with freshly ground black pepper. Serve with rabbit.

POLPETTONE DI PATATE
(Baked Mashed-Potato Loaf)

SERVES 6–8

8–10   medium potatoes, washed and peeled
   5   tablespoons lightly salted butter
  ½   cup unflavored fine dry bread crumbs
  ½   teaspoon chopped garlic
  ½   pound rich whole-milk ricotta cheese
  ½   cup freshly grated Parmesan cheese
  ¼   cup heavy cream

3   eggs, lightly beaten
    Salt and freshly ground black pepper to taste
    Sprinkle of dried oregano

Boil potatoes in lightly salted water about 20 minutes; do not overcook. Set aside to cool, then mash.

Preheat oven to 400°F.

Melt butter in saucepan and use 2 tablespoons of it to coat loaf pan. Sprinkle inside of pan with a thick layer of bread crumbs and set aside.

Sauté garlic to golden color in remaining butter. Remove from fire; stir in ricotta, Parmesan cheese, and heavy cream. Mix well. Add eggs and mashed potatoes, stirring to combine. Add salt and pepper to taste and a sprinkle of oregano. Pour mixture into prepared loaf pan. Smooth surface and place in oven. Bake until top has formed a deep golden brown crust. Serve immediately. (Leftovers are excellent served at room temperature with eggs).

INSALATA DI ZUCCHINE, POMODORI
E CIPOLLINE
(Zucchini, Tomato, and Scallion Salad)

SERVES 6–8

4   medium zucchini, washed and trimmed
2   large ripe tomatoes, cut into bite-size chunks
1   bunch slender scallions, roots and green parts cut off,
        washed, dried, and julienned
¼   cup of olive oil
    Strained juice of 2 lemons
    Salt and freshly ground black pepper to taste

Boil zucchini in salted water for 8 minutes; drain, then run cold water over them and cut into slices ¼ inch thick. Combine with tomatoes and scallions in serving bowl. Toss well with remaining ingredients.

SPUMANTI DI AMARETTI
(Amaretti Delight)

SERVES 6–8

1 pound amaretti, crumbled and soaked in ½ cup
Marsala wine or sweet sherry
3 tablespoons granulated sugar
6 egg yolks
3 tablespoons sweetened cocoa powder
4 very ripe peaches, peeled, stones discarded, cut into
small pieces
1 pint heavy cream
1 tablespoon Grand Marnier

Using a food processor, make a thick creamy paste of all the ingredients except the cream and Grand Marnier. Separately whip cream and add Grand Marnier to make a Chantilly. Pour creamy paste into stemmed fruit goblets, top with Chantilly, and serve.

Dining at
My Sister's Suitor's

It took Iolanda and me two weeks to talk our sister Ginetta into accepting the dinner invitation from Signor Gabriele Terelli, the widower who lived down the street from us. After all, the invitation had been extended to the whole family, Ginetta's honor was not at stake. And Signor Terelli had a superb reputation as a chef. In fact, he *was* the chef at the Grand Hotel Italia that stood in Piazza Mameli facing the monument to the Unknown Soldier.

Signor Gabriele Terelli had been a widower for the past two years, had no children, and I'm sure that at that time he was ready for a new wife. He had shown a keen interest in my sister Ginetta. True, Ginetta was his junior by a good fifteen years, and she wanted nothing to do with him. Certainly not because Signor Terelli was wanting in looks or manners or even position, but mainly because he was a *chef*. Silly reason.

"In any case, there is the fifteen years' difference in age to be considered—and he's a widower," my mother would point out without much conviction.

"I'm positive that he must perspire like a pig, being in front of the hot stoves all day long," Ginetta would object with disdain.

"And he might even smell of rancid fats and sauces," she would add for good measure.

"On the contrary," my sister Iolanda would reply, "he always looks so neat and extremely clean—he's elegant. And do you know that he wears silk shirts?" She was really impressed.

"I think it's foolish and above all selfish of you to deprive us all of a good meal," I'd say, truly indignant at Ginetta. I was fifteen at the time, and my interest in food had grown considerably.

"He probably serves the best since, in all probability, he steals the food from that hotel," my father the socialist would remark disapprovingly. In reality, he had always shown himself to be against the whole business.

This went on for two weeks after Signor Terelli had approached my sister Ginetta with the invitation. Finally she capitulated. On a Monday evening, his night off at the hotel, we set out for Signor Terelli's apartment. Ginetta walked several steps behind us, being the exploited one. Notwithstanding, she had made herself up to look positively terrific. Iolanda and I giggled all the way over. My father and mother, I believe, had begun to reconsider the matter a bit more seriously. That is to say, in favor of Signor Terelli.

Signor Terelli's apartment was immaculately clean for a single man's, and very well appointed. He showed excellent manners to us all, and eagerness to please Ginetta. The aromas of food in that apartment made me slightly dizzy with expectation.

Things did not go smoothly, however, during our first dinner at Signor Terelli's. Ginetta would twitch her nostrils very suspiciously whenever our host came near her at the table. And she went so far as to titter brazenly as he described the recipe for the veal we were about to eat.

I was totally enraptured with the meal and hoped that Ginetta would stop her carrying on. Instead, she ended the evening by saying with heavy-handed sarcasm:

"Oh, what a perfect wife you would make."

Signor Terelli showed a certain annoyance at that, but since my mother laughed, he chose to dismiss the insult by joining in the laughter. In any case, he was kind enough to invite us to a second dinner.

On that occasion, Ginetta made it even worse by telling him

at the end of the meal how she would have cooked it, plainly implying that the dinner could have been improved.

Signor Terelli, very obviously hurt, made light of it by suggesting that he was sure she would have done better, and that his kitchen was at her disposal at any time. To which Ginetta replied with hauteur that she wasn't accustomed to being a housewife. I was furious with her, my father was definitely annoyed, and Iolanda just looked at Ginetta with contempt. My mother dismissed it all.

Undaunted, our host invited us for yet another dinner. My father wanted to beg off. I prayed that we would accept. Ginetta, to our collective surprise, jubilantly accepted.

I thought then that she had begun to like Signor Terelli and was indeed ready to reconsider the entire matter. I couldn't have been more wrong.

During this final meal, Ginetta made the extravagant announcement, to our total astonishment, that she was about to leave Italy shortly, to be married and go live in France. She had the gall to mention where she was going in France, and to make up a completely fictitious name for the man she was to marry. We were speechless. Signor Terelli offered his congratulations, showing enormous grace. At the end of the dinner, we filed out of his apartment feeling like chastised dogs.

I hated Ginetta that evening. My father said that never before in his entire life had he ever been so deeply humiliated. Iolanda was outraged. My mother was merely amused.

These are the dinners we were served by Signor Gabriele Terelli. What a pity it had to come to such an end. (The authenticity of these recipes is, by the way, 100 percent, for Signor Terelli was also the author of a modest cooking manual, printed by a local typographer, a copy of which I used to own.)

✳ ✳ ✳

DINNER ONE

POMODORI FARCITI CON RISOTTO
(Tomatoes Stuffed with Risotto)

MOSTACCIOLI ALLA BARESE
(Mostaccioli Bari Style)

SCALOPPINE ARLESIANA
(Veal Scaloppine Arlesiana Style)

SUPPLI DI ZUCCHINE
(Zucchini Croquettes)

TALEGGIO E MELE CARLINE
(Taleggio Cheese and Apples)

Wines: Pomino Bianco Secco and Ghemme.

POMODORI FARCITI CON RISOTTO
(Tomatoes Stuffed with Risotto)

SERVES 6

3   ripe fresh medium tomatoes
4   tablespoons lightly salted butter
½   small onion, thinly sliced
½   cup rice, preferably imported Arborio rice
3   cups hot chicken consommé (see page 207)
½   cup tomato sauce (see page 211)
    Freshly ground black pepper

Sprinkle of freshly grated nutmeg
Sprinkle of ground ginger
½   cup freshly grated Parmesan cheese
1   can (14 ounces) Italian tuna packed in olive oil
3–4   fresh basil leaves, coarsely chopped, or ¼ to ½ tea-
     spoon dried basil

Cut tomatoes in half, then scoop out most of the pulp; set pulp aside. Melt 1 tablespoon butter in a saucepan and cook tomatoes for 5 minutes, uncovered, basting them with the butter. Set aside to cool while you prepare the risotto.

Melt remaining butter in clean saucepan and cook sliced onion to a translucency. Pour rice into pan and mix well with the onion and butter. Stir while cooking. Begin to pour in chicken consommé over the rice, a bit at a time, stir, cooking slowly over medium flame. Keep pouring in consommé until rice is almost cooked (rice should be *very* al dente). Still on the fire, add tomato sauce and mix well. Chop tomato pulp very fine, then add to rice. Stir in pepper, spices, and cheese. At this point, risotto should be perfectly cooked.

Remove from fire and let risotto cool for 30 minutes. Add tuna, which should be broken up into small chunks, and basil. Blend well. Let risotto cool to room temperature, then spoon into tomato halves. Serve immediately.

MOSTACCIOLI ALLA BARESE
(Mostaccioli Bari Style)

SERVES 6–8

1   bunch broccoli (about 2 pounds)
½   lemon
2   tablespoons olive oil
1   pound Italian sweet pork sausage, meat removed from
     casing and broken up into lumps

 4 tablespoons lightly salted butter
1½ teaspoons chopped Italian parsley
 ½ teaspoon chopped garlic
 5 anchovy fillets, drained
 5 pieces imported dried porcini, presoaked in lukewarm
      water at least 1½ hours in advance, drained, and
      soaking water reserved
    Sprinkle of dried oregano
    Freshly ground black pepper to taste
    Salt (optional)
 3 cups tomato sauce (see page 211)
1½ pounds imported mostaccioli, or a short pasta of your
      choice
 ½ cup freshly grated pecorino cheese

Select a bunch of broccoli with the least leaves and the slenderest stems. They will be the tenderest.

Bring to boil a large pot of salted water. Squeeze juice of ½ lemon into it, then add rind. Wash bunch of broccoli under cold water and immerse in boiling water. Cook 3 minutes. Remove broccoli and cool thoroughly under cold water. Cut broccoli into florets, including part of the tender stems, which you will cut into bite-size pieces. Set aside.

Heat the oil in a skillet and cook sausage meat until brown. Set aside without draining.

Melt butter in a large deep saucepan, then add parsley, garlic, and anchovy fillets. Sauté, stirring, until anchovies have melted. Add presoaked porcini, which you should have chopped into coarse pieces. Sauté 2 minutes. Add the strained water in which you soaked porcini; add oregano and black pepper. Taste, and if necessary add salt. Add the sausage meat, including oil from the pan. Cook, uncovered, 5 to 6 minutes. Stir in tomato sauce; cook 10 minutes. Add broccoli and blend well, being careful not to mush up broccoli. Cook 5 minutes.

In a large pot of salted boiling water, cook mostaccioli or pasta of your choice for 10 to 12 minutes. Drain pasta and sauté in broccoli sauce, tossing until well coated. Serve with the pecorino cheese on the side. The sharpness of the pecorino will bring out the flavor of the sauce better than the milder Parmesan.

SCALOPPINE ARLESIANA
(Veal Scaloppine Arlesiana Style)

SERVES 6

12   slices tender veal, clean and free of sinews
1   medium eggplant, unpeeled, sliced into rounds approximately ⅛ inch thick (12 to 14 slices)
   Coarse salt
1   cup vegetable oil
¾   cup all-purpose flour
2   eggs
2   tablespoons heavy cream
1   tablespoon freshly grated Parmesan cheese
½   pound lightly salted butter
2   whole cloves garlic, peeled
   Small sprig fresh rosemary, if obtainable
2   leaves fresh sage or ¼ teaspoon dried sage
   Sprinkle of freshly grated nutmeg
   Salt and freshly ground black pepper to taste
½   cup red wine
12–14   fresh medium mushrooms, caps only but stems reserved (see note below)
12–14   slices, as thick as eggplant slices, Fontina cheese or fresh mozzarella

Your butcher can prepare the veal for you. If you do it yourself, place veal between 2 pieces of waxed paper or aluminum foil, and flatten with a meat pounder to rather thin slices.

Sprinkle eggplant slices with coarse salt on both sides, place in a flat shallow pan, cover with waxed paper, press down with some weight. Leave for about 2 hours in order to squeeze out bitter juice.

Heat half of the vegetable oil in a skillet. Pat dry eggplant slices, then dust lightly with flour. Fry to deep golden brown on both sides. Set aside to drain on paper toweling.

Prepare egg batter by beating together eggs, cream, and Parmesan cheese. Lightly dust veal scaloppine with flour, then dip in egg batter until well coated. Heat remaining vegetable oil in clean skillet. Sauté veal on both sides to a light golden color. Set aside to drain on paper toweling.

Melt butter in saucepan over low flame. Add cloves of garlic and sprig of rosemary; sauté, then discard both when garlic becomes golden brown. Add sage, nutmeg, and salt and pepper to taste; sauté 4 minutes. Add red wine and let evaporate approximately 10 minutes. Meanwhile, wash mushroom caps under cold water. Dry, add to butter, and sauté 3 minutes. Set aside.

Preheat oven to 350°F.

Pour half the butter sauce into a baking pan, keeping mushroom caps on the side. Place one slice of eggplant over each slice of veal. If eggplant slice is too large, trim off and keep trimmings (see note below). Place slices of Fontina cheese or mozzarella over eggplant. Trim cheese slices, if necessary, and keep trimmings.

Lay scaloppine slices in baking pan, then pour other half of butter sauce over. Bake until cheese has melted. Place one mushroom cap over each slice of veal; glaze under broiler 1 minute. Serve.

Note: Leftover trimmings of eggplant slices and cheese can be used in a salad or marinated in ¼ cup olive oil. Add to the trimmings the mushroom stems, sliced, red wine vinegar to taste, and serve as an appetizer or snack with good crisp bread.

SUPPLI DI ZUCCHINE
(Zucchini Croquettes)

SERVES 6–8

8   medium zucchini, trimmed and washed under cold
    water
2   egg yolks
2   tablespoons heavy cream
1   teaspoon chopped Italian parsley

3   tablespoons freshly grated Parmesan cheese
     Salt and freshly ground black pepper to taste
½   cup all-purpose flour
½   cup unflavored bread crumbs, sifted very fine
½   cup vegetable oil

Shred zucchini to a fluffy consistency using shredding blade of food processor. Let moisture from shredded zucchini be absorbed by paper toweling. Whip up a batter with the egg yolks, heavy cream, parsley, cheese, and salt and pepper to taste. Roll shredded zucchini in flour, shape into balls the size of a large walnut, and pack firmly. Dip zucchini balls (*supplì*) in batter and soak well. Roll *supplì* in bread crumbs. Set aside.

Heat vegetable oil in skillet. Test oil temperature with a few drops of batter; when sizzling, gently place zucchini *supplì* in it. Fry to a deep golden color. Remove *supplì* from pan and drain on paper toweling. Serve hot.

TALEGGIO E MELE CARLINE
(*Taleggio Cheese and Apples*)

Taleggio is a cheese very similar in taste to Fontina, Bel Paese, and Port-Salut. *Mele Carline* are the closest equivalent of Granny Smith apples. Serve with very fresh, crisp *grissini* (breadsticks).

❋ ❋ ❋

DINNER TWO

CROSTINI DI FEGATO DI POLLO
(Chicken Liver Pâté on Toast)

FETTUCCELLE CON CARCIOFINI
(Fettuccelle with Baby Artichoke Sauce)

POLLO AL VINO BIANCO
(Chicken in White Wine)

CAROTE, ZUCCHINE E RAPE ROSSE
(Carrots, Zucchini, and Red Beets)

POMPELMO AL MARSALA,
MIELE E AMARETTI SCHIACCIATI
(Grapefruit with Marsala Wine, Honey, and Crushed Amaretti)

Wine: Grignolino from Piemonte.

CROSTINI DI FEGATO DI POLLO
(Chicken Liver Pâté on Toast)

SERVES 6–8

½   small onion, peeled
1   medium carrot, washed and scraped
1   stalk celery, washed and scraped
1   clove garlic, peeled
6   leaves fresh basil or ½ teaspoon dried basil
1½ tablespoons olive oil
¾   pound chicken livers, cleaned

10 pieces imported dried porcini, presoaked in lukewarm
    water at least 1½ hours in advance, drained, and
    some of the soaking water reserved
5   tablespoons lightly salted butter
2   tablespoons Marsala wine or sweet sherry
1   tablespoon freshly grated Parmesan cheese
    Salt and freshly ground black pepper to taste
    Strained juice of ½ lemon
1   loaf crisp Italian bread

Chop by hand or shred in food processor the onion, carrot, celery, garlic, and fresh basil leaves. Heat olive oil in skillet and sauté shredded vegetables 6 to 7 minutes. Set aside.

Chop chicken livers very fine; also chop porcini very fine. Sauté livers and mushrooms in 3 tablespoons of the butter in separate skillet for 6 minutes. Add livers and mushrooms to cooked vegetables. Place pan over low flame. Add wine and cook, uncovered, 5 minutes, or until wine evaporates. Add some of the mushroom water, strained. Add cheese and salt and pepper to taste. Add lemon juice. Cook 3 more minutes, mixing with wooden spoon to a smooth, soft pâté. Set aside.

Slice loaf of bread into ⅛-inch-thick rounds. If too large, cut rounds in half. Sauté bread slices in remaining 2 tablespoons butter in clean skillet until golden. Add more butter if necessary. Spread liver pâté over bread slices. Serve immediately.

FETTUCCELLE CON CARCIOFINI
(Fettuccelle with Baby Artichoke Sauce)

SERVES 6–8

½ lemon
2   pounds small, very fresh, very tender artichokes, if ob-
    tainable, or regular artichokes trimmed down to
    that size
½ cup olive oil

  1 teaspoon chopped garlic
1½ tablespoons chopped Italian parsley
    Salt and freshly ground black pepper to taste
1½ pounds fresh or dried fettuccelle, if you make your
      own (see page 228), or imported spaghettini
  2 tablespoons lightly salted butter
 ½ cup freshly grated Parmesan cheese

Bring to boil a large pot of lightly salted water, squeeze juice of ½ lemon into it, then add rind. Immerse artichokes, making sure to keep sinking them with wooden spoon. Cooking time depends on size: 8 minutes for small ones, 12 to 15 minutes for trimmed regulars.

Drain artichokes and shake water out of each one. Cut into bite-size sections and take out choke. Sauté in hot olive oil in skillet 1 to 2 minutes. Add garlic, parsley, and salt and pepper to taste. Sauté another 2 minutes. Set aside, leaving artichokes in oil. This is now the sauce for your pasta.

Cook fettuccelle in large pot of salted boiling water. If using fresh, cook 3 minutes; cook dried fettuccelle or spaghettini 5 to 7 minutes. Drain well. Melt butter in large skillet; add pasta and stir to coat. Add artichokes and sauce a little at a time. Blend well.

Serve with Parmesan cheese.

POLLO AL VINO BIANCO
(Chicken in White Wine)

SERVES 6–8

  2 broilers (about 2½ pounds each)
 ½ cup vegetable oil
 ½ pound lightly salted butter
 ½ small onion, peeled and thinly sliced
  1 shallot, peeled and sliced
  2 cloves garlic, peeled

 1　sprig fresh rosemary or sprinkle of dried rosemary
 3　bay leaves
 　　Salt and freshly ground black pepper to taste
 2　cups good dry white wine
 　　Sprinkle of freshly grated nutmeg
 　　Sprinkle of ground ginger
1½　teaspoons dry mustard and 1 packet of saffron, blended
 　　　in ¼ cup warm water
10　pieces imported dried porcini, presoaked in lukewarm
 　　　water at least 1½ hours in advance, drained, and
 　　　soaking water reserved
 6　slices prosciutto, julienned

Cut each chicken into 4 pieces; wash and pat dry. Heat vegetable oil in a large skillet. Sauté chicken pieces quickly on both sides for 10 minutes total. Place chicken pieces on paper toweling to drain.

Melt butter in large deep saucepan. Add onion, shallot, garlic, rosemary, and bay leaves. Sauté 6 minutes. Arrange pieces of chicken in pan. Cook, uncovered, 5 minutes, turning often. Add salt and pepper to taste. Add wine and cook, uncovered, until wine evaporates. Add nutmeg and ginger and the blend of mustard and saffron. Cook a few more minutes. Add porcini and 2 tablespoons of the soaking water, strained. Cook 10 minutes. Add julienne of prosciutto.

Arrange pieces of chicken on serving platter. Spoon sauce over and serve.

CAROTE, ZUCCHINE E RAPE ROSSE
(Carrots, Zucchini, and Red Beets)

SERVES 6–8

 4　carrots, washed and scraped
 4　zucchini, washed and trimmed
 2　medium red beets, leaves cut off

⅓ cup olive oil
1 tablespoon chopped fresh coriander
½ teaspoon chopped garlic
   Salt and freshly ground black pepper to taste
1 tablespoon red wine vinegar

In pot of salted boiling water, cook carrots, zucchini, and beets. Take vegetables out of water according to their cooking time. In any case, leave vegetables very crisp. Cool under cold running water. Julienne carrots and zucchini. Peel and slice beets into ⅛-inch rounds.

Heat oil in large skillet. Add coriander and garlic and sauté 4 minutes. Add vegetables. Sauté gently over low flame. Season to taste, then add vinegar and sauté 2 minutes. Serve.

POMPELMO AL MARSALA, MIELE E AMARETTI SCHIACCIATI
(Grapefruit with Marsala Wine, Honey, and Crushed Amaretti)

SERVES 6–8

3–4 ripe medium pink grapefruit
1 cup Marsala wine or sweet sherry
2 tablespoons honey
6–7 amaretti, coarsely crushed

Cut grapefruit into halves, partition, and remove membranes. Keep grapefruit halves refrigerated until you have made the sauce.

Heat up Marsala wine or sweet sherry in saucepan; add honey and bring to boil. Blend well. Take grapefruit halves from refrigerator and sprinkle crushed amaretti over them. Pour hot wine and honey sauce over fruit. Serve immediately.

Note: For a special treat, use Calvados instead of Marsala or sherry.

❅ ❅ ❅

DINNER THREE

PASTA IN BRODO DI PESCE
(Pasta Cooked in Fish Broth)

TRIPPA ALLA GENOVESE
(Tripe Genoa Style)

TORTA PASQUALINA
(Easter Pie)

FRAGOLONI CON LIMONE, ZUCCHERO E PEPE NERO
(Strawberries with Lemon, Sugar, and Freshly Ground Black Pepper)

Wines: Barbera d'Asti and Moscato d'Asti.

PASTA IN BRODO DI PESCE
(Pasta Cooked in Fish Broth)

SERVES 6–8

1 striped bass, 3 to 4 pounds, cleaned and scaled, head
    and tail left on
1 small onion, peeled and cut in half
1 small bunch Italian parsley
1 sprig fresh rosemary
    Sprinkle of dried marjoram
2 stalks celery, washed
    Rind of 1 lemon
    Salt to taste

¼ cup virgin olive oil
1 pound short pasta, such as tubettini or anicini
   Sprinkle of freshly grated nutmeg

Wash fish well under cold running water. Place in a poacher large enough to accommodate it without crowding. Fill with 2 quarts of cold water. Add all ingredients but oil, pasta, and nutmeg. Set poacher over medium flame. Bring to boil, then cook 4 minutes.

Remove fish gently and set aside. When fish has cooled to room temperature, skin it, cut off head and tail, and add both to broth. Keep rest of fish aside. Cook fish broth for another 10 minutes over low flame.

Strain broth through fine wire strainer lined with layers of cheesecloth. Set strained broth over fire again. Add virgin olive oil and bring to boil. Add pasta and cook 7 to 8 minutes.

Serve in soup bowls, garnished with chunks of bass. Grate or sprinkle a bit of nutmeg over each plate.

Reserve the remaining fish, if any, for later use, such as in a salad, or sauté in butter, parsley, saffron, and garlic.

TRIPPA ALLA GENOVESE
(Tripe Genoa Style)

SERVES 6–8

4 pounds fresh honeycomb tripe, which you can obtain from your butcher already blanched (do not use frozen)
1 lemon
3 tablespoons olive oil
6 tablespoons lightly salted butter
2 medium carrots, washed, scraped, and minced
2 stalks celery, washed, scraped, and minced

1   small onion, peeled and finely chopped
½   teaspoon chopped garlic
1   tablespoon chopped Italian parsley
      Generous grating of nutmeg
      Pinch of dried sage
1   sprig fresh rosemary, if available
4   bay leaves
      Generous sprinkle of hot paprika or cayenne pepper
      Salt and freshly ground black pepper to taste
12–15   pieces imported dry porcini, presoaked in warm water
         at least 1½ hours before use, drained, and soaking
         water reserved
3   fresh basil leaves, coarsely chopped, or ½ teaspoon
         dried basil
1   tablespoon pignoli (pine nuts)
1½   cups robust red wine
1   tablespoon tomato paste diluted in ½ cup warm water
2½   cups tomato sauce (see page 211)
1   cup freshly grated Parmesan cheese

Cook tripe for one hour in 8 quarts of lightly salted, boiling water to which you have also added the juice and rind of one lemon. Drain tripe and let cool at room temperature.

Heat olive oil and butter in large Dutch oven over medium flame. When sizzling, add carrots, celery, onion, and garlic. Sauté approximately 8 minutes. Add parsley, nutmeg, sage, rosemary, bay leaves, paprika or cayenne pepper, and salt and pepper to taste. Sauté 5 minutes, stirring all the while. Add porcini and 3 tablespoons of the soaking water, strained. Sauté 3 minutes. Add basil leaves and pignoli; sauté 3 minutes longer. Add wine and let evaporate approximately 10 minutes. Add diluted tomato paste. Cook a few more minutes, then take off the fire.

At this point, tripe should be cool enough to be sliced into strips 3 inches long by ¼ inch wide. Add sliced tripe and tomato sauce to Dutch oven; mix well. Cook over medium flame for 15 minutes, uncovered.

Preheat oven to 350°F.

Mix ½ cup of the cheese into the tripe and place in oven. Bake, uncovered, 25 minutes. Sprinkle remaining cheese over it and serve.

TORTA PASQUALINA
(Easter Pie)

SERVES 8–10

2½ cups plus 2 tablespoons all-purpose flour
    Sea salt or kosher salt to taste
⅓ cup olive oil
3 bunches fresh Swiss chard
1½ cups freshly grated Parmesan cheese
½ teaspoon dried marjoram
1 pound whole-milk ricotta
1 cup heavy cream
5 tablespoons lightly salted butter
6 eggs
    Freshly ground black pepper to taste

Make a mound of the 2½ cups flour on your work table as if you were making fresh pasta. Make a well in center of mound, and gradually pour in ½ cup lukewarm water, salt, and 1 tablespoon of the olive oil. As if making pasta, work mound of flour until it turns into a soft, well-amalgamated dough ball. Divide ball into 15 equal pieces. Lightly sprinkle some flour over each piece of dough, and cover with a slightly damp cloth.

Clean Swiss chard leaves under cold running water, cut off hard spines. Roll leaves together tightly. Cut leaves into ribbons the size of narrow fettuccine. Cook Swiss chard ribbons, covered in a little bit of water, for 2 to 3 minutes; drain well. Arrange Swiss chard ribbons loosely on a platter and sprinkle salt, 3 tablespoons of the Parmesan cheese, and marjoram over them.

Wrap ricottta in a piece of cheesecloth and squeeze all liquid out of it. Place ricotta in a bowl, add 2 tablespoons flour, salt, and heavy cream. Blend well and set aside, covered.

Begin to roll out the pieces of dough, one at a time, into *very thin* round sheets, or *sfoglia*. Coat a deep 9-inch pie plate lightly with olive oil by using a pastry brush. Drape sheet of dough over pie plate, covering bottom and sides completely, making sure ½ inch of sheet overlaps border of plate. Make another sheet of dough as thin as the first one. Coat first layer of dough in pie plate with olive oil, then lay second sheet over it. Repeat same operation 7 times so you will end with 7 sheets of dough in pie plate. The top of the seventh layer should not be coated with oil but evenly covered with the Swiss chard, which should be moistened with olive oil.

Spoon ricotta mixture over Swiss chard and smooth uniformly. Use your thumb to make six small wells in surface of ricotta. Place a ½ tablespoon of butter in each well, then carefully break an egg into well over each lump of butter. Sprinkle top of eggs with salt, pepper, and rest of Parmesan, Continue making sheets, one at a time, using remaining 8 pieces of dough. Drape one sheet over stuffing and coat with olive oil. Continue to do so until you have used up all 8 sheets of dough, coating each layer but the top one with oil. Make a fluted border all around rim of pie plate, cutting off surplus dough. Melt remaining butter and pour evenly over top of pie.

Preheat over to 350°F.

Pierce pie deeply with a fine skewer, making sure not to hit spots where you have placed eggs. Bake 1 hour. Let pie cool to room temperature. Cut into slices and serve.

FRAGOLONI CON LIMONE, ZUCCHERO E PEPE NERO

(Strawberries with Lemon, Sugar, and Freshly Ground Black Pepper)

SERVES 6–8

2   pints large, ripe, sweet fresh strawberries
    Juice of ½ lemon, strained
1   tablespoon granulated sugar
    Freshly ground black pepper

Wash strawberries well under cold running water, then hull. Marinate berries in lemon juice and sugar in a large bowl. Let stand for 30 minutes. Serve in stemmed glasses, showering each portion of strawberries with two turns of the peppermill.

Monsignor
Stefano Betti's
Typewriter

I met Celestina—she never allowed anyone to call her *signorina* and least of all *signora*—on a perfect spring morning. She was laboriously trudging her way up the incline of Sant'Andrea, overloaded with packages and a heavy cardboard box. I came up alongside her and offered my help. She stopped, gave me a thin-lipped smile, and said, "Thank you, *ragazzino*. How very kind."

I returned the smile. *Ragazzino*, indeed—I was seventeen years old at the time. I took the cardboard box and one of the packages from her. We made our way up to the massive Quattrocento Ligurian *palazzotto*. It stood three stories high on the Piazzetta di Sant'Andrea, facing the *barocco romanesco* church named after the same saint. Here lived Monsignor Stefano Betti and Celestina, his one and only personal servant and cook.

Celestina was a short, delicate woman well into her sixties, extremely neat and dapper, dressed in black from neck to toes. We stopped in front of the heavy, dark green door to the *palazzotto*. Celestina pushed the door open with her little shoulder. That door was never locked, day or night. She made room for me to pass, obviously expecting me to help her all the way into the house.

An impressive marble stairway faced me, but Celestina motioned her head to one side along the ground floor. We entered what must have been a pantry or storage room. I deposited the box and package where she told me. She smiled again, thanked me again, and asked if I would like a glass of water. I accepted because I wanted to prolong my stay in that great house. Celestina fetched the water and commenced to ask me questions, fast, like an interviewer. Who was I, my name, my age, where I lived, who my parents and any other members of my family were. And finally, for some reason, what I intended to do with my life. I answered all her questions just as rapidly. ". . . and I want to become a writer," I concluded.

"Oh . . ." she remarked.

Then, I don't know what prompted me to add, "But I don't have a typewriter to write with. . . ."

Celestina seemed to understand my problem. She went to refill my glass with water and said very seriously, "Come back day after tomorrow at two o'clock, here, ring the bell by the stairs. I'll ask the Monsignore."

Not knowing what to make of it, I drank the second glass of water and assured her that I would be back.

And so I did go back. I rang the bell at the foot of the stairway, and a few minutes later Celestina appeared at the top of it. She motioned me upstairs. On the wall at the top hung a most beautifully carved Sicilian crucifix. Celestina ushered me through a dark wooden door and whispered, "You'll get the typewriter." I wanted to say something, but she silenced me by lifting her finger.

We entered a large room lit only by two enormous windows that opened on to the Piazzetta. The room was almost bare aside from wooden benches along its walls and several naïve and not very good Cinquecento religious paintings. She instructed me to sit and moved silently away through another door. This had to be the supplicants' room, I thought. Everything here smelled of needs and favors and traces of incense.

Soon thereafter, Monsignor Stefano Betti entered the room, followed by Celestina. I stood. She introduced me to a benevolent-looking, rotund man. He had very fat hands and asked me many questions in a very rich voice. Celestina stood, smiling. The two of them exchanged a few words in a dialect I couldn't make out. Finally, the Monsignore took me into a small room where there was an old desk with an aged Remington on it (Olivetti wasn't yet The Word in Italy in those days), a few books on shelves, a chair, and a small, black crucifix on the wall behind the chair.

Monsignor Betti informed me that I could work here every day from 2:00 to 4:00 P.M.—including Sundays after Mass. He seemed to agree totally that one couldn't be a writer without the use of a typewriter. However, the Monsignore also made clear to me his desire to read my work every now and again.

So, happily, I started working in the little room, making sure to type one or two extra pages every so often on noncompromising, religious-leaning subjects for the Monsignore's possible inspection. My real writing was devoted to anti-Fascist protests (it was 1938, the time of Mussolini's Italy) and I did not know the political views, if any, of Monsignor Betti.

Every day on leaving the *palazzotto*, as I reached the bottom of the stairway, the most delicious aromas of food cooking would hit my nose, making me insanely hungry. Later, I discovered that the kitchen was located on the ground floor off the pantry or storage room of my first visit. In any event, Celestina never offered me anything other than water and reminders of the Monsignore's generosity.

This arrangement went on for months. I felt greatly privileged to be able to type my work in a Quattrocento Ligurian *palazzotto*, and all in return for my Christian good deed.

One afternoon in the fall, as I was about to leave as usual at four o'clock, Celestina met me at the bottom of the stairway. She looked annoyed, upset. At first I thought that my tenure as writer in residence was over. Carefully, I asked her if something was the matter. She shook her neat little white head. We stood in silence. Finally she informed me, in the complaining tone of a wife whose husband has called to tell her that he couldn't be home for dinner that evening, that Monsignor Stefano Betti was being detained at the Sanctuary of Sassello until the following morning. Celestina had cooked his meal as usual, ready to be served at five-thirty punctually. What was she to do now?

I inhaled a noseful of the delicious scent filtering from the remote kitchen. I must have shown the look of a beggar on my face, because after a moment she said, "Maybe you would like to share the dinner with me?"

Of course I would.

We dined in an old-fashioned, immaculately clean kitchen. That is when I discovered that both the Monsignore and Celestina were natives of the Veneto region. I could tell from her cooking. Despite the fact that she was Venetian, she still offered only plain water with that wonderful dinner.

And this was the menu for that fortunate evening:

FUNGHI CRUDI E BIANCHETTI
(Raw Mushrooms Stuffed with Whitebait)

LINGUINE E CAPESANTE ALLA VENETA
(Linguine and Bay Scallops Veneto Style)

AGNELLO ALL'AGLIO
(Lamb Cooked with Garlic)

VERZE ALL'AGRO
(Green Cabbage in Vinegar)

ZABAGLIONE DI CREMA E CIOCCOLATO
(Zabaglione of Cream and Chocolate)

Wine: The wine that was not served at that dinner should have been a chilled Pinot Grigio from the Friuli region for the first two courses, and a fine Merlot from the Veneto region to go with the lamb and cabbage course.

FUNGHI CRUDI E BIANCHETTI
(Raw Mushrooms Stuffed with Whitebait)

SERVES 6–8

10   large fresh mushrooms
 1   clove garlic, peeled and cut in half
½   pound fresh whitebait fish
¼   cup olive oil
1½   teaspoons chopped Italian parsley
     Juice of 1 lemon, strained
     Salt and freshly ground black pepper to taste
     Sprinkle of paprika

Very carefully separate mushroom caps from stems. Keep stems for other uses by wrapping in foil and refrigerating. Wash caps under cold water and let dry. Gently rub caps inside and outside with the two half cloves of garlic; see that caps get enough garlic flavor. Set aside.

Wash whitebait thoroughly in cold water. (Do not attempt to remove heads or tails of fish, least of all to clean the insides. It would be absolutely insane.) Let fish drain. Dip whitebait, in a wire strainer, into large pot of boiling water. Keep fish submerged in boiling water no longer than 1 minute; the fish will now turn milk-white. Drain well, being careful not to break fish up. Set aside to cool.

Mix together oil, parsley, and the lemon juice. Add salt and pepper to taste. Pour dressing over fish and see that whitebait is well soaked. Proceed to stuff mushroom caps with it. Sprinkle paprika over each stuffed cap. Serve one cap per person as an appetizer.

LINGUINE E CAPESANTE ALLA VENETA
(Linguine and Bay Scallops Veneto Style)

SERVES 6–8

1½ pounds fresh bay scallops
    Juice of 1 lemon, strained
1½ teaspoons chopped Italian parsley
    Salt and freshly ground black pepper to taste
¾   cup lightly salted butter
1   whole clove garlic, peeled
    Sprinkle of freshly grated nutmeg
2   tablespoons heavy cream
½   cup tomato sauce (see page 211)
1½ pounds imported linguine or long pasta of your choice
    Freshly grated Parmesan cheese (optional)

Wash scallops thoroughly under cold water. Drain well, place in a dish, and pour lemon juice over them. Mix, then add parsley and salt and pepper to taste. Let scallops marinate in this dressing for 30 minutes at room temperature.

Melt butter in a skillet over low flame. Add garlic to butter; let it become golden, then discard. Meanwhile, bring to boil a large pot of salted water.

Drain scallops of all juices, then sauté them in hot butter for approximately 2 minutes. Add nutmeg and heavy cream and sauté an additional minute. Add tomato sauce, mix well, and cook briefly. Set aside and keep warm.

Cook linguine in the salted boiling water approximately 7 minutes. Drain pasta. Put a few spoonfuls of the scallops and sauce in a large bowl. Add linguine a bit at the time and mix well. Repeat operation until the sauce is all used. This step shouldn't take more than half a minute.

Serve with grated Parmesan, if you wish, and freshly ground black pepper.

AGNELLO ALL'AGLIO
(Lamb Cooked with Garlic)

SERVES 8–10

1	tablespoon chopped fresh or 1 teaspoon dried rosemary
3	fresh sage leaves or ½ teaspoon dried sage
	Salt and freshly ground black pepper to taste
1	leg of young lamb (about 10 pounds), boned, most of fat and hard fell (paperlike skin) removed
1½	cups robust red wine
½	cup olive oil
3	bay leaves
12	whole cloves garlic, peeled
½	cup lightly salted butter

Mix together rosemary, sage, and salt and pepper to taste. Make small incisions in leg of lamb and stuff with rosemary mixture. Set lamb in a pan large enough to accommodate it. Pour wine over it, roll meat in it several times, and marinate for 1½ hours. Keep basting lamb with wine during this time.

Preheat oven to 400°F.

Take leg of lamb out of marinade. Set marinade aside. Place lamb in roasting pan, pour olive oil over, and sprinkle with salt and pepper. Add bay leaves. Roll meat in the oil so the whole leg is well coated. Place garlic cloves all around meat.

Place pan in oven and cook lamb 1 hour, making sure to remove cloves of garlic as soon as they become golden brown. Set aside. Add butter to roasting pan; let it melt and blend with olive oil and other juices. Add wine marinade. Cook lamb another 25 minutes. (Overcooked lamb is a criminal act in my view; however, in this particular recipe, as in a lamb stew, the meat should be rather well done.)

Remove lamb from oven. Strain sauce. Cut lamb into 1-inch-thick slices. Place cooked garlic cloves over slices of lamb, spoon hot strained sauce over, and serve.

VERZE ALL'AGRO
(Green Cabbage in Vinegar)

———— · ❀ · ————

SERVES 6

1   medium-large head Savoy cabbage
2   tablespoons olive oil
    Salt and freshly ground black pepper to taste
¼   cup strong red wine vinegar

Take leaves of cabbage apart one by one and wash well under cold water. Steam leaves, covered, in a small amount of water for a very short time, maximum of 2 to 3 minutes. Drain well. Heat oil in sauté pan. Sauté cabbage in it very briefly. Add salt and pepper; it should taste rather peppery. Add vinegar and cook 3 minutes longer. Mix well. Serve immediately.

ZABAGLIONE DI CREMA E CIOCCOLATO
(Zabaglione of Cream and Chocolate)

SERVES 8

10   egg yolks
1½   quarts heavy cream
½   cup confectioners' sugar
     Sprinkle of ground cinnamon
 4   drops vanilla extract
¼   cup grated bittersweet chocolate

Beat egg yolks with cream, sugar, cinnamon, and vanilla until well amalgamated. Pour into deep saucepan and set over medium flame. Beat mixture with a wire whisk until it thickens. Add chocolate. Keep beating until mixture reaches a smooth, creamy zabaglione consistency; do not let it boil. Set aside to cool. Serve at room temperature in stemmed glasses. This is truly a Venetian delight.

Donna Concetta

The city of Messina in Sicily has seen it all—invasions, earth-quakes, plagues, fires, and the implacable devastation from the sky during World War II.

Donna Concetta came to Messina across the Strait from her native Calabria seven years before the start of the war, gave birth to the last of her three sons, Turi, and stayed. She opened a *lavanderia* (laundry shop) on the wide, sunny Via Giuseppe Garibaldi and prospered. Her older sons, Calo and Alfio, helped her with the chores of the shop. Then the war came.

It was just before the Allied landing in Sicily that I first met Donna Concetta. It happened by mere chance, as I walked into her shop, laden with dirty clothes. She looks like a queen of the Greek tragedies, I thought when I first saw her. And later on, when we became good friends, I enjoyed her splendid laughter, her delightful, beautiful personality. But in her grief she was grim, ancient-Greek grim. Her silences were pure Sicilian.

Donna Concetta and her three sons lived in back of the store in one big room, which she had transformed into a neat, ade-quately appointed living quarter, with a small spotless kitchen that still retained the delicious odors of cooking even in those days of bleak hunger. Side by side above her massive, dark-wood matrimonial bed hung an oleograph of the Madonna and a large, sepia-tinted photograph under glass of a fierce-looking but very handsome man—her late husband, Orlando.

Orlando had been a well-known Calabrese mafioso, and one night, when the family was still living in Calabria, a voice called twice, loudly, from outside:

"Donna Concetta! Donna Concetta!"

When she came out onto the little balcony and looked down, she saw Orlando standing in the middle of a circle of eight tough-looking men. She and her husband looked at each other, fear and desperation in her eyes, courage and defiance in his. Orlando smiled and threw her a kiss from the tips of his fingers. Then, the eight knives plunged deep into his body.

"It had to happen that way." She shrugged as she finished her story, the horrid vision still alive in her dark eyes after so many years.

At that time I was barely twenty, one of thousands of desperate and hungry people living in Messina. Destruction and death rained on us from the sky every day at noon, delivered by the awesome American bombers swooping low over the lovely city.

I was stationed in Messina, part of the crew of the Decima MAS—the Tenth PT Boat Squadron. For all intents and purposes, we were destined to die. It had been written in Mussolini's grandiose operetta scenario. That perhaps accounted for our total freedom to do as we pleased when on leave about the city. The citizens of Messina would look upon us, dressed in our flamboyant white jumpsuits with all those metal buttons and the large round blue emblem of a viciously twisted shark on our breasts, as the doomed pitying those about to die.

In any case, my seven months of friendship with Donna Concetta and her children were glorious, a wonderful gift from destiny. We laughed and loved each other and shared whatever bit of food any of us could lay hands on.

Donna Concetta would now and then say, "Ah, what I wouldn't do for a slice of fresh swordfish from Ganzirri up the road. O Dio!" Then she'd look at the cold stove and shake her head.

One day, after a noon bombing, the news spread quickly about the city that a ship at anchor in the harbor had been hit and was capsizing. The ship's cargo was thousands of sacks of flour.

"Flour . . . flour . . . flour," was the general whisper in the streets of Messina. The sacks, floating around the listing, sinking ship, looked like a bed of rocks. One had to rescue the sacks quickly. Once water-logged they, too, would sink, forever.

Calo, Alfio, little Turi, and I were quick enough in securing two sacks of flour and carrying them over to the shop. Donna Concetta's sunny laughter broke loose when she saw us.

"Good God, it is not swordfish, but we'll have lots of pasta and bread, instead."

We did have lots of pasta and bread. Here are some of the pasta dishes she made in the few weeks that followed. The ingredients necessary in Donna Concetta's sauces were obtained by exchanging some of our flour with those people who had an onion or a few tomatoes.

❊ ❊ ❊

LASAGNETTE ALLA PALERMITANA
(Pasta Palermo Style)
Wine: Corvo Red di Salaparuta

TORCELLI CON CECI
(Pasta Twists with Chick-peas)
Wine: Corvo White di Salaparuta

FARFALLE DI TAORMINA
(Bowties or Butterfly Pasta Taormina Style)
Wine: Rapilatà Red

TAGLIARINI CON SARDINE
(Pasta with Sardines)
Wine: White wine from Etna

QUADRETTINI MESSINESI
(Little Squares of Pasta Messina Style)
Wine: Corvo White di Salaparuta

LASAGNETTE ALLA PALERMITANA
(Pasta Palermo Style)

SERVES 6–8

Fresh lasagnette made with 3 cups flour, 4 eggs, ¼ cup
    olive oil, and a sprinkle of salt (see page 228) or
    1½ pounds imported dried lasagnette
2   medium eggplants
¾   cup olive oil
3   cloves garlic, peeled
    Salt and freshly ground black pepper to taste
¼   teaspoon crushed red pepper
1   small onion, peeled and thinly sliced
2¼ teaspoons chopped Italian parsley
4   anchovy fillets, drained
    Sprinkle of dried oregano
3   fresh basil leaves, finely chopped, or ¼ teaspoon dried
    basil
3   cans (20 ounces each) imported Italian peeled toma-
    toes, drained
12 slices (each ⅛ inch thick) pancetta or bacon, cut
    coarsely into pieces
1   tablespoon vegetable oil
½   cup freshly grated pecorino cheese

After you have made lasagnette, preheat oven to 375°F.

Cut eggplants into cubes the size of a bouillion cube, mix with
¼ cup of the olive oil, and place in baking pan. Add garlic, salt,
pepper, and crushed red pepper. Mix well. Bake 20 minutes.

Purée eggplant and garlic in food processor. Set aside in pan
juice while you begin to make your sauce.

Heat remaining ½ cup olive oil in saucepan. Add sliced onion
and sauté until translucent. Add parsley and anchovies and sauté
4 minutes. Add oregano, basil, and peeled tomatoes. Cook 30
minutes, uncovered. Check your seasoning balance; don't forget
that you have crushed red pepper in eggplant.

Process tomato sauce through food mill; the consistency should be that of thick tomato soup. Set sauce over low flame. Add puréed eggplant and cook 20 minutes. Keep hot.

Fry pancetta or bacon in vegetable oil approximately 6 minutes. Drain; add pancetta or bacon to sauce. Blend well.

Bring to boil a large pot of salted water. Cook lasagnette 3 minutes if using fresh, 7 minutes if dried. Drain. Add lasagnette to sauce and mix well. Serve with grated pecorino cheese.

TORCELLI CON CECI

(Pasta Twists with Chick-peas)

SERVES 6–8

    Fresh pasta (see page 223) or 1½ pounds short fusilli
4 cups olive oil
¼ pound prosciutto fat (from your pork store or grocer)
1 small onion, peeled and thinly sliced
1 stalk celery, washed and scraped, very finely chopped
2½ cups tomato sauce (see page 211)
    Crushed red pepper to taste
2 cans (20 ounces each) chick-peas, drained
¼ cup freshly grated caciocavallo or fresh pecorino
    cheese

If using fresh pasta, roll out to double the thickness of lasagnette (see page 228). Cut sheets into strips, 1½ inch long by ½ inch wide, then twist each strip twice. Sprinkle with flour, cover with a towel, and set aside.

Heat olive oil in saucepan. Add prosciutto fat and sauté 10 minutes. Add sliced onion and celery; sauté until onion is golden brown. Add tomato sauce and crushed red pepper to taste. Cook, uncovered, 15 minutes. Add chick-peas and simmer 6 to 8 minutes longer.

Cook pasta in salted boiling water the usual way: 2 to 3 minutes for fresh, 8 minutes for dried. Drain. Add pasta to sauce. Turn onto a serving platter and serve with either of the two cheeses.

FARFALLE DI TAORMINA
(Bowties or Butterfly Pasta Taormina Style)

SERVES 6–8

Fresh pasta (see page 223) or 1½ pounds imported
   dried butterfly-shaped pasta
1 large head cauliflower, leaves and hard center removed
½ cup olive oil
1 teaspoon chopped garlic
   Sprinkle of crushed red pepper
   Salt and freshly ground black pepper to taste
1 tablespoon chopped Italian parsley
3 fresh basil leaves or ¼ teaspoon dried basil
½ pound caciocavallo or fresh pecorino, diced the size
   of salad croutons
2 tablespoons lightly salted butter
¼ cup freshly grated Parmesan cheese

If using fresh pasta, roll out as thin as possible. Cut sheets into ribbons 2 inches long by 1½ inches wide, using serrated wheel cutter. Pinch each piece of pasta in the middle in order to shape into a bowtie or butterfly. Sprinkle flour over them and cover with a towel.

Cook head of cauliflower in salted boiling water 10 minutes. Drain and run cold water over cauliflower, then cut into small florets.

Preheat oven to 375°F.

In a baking pan, heat olive oil; add garlic, crushed red pepper, and salt and black pepper to taste. Add cauliflower florets and mix well. Add parsley, basil, and diced cheese. Bake 15 minutes.

Cook pasta in salted boiling water the usual way: 3 minutes for fresh, 9 minutes for dried. Drain. Melt butter in sauté pan. Add pasta and sauté 30 seconds. Add cauliflower sauce and toss pasta. Serve with Parmesan cheese.

TAGLIARINI CON SARDINE
(Pasta with Sardines)

SERVES 6–8

Fresh pasta (see page 223) or 1½ pounds imported
dried tagliarini or spaghettini
¼ cup fennel seeds
¾ cup olive oil
1 onion, peeled and very thinly sliced
2 tablespoons sultana raisins
2 tablespoons pignoli (pine nuts)
Freshly ground black pepper to taste
1 cup tomato sauce (see page 211)
1 pound fresh or frozen sardines; if frozen, defrosted at
room temperature, heads and tails cut off
3 anchovy fillets, drained
1 packet saffron dissolved in 3 tablespoons warm water

If using fresh pasta, roll out as thin as possible. Cut sheets into tagliarini. Sprinkle with flour and cover with towel.

Cook fennel seeds in salted boiling water 15 to 20 minutes. Drain. Mash fennel seeds and set aside.

Heat ½ cup of the olive oil in a saucepan. Add onion. When golden, add raisins, pignoli, and pepper. Sauté 6 minutes. Add mashed fennel seeds and sauté 2 minutes. Add tomato sauce and cook, uncovered, 5 minutes. Keep warm.

Clean out insides of sardines and wash fish well under cold running water. Let fish drain. Heat remaining ¼ cup olive oil in large sauté pan. Add anchovy fillets and sauté 2 minutes. Place sardines in pan, sauté quickly on both sides. Add dissolved saffron. Cover pan and cook 5 minutes.

Meanwhile, cook pasta in salted boiling water the usual way: 3 minutes for fresh, 6 to 7 minutes for dried. Drain. Remove half the tomato sauce from saucepan. Sauté pasta quickly in sauce, then turn onto serving platter. Arrange sardines and juice from sauté pan over the pasta. Spoon remaining tomato sauce over pasta and sardines and serve. This pasta is also excellent served at room temperature.

QUADRETTINI MESSINESI
(Little Squares of Pasta Messina Style)

SERVES 6–8

Fresh pasta (see page 223) or 1½ pounds imported dried, wide egg tagliatelle

8 tablespoons olive oil
3 whole cloves garlic, peeled
4 ounces imported dried porcini, presoaked in lukewarm water at least 1½ hours in advance, drained, and soaking water reserved. Chop porcini coarsely
1 tablespoon chopped Italian parsley
¼ teaspoon dried marjoram
   Freshly ground black pepper to taste
1 pound Italian hot pork sausages, meat removed from casing
2 tablespoons all-purpose flour
2 eggs
   Salt to taste
½ cup freshly grated pecorino cheese
3 tablespoons lightly salted butter

If using fresh pasta, roll out as thin as possible. Cut sheets into squares 1 inch by 1 inch. Sprinkle flour over them and cover with a towel. If using dried tagliatelle, break up into approximate squares.

Heat 5 tablespoons of the olive oil in a saucepan. Add garlic and cook until golden, then discard. Add porcini and cook 4 minutes. Add a few tablespoons of soaking water, strained. Add parsley, marjoram, and pepper to taste. Stir, taste, then cook 3 more minutes. Set aside.

Make little balls of the sausage meat. Roll balls lightly in flour. Beat eggs, with salt and ¼ cup of the pecorino cheese; blend well. Heat remaining 3 tablespoons oil in skillet. Dip sausage balls in egg batter, coating very well. Fry until golden brown on all sides. Scoop balls out of hot oil and add to porcini. Scramble remaining batter in hot oil in which you fried sausage balls. Break up scrambled egg batter into smaller pieces and add, along with oil, to porcini and sausage balls. Set pan over low flame and stir contents well. Cook, uncovered, 3 minutes. Keep hot.

Cook pasta in salted boiling water the usual way: 2½ minutes for fresh, 6 to 7 minutes for dried. You should add a tablespoon of vegetable oil to boiling water to prevent fresh quadrettini from sticking together. Drain.

Melt butter in sauté pan and toss quadrettini in it. Turn pasta onto a serving platter, spoon sauce over, and shower with remaining ¼ cup of pecorino cheese. Toss well and serve immediately.

7

Villa Sorriso

On the fourth of July, 1942, I was twenty-one years old. On that morning I got a ride on an army truck to the tiny strip of beach five kilometers from Messina. I wanted the sun and to be alone.

Perilously reclining to portside, an old-fashioned destroyer hit a week earlier by RAF bombers stood like a dying elephant in the little bay, five hundred meters offshore. World War II raged in Sicily still. It was one of those surplus double-smokestack warships the United States had given to the Royal Italian Navy after World War I for its valiant cooperation in that conflict. Now we were enemies.

The sea, calm, of the most delicate blue, was hardly audible. The sun was hot, and a slow sirocco blew like a bad omen from the shore of not-so-distant Africa. I lay there in my swimming trunks, elbows sunk into the sand, my eyes fastened on the mortally wounded, abandoned ship. Certainly not an encouraging sight for a young man on his twenty-first birthday. I finally switched off the view in front of me and let my mind wander to less depressing memories.

Then, a voice shouted near me, "King, come back here!" I turned to face a big, tawny Great Dane bounding toward me, barking. I remained still—afraid. Next I saw the source of the voice—a short, dark-haired woman in a bathing suit. The monstrous dog came to a stop a few inches from the neat pile of my clothes next to me, busy sniffing. I gave him an ingratiating smile just to make sure. The Great Dane looked down at me with friendly, liquid eyes. So far, so good, then.

The dark-haired woman approached, saying with concern, "I am sorry. I hope he did not scare you." I looked up at her. She looked thirtyish, rather pretty, and well proportioned. She smiled. She looked prettier.

"Here, King," she ordered the dog, who paid her no mind at all but started running away from us. "King!" she shouted again. "He is young and out of control," she apologized. I nodded, concurring. "Glorious day," she said and, pointing at the crippled ship, went on, "If it wasn't for that, you'd think we were not at war." Her Italian had the particular, precise diction of the well-educated Sicilian. I nodded again, admiring her tan body. She glanced at the pile of my clothes, recognized the uniform. "MAS," she whispered, shaking her head. "Poor child," she added feelingly. Her calling me a child brought a lump to my throat.

"This is not a private beach, is it?" I asked, trying to cover up my emotion.

"What if it was"—she shrugged—"you are certainly welcome to it." I got up and introduced myself.

"Titina Pellegrini," she said, and shook my hand. "What are you doing here alone?"

"Today is my birthday," I felt compelled to tell her.

"Ah, *buon compleanno*," she said, smiling. "Where are you from?"

"Up north."

"Yes, your eyes are blue," she stated matter-of-factly. We both sat on the sand. We watched the dog galloping merrily along the beach.

"Big dog—must eat as much as a man," I remarked, thinking the matter over seriously.

She laughed. "Or as a woman." Now she looked very pretty. "No friends to celebrate your birthday with?" she asked.

"I like to be alone."

"How old are you today?"

"Twenty-one."

"Oh, my God!" She pointed at the pile of my uniform almost with anger, obviously wanting to say more.

"Are you from around here?" I changed the subject.

"I live up there." She turned around and pointed at the hills on the other side of the road that ran above the beach. The dog finally came back and stretched at her feet.

"Why did you name the dog King? Isn't that an English name? Nowadays . . . I would think . . ." I trailed off.

"Yes, it means Rex in English. In Sicily we do what we want— you know?" she replied defiantly. "Come on up to the house. You deserve a birthday glass of wine and some food. You are too young to be alone." She got to her feet. So did the dog and I. "I can't stand looking at that," she went on, pointing at the re- clining ship again. I picked up my uniform to put it on. She stopped me.

"Carry it. It's just across the road."

The sign over the old iron gate said VILLA SORRISO. Ivy, bougain- villea, morning glories, sunflowers, and other vegetation spilled over the old walls and flourished everywhere along the narrow path to the villa. The war felt years away, or as if it never had happened. Titina walked in front, King trotting behind her. I walked behind the dog in my swimming trunks, carrying the bundle of clothes under one arm.

The house, perched on a knoll on the side of a hill, and made of the local stone, was very impressive, not unlike a modest Saracen castle, centuries old. It was spacious and cool, crowded with ancient, dark pieces of furniture, and shadowy. It made a visitor feel welcome, yet on the alert. It was very Sicilian.

Two elderly women came out of a room at the same time, both smiling. They looked gentle, yet overly proud, the way the gentry of this land look. Titina made the introductions—"Aunt Ignazia and Aunt Corrada." The three women looked alike, the elderly two dressed to the neck in black. I felt conspicuous in my bathing trunks and bare feet. They guided me into another room and invited me to sit on a large chair of Spanish origin. The whole history of the island seemed to be told by the pieces of furniture and artifacts in the room. Not knowing what to do with my bundled-up uniform and shoes, I placed them on the floor next to the chair. Titina, on the other hand, made no effort to get dressed, and the old aunts paid no mind to that. King had dis- appeared somewhere.

One of the aunts left the room and came back shortly carrying a rococo silver tray holding four glasses and a bottle of Faro wine.

"It's his birthday today. We must wish him well," announced Titina. Once again I realized how much I loved that island and its people. Aunt Ignazia, who seemed to be the elder, began to ask me many questions most tactfully. With brio, Aunt Corrada kept on refilling the glasses with that delicious Faro. In the course of our conversation, I learned that the aunts were spinsters and Titina on the way to becoming one. She was a teacher of mathematics at one of Messina's high schools, and bicycled all the way to the city and back every day. Titina made bitter comments on the war, the Fascist and German rulers, and cursed the Allies and their wanton bombing. Aunt Corrada interrupted her and asked me if I wanted to get dressed before I caught cold. I agreed promptly, relieved. Titina remarked that that uniform gave her goose pimples, and openly called Mussolini "the megalo-maniacal operetta impresario with macabre designs to kill our children." The two old ladies reproached her in unison, "Titina!" She shrugged.

I picked up my uniform and shoes, looking at the three women questioningly. They were silent. I slipped into the white jump-suit that was my uniform, and remained barefooted because I couldn't bring myself to put on socks and shoes in front of them.

Titina looked at the flamboyant uniform and commented angrily, "Uniforms, uniforms, stupid uniforms." She looked at me and said, sadly, "Don't wait—run away—don't let them kill you, child!" Her words had the sound of Greek tragedy. She then left the room. I began to perceive that my birthday was turning into something that I hadn't expected.

Titina returned wearing a housecoat and carrying a book, which she handed to me. "*Buon compleanno*," she said. It was a paperback edition published by Mondadori, an Italian translation of *David Copperfield*. The aunts looked relieved, and so did I. More wine was poured. I was asked to stay for a late lunch, which evidently they had prepared for themselves. I put up less than a half-hearted resistance in trying to impress them that I wasn't hungry, and did not intend to be that much trouble. Those three wonderful women dismissed my feeble excuses with a shrug of their shoulders.

"It's your birthday. You must eat," said Titina with finality.

"We very seldom have men to share our meals with," Aunt Corrada giggled.

"There is plenty of food and another mouth is blessed," declared Aunt Ignazia judiciously. I gave in gladly to my good fortune of the day.

We moved to the back of the house and into the open, under a grape arbor that, at this time of day, was almost in complete shadow. A rustic outdoor table was quickly set up and more cold Faro poured. While the women were busy elsewhere, I took the opportunity to put on my socks and shoes.

It felt festive, peaceful, in this hospitable home. If what they served that day at lunch reflected their daily diet, they certainly had no worries about war rations. I still vividly recall the meal, and later, years later, through memory and experiment, was able to reconstruct the recipes and give them names.

Later, toward early evening, when I announced that I had to return to the naval base in Messina, Titina offered to take me back on her bicycle. I tried to assure her that I could hitchhike a ride on some army truck easily, as I had done in the morning. She dismissed that idea quickly, and went to fetch her bike. It was a shiny Legnano man's bike, with white painted fenders as prescribed by the curfew law. She rode seated on the crossbar. I pedaled all the way to Messina.

We laughed and even sang on our way to the city. That day the war seemed to have taken a holiday in celebration of my birthday. Before she left for home, Titina made me renew my promise to return to Villa Sorriso on the following Sunday to have dinner with her and her aunts—a promise I promptly kept.

This turned out to be a meal I shall never forget, because on the following day the PT boat or MAS, of which I was part of the crew, was sunk by a British submarine twenty-five miles southwest of Taormina. After five hours of floating at sea as best we could, some of us survivors were picked up by an Italian navy vessel and brought ashore to a hospital in Calabria.

I never saw Titina and her aunts again, or the copy of *David Copperfield*.

❈ ❈ ❈

DINNER ONE

FICHI RIPIENI CON FORMAGGIO INCANESTRATO
(Figs Stuffed with Soft Goat Cheese)

POLLASTRINA E MELANZANE
(Young Pullet with Eggplants)

INSALATA VILLA SORRISO
(Villa Sorriso Salad)

Wine: Since the white Faro wine from Messina may prove impossible to find at your wine merchant's, use white Corvo di Salaparuta and serve cold throughout the whole meal.

FICHI RIPIENI CON FORMAGGIO INCANESTRATO
(Figs Stuffed with Soft Goat Cheese)

Formaggio incanestrato—literally "basketed"—is a soft goat cheese very popular in Sicily. In consistency and taste it is very similar to the French chèvres. It is pressed into wicker baskets, hence the name.

SERVES 6

1 pound soft goat cheese of your choice
2 tablespoons virgin olive oil
  Freshly ground black pepper to taste
2 dozen fresh, very ripe green figs, split open

Combine cheese and oil in a mixing bowl, and shower generously with black pepper. Mash and blend well together. Place ½ tablespoon or less of the mixture on half of each fig. Cover with other half fig. Refrigerate 10 minutes before serving.

POLLASTRINA E MELANZANE
(Young Pullet with Eggplants)

SERVES 6

2   small young broilers (about 4 pounds total)
2   medium eggplants
2   tablespoons sea salt or kosher salt
1   cup olive oil
1   whole clove garlic, peeled and crushed
    Salt and freshly ground black pepper to taste
1   cup dry white wine
1   pound fresh, ripe tomatoes
1   pound pancetta or bacon, finely chopped
    Chicken consommé (see page 207), if necessary
1½   teaspoons finely chopped Italian parsley

Cut each chicken into 4 pieces. Set aside. Wash eggplants and dice into small cubes without peeling. Sprinkle with sea salt or kosher salt and place in a colander for 1 hour to drain off bitter moisture. Dry chicken well.

Heat ⅓ cup of oil in a casserole. Sauté garlic until brown, then discard. Place pieces of chicken in hot oil. Fry evenly until golden brown. Sprinkle with salt and black pepper to taste. Drain off most of the oil, then add wine and cook, uncovered, over a medium flame until wine evaporates—about 10 minutes.

Chop tomatoes coarsely and add to casserole. Add pancetta or bacon. Taste for seasoning, then cook 20 minutes, uncovered, moistening with 1 to 2 tablespoons chicken consommé, if necessary. Lower flame. Let simmer.

Heat remaining ⅔ cup oil in another pan. Fry eggplant cubes over high flame about 10 minutes, tossing. Shower with black pepper and parsley. Drain off most of oil. Gently stir eggplant into casserole, mixing with chicken pieces. Cook an additional 5 minutes. Serve very hot.

INSALATA VILLA SORRISO
(Villa Sorriso Salad)

SERVES 6

6 large, firm, ripe tomatoes, quartered
1 pound fresh mushrooms, washed, sliced thickly through
    caps and stems
½ pound Gaeta olives, pitted
1 tablespoon medium capers, drained
3 tablespoons shelled fresh peas, left raw
5 anchovy fillets, drained and finely chopped
½ teaspoon chopped garlic
2 fresh mint leaves, coarsely chopped
½ cup virgin olive oil
4 tablespoons balsamic vinegar
    Salt and freshly ground black pepper to taste

Combine all the ingredients except oil, vinegar, salt, and pepper in a large salad bowl. Refrigerate while you prepare dressing.

Blend oil, vinegar, salt, and pepper. Mix well. Spoon dressing over salad, 1 spoonful at a time, tossing well and gently until you have used up all the dressing. Serve.

❀ ❀ ❀

DINNER TWO

MINESTRA DI PISELLI FRESCHI E CARCIOFI
(Fresh Pea and Artichoke Soup)

PESCESPADA DI GANZIRRI
(Swordfish Ganzirri Style)

CAPONATA
(Eggplant Niçoise)

Wine: Val di Lupo from Etna is excellent with fish. But since you won't be able to buy it at your wine merchant's, serve Corvo di Salaparuta red. Chill slightly before serving.

MINESTRA DI PISELLI FRESCHI E CARCIOFI
(Fresh Pea and Artichoke Soup)

SERVES 6

3 fresh artichokes, preferably small
    Juice of 1 lemon, strained
¼ cup olive oil
1 whole clove garlic, peeled and crushed
1½ teaspoons finely chopped Italian parsley
    Freshly ground black pepper to taste
7½ cups chicken consommé (see page 207)
    Salt (optional)
1 pound fresh peas, shelled
    Freshly grated Parmesan or pecorino cheese

Take off tough leaves from artichokes, trim and wash, then drain well. Quarter artichokes; douse with lemon juice. Heat oil in a soup pot. Sauté garlic until brown, then discard. Add artichokes and parsley to pot. Sauté 5 minutes. Add black pepper and consommé. Taste for salt. Cover pot and cook 25 minutes over medium flame, adding peas during the last 5 minutes.

Serve with plenty of Parmesan or pecorino cheese, grated at the moment over each serving.

PESCESPADA DI GANZIRRI
(Swordfish Ganzirri Style)

Ganzirri is a little fishing town on the extreme northeast point of the island of Sicily on the Strait of Messina, and it is well known for the swordfish caught in its waters.

SERVES 6

1 pound fresh swordfish, skinned and cut into small pieces, plus 6 thin slices swordfish, also skinned
1 small onion, peeled and finely chopped
1 cup olive oil
2½ tablespoons brandy
Salt
2½ tablespoons unflavored bread crumbs
6 thin slices mozzarella cheese
4–5 fresh basil leaves, finely chopped, or ½ teaspoon dried basil
Sprinkle of dried thyme
Crushed black pepper to taste
1–2 lemons, cut into wedges

Wash and dry small pieces of swordfish. Mix with onion. Heat oil in a pan, then sauté fish and onion until onion begins to brown.

Add brandy and a sprinkle of salt. Let brandy evaporate, 2 to 3 minutes approximately. Remove pan from fire. Stir in bread crumbs.

Wash and dry thin slices of swordfish. Spread cooked fish mixture evenly over each slice. Top with a slice of mozzarella. Sprinkle with herbs and pepper. Roll up slices and fasten with round, wooden toothpicks. Grill swordfish rolls about 10 minutes, basting with the fish drippings. Grill flame must not be too high.

Serve immediately, garnished with lemon wedges.

CAPONATA
(Eggplant Niçoise)

———— · ❀ · ————

SERVES 6

2   medium eggplants
     Sea salt or kosher salt
1   cup olive oil
1   small bunch celery
1   red onion, peeled and sliced
1   can (4 ounces) tomato paste
3   tablespoons warm water
     Crushed black pepper
2   teaspoons granulated sugar
1½ cups very good red wine vinegar (essential to recipe)
1½ tablespoons capers, drained
4   ounces imported green olives

Wash eggplants and dice without peeling. Sprinkle with sea salt or kosher salt and place in a colander for about 1 hour to drain off bitter moisture.

Heat ½ cup of the olive oil and fry eggplants until brown on all sides. Drain on paper toweling, keeping oil in skillet.

Wash celery very well under cold water. Trim and discard

tough stalks. Cut tender stalks into short sticks. Fry celery sticks until light brown in oil you used for eggplant. Drain on paper toweling.

Heat remaining ½ cup olive oil in a sauté pan. Sauté onion until translucent. Dilute tomato paste in the warm water. Combine with onion. Season with salt and crushed pepper to taste. Cook about 15 minutes over medium flame. Stir in the sugar, vinegar, capers, olives, eggplant, and celery. Shower with more crushed pepper to taste. Simmer, uncovered, about 10 minutes. Let cool. Serve at room temperature.

8

Porto Ercole

In 1965 my wife, Jane, and I moved to Porto Ercole on the Argentario peninsula in Italy, to stay. We left New York actually to start anew. I was, on the advice and prompting of my dear friend and once my literary agent, René de C., to build a deluxe, very exclusive "compound" to feed and entertain the super-elegant set.

At the time, only one hotel existed in Porto Ercole, the Pellicano, with nine splendid rooms, each different from the other; Charlie Chaplin, Sophia Loren, royalty, millionaires, and the Italian aristocracy were its patrons.

Principe Alessandro (Tinti) Borghese graciously offered me a handsome octagonal thirteenth-century Moorish lookout tower to be used as the main building of the "compound." This came about when he learned that I had served under his uncle Principe Valerio Borghese, commander of the Decima MAS during the war. What I had to provide to make the superb structure functional was to cut a road into the wilderness of the promontory on which it stood, for there was no other way to reach it, and bring in water supplies, electricity, telephone lines, and gas pipes. In sum, a barrel of money was needed. However, the project still looked plausible and possible. At that time, Porto Ercole was still thought of as the most desirable and most accessible spot on the Tyrrhenian seacoast along with the island of Sardinia. In reality, Porto Ercole is a lot easier to reach than the island, because it lies between Rome and Florence—two hours' drive from either city to Grosseto, then a short ten-minute ride to the promontory itself.

The Englishman and his American wife who ran the Pellicano hotel were happy to be relieved of the task of feeding and entertaining the famous, moneyed, titled, and demanding crowd. René felt dead sure that no one but I could provide what those wonderfully spoiled people wanted.

The talks, discussions, and planning began while sipping Negronis in the salon of the Pellicano, but, alas, every time I would ask when we were to start the work on cutting the road to the Moorish tower someone would interject merrily, "The road, okay, but tell me, Alfredo, what will you serve in the late afternoons when one comes in from the sea? That's important to know."

"Superbly fresh *frutti di mare* (shellfish) to dip in hot mustard, saffron, and sweet cream sauce. What else!" someone would answer for me.

"And ice-cold Russian vodka or champagne," another would add.

"No, no. Who wants *frutti di mare* after a morning at sea? Pizza! . . . the thinnest little *pizzette*, with fresh black olives, Stracchino or Gorgonzola on it. And the best Frascati," cut in another, with determination.

"For me, the best Scotch salmon and fresh-pressed caviar are the only sensible late-afternoon snacks. *Non c'è altro!*" a famous beautiful lady would put in.

"Ladies, gentlemen, please . . ." I'd try to stop them and bring them back to our discussion of the road.

"For supper, excellent pasta, sauced with fresh fish. Grilled carré of wild boar and extravagant salads," someone else would override my plea without the slightest qualm.

"Fish. Fish. Broiled, grilled, poached, raw. Fish is the food."

"Music and entertainment. Joy and fun. To bring life to this desert at night. That's what's needed," the heiress to a famous salami fortune would state, dead seriously.

They sounded as desperate as the last group of aristocrats isolated in a castle and besieged from outside by an angry rabble.

"Ladies, gentlemen. Please, let's return to the road. First we must solve all our technical problems." My eyes would meet those of the handsome, superbly mannered lady from Connecticut now residing at Porto Ercole, via marriage, as Contessa Gerini. She'd smile at me and shrug imperceptibly.

"The road is no problem. Bulldozers, money, and workers would cut that blessed road. The road is not the end of the world. *Mio Dio!*" someone would invariably say, then ask for another Negroni. *But . . .* I was getting nowhere.

So, René, Jane, Contessa Gerini, and I decided that I should present them with a series of the most tantalizing menus before I submitted my construction plans, costs, and all the other various building items.

In the following pages I will share with you the menus for the most chic, elegant place that was never built in Porto Ercole on the Argentario. Along with those menus I will also share with you the menus of the dinner at Principe Alessandro Borghese's and the luncheon at Contessa Gerini's magnificent villa perched on the rocky cliff to which shore Agrippina was forcibly ordered to swim by her devoted son, the Emperor Nero—while he fiddled, sitting on the bow of his imperial trireme. In any event, the indomitable mommy Agrippina made it safely to shore.

❀ ❀ ❀

LATE-AFTERNOON MENUS

These recipes are also suitable for dinners or luncheons, and some, as you will see, are perfect for cocktail parties. (Is anyone giving cocktail parties any more?)

BISTECCA RUSTICA
(Shell Steak Rustic Style)

ROLLATINE DI MELANZANE FRITTE
CON PROSCIUTTO
(Fried Eggplant Rolls with Prosciutto)

TRAMEZZINI ALLA MOSCOVITA
(Muscovite Toasts)

INSALATA DELL'ARGENTARIO
(Argentario Salad)

PATATE RIPIENE
(Stuffed Potatoes)

PIZZETTE CAPRICCIOSE
(Small Pizzas "to Please Your Whim")

UOVA A CAVALLO
(Eggs on Horseback)

Wines:

WHITE: Orvieto Secco, Frascati, Sauvignon Blanc, Sancerre, Saran Nature

RED: Sfursat from Valtellina, Nebbiolo, Zinfandel, Merlot

BISTECCA RUSTICA
(Shell Steak Rustic Style)

SERVES 6

6   tender, lean shell steaks, each ½ inch thick, all fat removed
¼   cup good walnut oil
    Coarsely crushed black peppercorns
2   large, plump red or yellow sweet peppers
¼   cup olive oil
4   anchovy fillets, drained
2   whole cloves garlic, peeled and thinly sliced
3   fresh sage leaves, chopped, or sprinkle of dried sage
    Sprinkle of freshly grated nutmeg
    Sprinkle of hot dry mustard

Pound each steak between two pieces of aluminum foil down to half their thickness. Marinate for 2 hours in walnut oil and coarsely crushed black peppercorns. Make sure to marinate steaks on both sides.

Core peppers, discard seeds, and cut into matchstick-size pieces. Set aside.

Heat oil in skillet. Add anchovies and garlic and sauté over low flame until anchovies have melted. Do not let garlic burn. Add sage, nutmeg, and mustard. Stir. Add peppers and cook slowly, stirring often—about 10 minutes. Keep hot.

Grill steaks over charcoal to very rare, or to your preference. Add walnut oil marinade to peppers. Stir, then taste for seasoning. Spread pepper sticks over each steak and serve.

ROLLATINE DI MELANZANE FRITTE CON PROSCIUTTO
(Fried Eggplant Rolls with Prosciutto)

SERVES 6

3 medium eggplants
Sea salt or kosher salt
Juice of 1 lemon, strained
½ cup all-purpose flour
½ cup olive oil
1 whole clove garlic, peeled
1 dry red chili pepper, cut in half
¾ pound thinly sliced prosciutto, Black Forest ham, or Virginia ham
3 tablespoons lightly salted butter

Slice eggplant into ⅛-inch slices, leaving skin on. Sprinkle each side of each slice with sea salt or kosher salt and a few drops of lemon juice. Cover with waxed paper, then with a heavy chopping board. Let stand 1½ to 2 hours, to let out bitter moisture from eggplant.

Carefully dust eggplant slices with flour. Heat oil in frying pan, then add garlic and the two chili pepper halves. When garlic becomes golden brown, discard, along with chili pepper. Fry eggplant slices, in batches, on both sides until golden. Remove from oil, place on paper toweling. Spread a slice of prosciutto (or ham) over each slice of eggplant. Roll loosely and secure with a wooden toothpick.

Melt butter and coat with it a shallow fireproof serving plate. Arrange eggplant rolls in plate. Set over low flame for 2 to 3 minutes. Serve hot.

TRAMEZZINI ALLA MOSCOVITA

(Muscovite Toasts)

SERVES 6

¼   cup virgin olive oil
12   thin slices fresh white bread, crusts trimmed off (you can also use sliced pumpernickel bread or Russian-style sliced black bread)
     Freshly ground green peppercorns to taste
1   pound double-ground lean sirloin of beef
9   ounces fresh, lightly salted caviar, such as golden white-fish caviar from the Great Lakes

Heat oil in skillet. Sauté slices of bread lightly on both sides. Shower each side with green pepper. Cut each slice of bread into two triangles. Spread ground sirloin of beef over each triangle. Add touch of green pepper. Spread caviar over meat.

Serve with ice-cold (but un-iced) vodka.

INSALATA DELL'ARGENTARIO
(Argentario Salad)

SERVES 6

2   oranges, preferably Seville
2   large crunchy apples
2   medium Belgian endives
1¼   pounds shrimp (size 25 to 30). Your fish merchant will
     know what to give you.
¼   cup Cognac
¼   cup Marsala or port wine
2   cups mayonnaise (see page 218)

Squeeze and strain juice of 1 orange. Peel the other orange and slice thin. Set aside in refrigerator. Peel and core apples; cut into julienne sticks. Set aside in refrigerator. Cut endives lengthwise into ribbons, then wash well under cold water and drain well.

Boil shrimp in 4 quarts of lightly salted water 2 to 3 minutes. Drain. Run cold water over shrimp. Shell shrimp, then devein. Refrigerate 10 minutes.

In a large salad bowl, combine Cognac, Marsala or port, and orange juice. Mix well, then add shrimp. Marinate 1 hour in refrigerator. Fold mayonnaise and apple sticks into salad bowl. Blend well with your hands.

Place an equal amount of endive ribbons on each serving plate. Spoon shrimp salad over endive and decorate with slices of Seville orange. Serve immediately.

PATATE RIPIENE
(Stuffed Potatoes)

SERVES 6

12 medium potatoes, scrubbed well under cold running water
1 live lobster (1¼ pounds)
1 packet saffron diluted in 3 tablespoons Cognac
2 egg yolks
¼ cup heavy cream
¼ cup grated pecorino cheese
1 teaspoon very finely chopped fresh basil leaves or ¼ teaspoon dried basil
  Salt and freshly ground black pepper to taste
8 tablespoons lightly salted butter
¼ pound Fontina cheese, cut into 12 strips
¼ cup dry sherry

Boil potatoes in their skins in salted water for 25 minutes, making sure not to puncture or break skins. Drain. Make an incision in the skin of each potato and scoop out as much as possible of the insides without damaging skins. Mash inside of potatoes coarsely while hot. Leave to cool to room temperature, as well as the skins.

Boil the lobster 4 to 5 minutes. Take meat out of shell and let cool; you should have about ½ pound of meat. Chop lobster meat coarsely. Marinate in saffron and Cognac. Set aside.

Beat together egg yolks, cream, grated pecorino, basil, salt and pepper, and 2 tablespoons of the butter, melted. Blend well. Taste for seasoning. Mix in potatoes and lobster meat, including whatever is left of marinade. Amalgamate thoroughly. Proceed to stuff potato skins with mixture, sealing original incisions with strips of Fontina cheese.

In a casserole large enough to contain the 12 potatoes, melt remaining butter over medium flame. Add sherry. Arrange potatoes in casserole, incision sides up. Let sherry evaporate, approximately 10 minutes. Baste stuffed potatoes with sauce. Cook, uncovered, 15 minutes longer, then place under grill 1½ minutes. Spoon hot sauce over each serving and serve immediately.

PIZZETTE CAPRICCIOSE
(Small Pizzas "to Please Your Whim")

MAKES 10 PIZZAS

Pizza Dough:
1   package active dry yeast
1   teaspoon salt
1¼   cups warm water
6   tablespoons olive oil
3½   cups all-purpose flour

Topping:
2½   cups tomato sauce (see page 211)
½   pound creamy imported Gorgonzola or blue cheese, cut
        into thin strips
½   pound sliced mortadella, cut into thin strips
½   pound Fontina cheese or mozzarella, cut into thin strips
2   teaspoons finely chopped fresh basil leaves or ½ tea-
        spoon dried basil
¼   cup crushed walnuts
½   cup pitted Gaeta olives, halved

In a mixing bowl combine yeast, salt, and ½ cup of the warm water. Let yeast dissolve. Add rest of water and 3 tablespoons of the oil to mixture. Stir in flour and blend well with your hands until it becomes a rather stiff, sticky dough. Place dough on a well-floured board. Knead vigorously until satiny smooth, elastic yet firm. This takes about 10 minutes. Pour 1 tablespoon of the oil into a large bowl. Add the dough ball. Turn to coat well with the oil, then cover with a towel and set in a warm spot in your kitchen, away from drafts. Let dough sit 1 to 1½ hours, or until it doubles in size.

Meanwhile, make your tomato sauce.

Preheat oven to 450°F.

Press the dough down with your fists. Cut into 10 pieces. Roll out each piece on a lightly floured board to the thickness of 4 sheets of basic writing paper. Keep in round shapes not much larger than a coffee cup saucer.

Cover each pizza with Gorgonzola or blue cheese, then with tomato sauce. Cover with mortadella and Fontina cheese or mozzarella, then sprinkle on basil and walnuts. Add more tomato sauce. Smooth each pizza top. Add halved olives, dividing evenly. Coat a shallow baking pan large enough to contain the ten pizzas with the remaining olive oil. Arrange pizzas in pan. Bake 10 minutes in 450°F oven, then reduce heat to 400°F and bake pizzas an additional 5 minutes. Serve immediately.

UOVA A CAVALLO
(Eggs on Horseback)

The name of this dish makes no sense at all.

Serves 6

1–2   bunches of scallions
2   pounds asparagus, preferably thin ones, very fresh and very green
1   lemon, cut in half
10   tablespoons lightly salted butter
       Sprinkle of ground ginger mixed in 2 teaspoons dry vermouth
1   dozen large, very fresh eggs
       Freshly grated Parmesan cheese

Choose scallion bunches with long shoots. Reserving 12 shoots whole, chop the remainder and wash. Set aside. The bulbs of the scallions can be reserved to use in salads or some other recipe.

Trim and wash asparagus; divide into 6 equal bunches. Tie each bunch loosely (2 ties per bunch) with green scallion tops.

In a large pan that can accommodate asparagus horizontally, bring to boil 2 quarts lightly salted water, squeeze lemon into water and drop in rind. Arrange asparagus bunches in water, making sure they are completely submerged. Cook 3 minutes. Remove bunches from water. Run cold water over asparagus until they reach room temperature.

Preheat oven to 350°F.

Melt 7 tablespoons of butter in a saucepan. Add ginger and vermouth mixture. Transfer bunches of asparagus to a baking pan. Pour melted butter over them, making sure to cover every stalk as much as possible.

Place pan in oven. Bake 5 minutes, basting.

Meanwhile, fry eggs, sunnyside up, lightly in remaining butter. Place a pair of fried eggs over each bunch of asparagus, being very careful not to break egg yolks in the process. Shower with freshly grated Parmesan. Return baking pan to oven for 1 minute, then remove and place under broiler 1 minute.

Serve 1 bunch of asparagus per person. Spoon hot butter from the pan over each serving. Parmesan cheese and a peppermill should be served on the side.

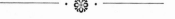

DINNER MENU

From the restaurant that never was.

ANTIPASTI

PROSCIUTTO DI MONTAGNA
(Mountain Prosciutto)

ZUCCHINE RIPIENE AL TEGAME
(Baked Stuffed Zucchini)

BIGNES DI JANE WHITE

SUPPLI AL RISOTTO DI MARE
(Rice Croquettes with Seafood)

PASTA

PASTA PRIMAVERA
(Pasta of Spring)

TAGLIARINI AL SALMONE
(Pasta in Salmon Sauce)

FARFALLE BENTIVOGLIO
(Bowties Pasta Bentivoglio)

MELANZANE IMBOTTITE DI PASTA
(Pasta-Stuffed Eggplants)

CARNE ° PESCE

VITELLO CONTADINA
(Veal Farmer's Style)

ARISTA DI CINGHIALE
(Roast Saddle of Wild Boar)

MANZO ''A QUEL DIO BIONDO''
(Beef Fit for a Blond God)

BRANZINO CON FINOCCHIO E PERNOD
(Striped Bass with Fennel and Pernod)

VERDURE

SEDANO AL FORNO
(Braised Celery)

PISELLI MANGIATUTTO CON TARTUFI
(Snow Peas with Truffles)

CAVOLINI DI BRUXELLES FRITTI
(Fried Brussels Sprouts)

CETRIOLI ALLA PANNA
(Cucumbers with Whipped Cream)

PROSCIUTTO DI MONTAGNA
(Mountain Prosciutto)

Prosciutto di montagna is a specially cured ham from Abruzzi and from the Roman countryside. It is darker in color than the usual prosciutto, and drier. Its texture is similar to that of dried beef, such as *bresaola* or Grison. It is not an item easily found in our markets; however, you can substitute various other hams, such as an excellent baked Smithfield ham, sliced not too thin, or a Kentucky ham also baked and sliced the same way, or Westphalian ham.

SERVES 6

1 pound of whichever ham you choose, in 12 slices
2 cloves garlic, peeled and coarsely chopped
1 tablespoon chopped Italian parsley
1½ teaspoons chopped fresh basil or ½ teaspoon dried basil
Juice of 1 lemon, strained
Freshly ground black pepper to taste
2 tablespoons vodka

Arrange ham slices in a serving platter. Combine remaining ingredients to make the dressing for your ham. Blend well. Spoon over slices of ham and serve immediately. (It's terrific!)

ZUCCHINE RIPIENE AL TEGAME
(Baked Stuffed Zucchini)

SERVES 6

9 small zucchini
¼ loaf Italian or French bread, fresh or stale, broken into
   pieces
1 cup heavy cream
10 pieces imported porcini, presoaked in lukewarm water
   at least 1½ hours in advance, drained
1 tablespoon chopped Italian parsley
   Sprinkle of dried marjoram
   Sprinkle of freshly grated nutmeg
¼ cup grated Gruyère cheese
¼ cup freshly grated Parmesan cheese
¼ cup freshly grated pecorino cheese
2 egg yolks
   Salt and freshly ground black pepper to taste
5 tablespoons lightly salted butter
¼ cup dry unflavored bread crumbs, sifted very fine
3 tablespoons olive oil
   Chicken consommé (see page 207)

Wash and trim zucchini; halve lengthwise. Scoop out insides (not
too much) and set shells aside. Keep ¾ cup of insides, discarding
the rest.

Soak bread in cream in a large mixing bowl. Break up with your
hands until reduced to a mushy mixture. Chop porcini coarsely;
add to mixing bowl. Add parsley, marjoram, and nutmeg. Blend
well. Add cheeses and egg yolks. Whip with wire whisk until well
amalgamated. Add salt and pepper to taste. Set aside.

Preheat oven to 400°F.

Chop the ¾ cup zucchini pulp coarsely. Melt 1 tablespoon of
the butter in small pan. Sauté zucchini pulp 3 to 4 minutes, then
blend into mixture in mixing bowl. Proceed to stuff zucchini
shells with mixture. Sprinkle bread crumbs over stuffing, making
sure to cover each half zucchini completely.

In a round (if possible) baking tin large enough to accommodate all the zucchini, melt remaining 4 tablespoons butter. If you are using a round baking tin, arrange zucchini like spokes of a wheel. Drizzle olive oil over stuffing. Place tin in oven and bake 20 minutes. Baste zucchini with consommé. Reduce oven to 350°F and bake 10 minutes longer. Serve immediately, from baking tin.

BIGNES DI JANE WHITE

SERVES 8

Bignès:

3 tablespoons active dry yeast
   Warm water
3 cups all-purpose flour
2 tablespoons salt
1 tablespoon olive oil
1 teaspoon granulated sugar
½ cup milk
½ cup hot water

Cover the yeast with a bit of warm water—just barely. Let sit in warm place 5 minutes.

Combine flour, salt, and oil in large bowl. Add sugar to yeast, then add milk and hot water. Pour into flour mixture and amalgamate to a soft dough with your hands. Drape a towel over dough and let rise in a warm spot in your kitchen, away from drafts, until it doubles in bulk, approximately 1 hour.

Punch dough down on a floured board and knead into a smooth ball. Cut into 18 pieces, rounding each into a ball the size of a large lemon. Place dough balls on a greased baking sheet to rise for 20 minutes in same warm place.

Meanwhile preheat oven to 400°F.

Bake bignès for about 15 to 18 minutes, then remove from oven to rack to cool.

Stuffing:

10 slices of pancetta or regular bacon
1   pound fresh or frozen crabmeat; if frozen, defrosted,
        dry (using no water), at room temperature
1   tablespoon olive oil
2   tablespoons freshly grated Parmesan cheese
1½ teaspoons chopped fresh basil or ¼ teaspoon dried
        basil
    Salt and freshly ground black pepper to taste
    Sprinkle of ground ginger
2   drops Tabasco sauce

Make stuffing for bignès. Sauté pancetta in dry skillet, until crisp. Drain and chop coarsely. Sauté crabmeat in the olive oil in a skillet 2 minutes. Remove to a mixing bowl and blend with remaining stuffing ingredients, using your hands. Taste for seasoning, then set aside.

Batter for Bignès:

2   whole eggs, beaten lightly
    Salt and freshly ground pepper to taste
    Sprinkle of saffron (optional)
½   cup olive oil

Combine all batter ingredients (except oil) in separate bowl; beat lightly. Set aside.

Proceed to stuff bignès by first slicing off bignè tops. Set tops aside. Scoop out about 2 teaspoons of insides of each bignè and stuff with stuffing mixture, dividing evenly. Replace tops.

Heat oil in a large skillet. While oil heats, soak bignès in batter. Carefully place bignès in hot oil. Fry until deep golden brown on every side. Remove bignès from oil and drain quickly on paper toweling. Serve as hot as possible.

SUPPLI AL RISOTTO DI MARE
(Rice Croquettes with Seafood)

SERVES 8 (16 SUPPLI)

20　very fresh mussels, thoroughly cleaned and debearded
12　very fresh littleneck clams or oysters
4　tablespoons lightly salted butter
1　tablespoon finely chopped onion
1¼　cups rice, preferably Arborio
1　tablespoon very dry sherry
3　cups chicken consommé (see page 207), kept warm
　　over very low flame (you might not need it all)
　　Freshly ground white pepper to taste
¼　pound Fontina or mozzarella cheese, grated rather fine
2　tablespoons freshly grated Parmesan cheese
¾　cup tomato sauce (see page 211)
　　Sprinkle of freshly grated nutmeg
½　cup fine dry unflavored bread crumbs
¾　cup olive oil

Steam mussels open in lightly salted boiling water. Take mussels out of shells and rinse under cold water. Set aside, discarding shells.

Remove clams or oysters from shells. Set aside in their juice, discarding shells.

Melt butter in a skillet over a medium flame. Sauté onion until translucent. Fold in raw rice and blend well with a wooden spoon. Add sherry. Cook, stirring, 2 minutes. Add chicken consommé, a little at a time. Keep stirring with wooden spoon. Add pepper to taste. Keep adding chicken consommé until grains of rice start to soften. Add cheeses and blend well. Add tomato sauce and stir. Add nutmeg.

While risotto is cooking, chop mussels and clams or oysters roughly, just once or twice. Add, along with juices, to risotto. Blend well. Cook until rice is al dente and has become almost dry. Remove from fire and let cool at room temperature. As soon as you can handle risotto with your hands, shape into ovals 4 inches long by 1½ inches round. Roll *supplì* (rice balls) lightly in bread crumbs.

Heat oil to very hot. Fry *supplì* in it until deep golden on all sides. Remove from oil. Serve very hot.

PASTA PRIMAVERA
(Pasta of Spring)

SERVES 6

Fresh pasta (see page 223) or 1½ pounds imported
　　dried tagliarini or spaghettini
6　fresh ripe tomatoes
　　Salt and freshly ground black pepper to taste
6　fresh basil leaves, coarsely chopped, or ¼ teaspoon
　　dried basil
6　tablespoons lightly salted butter
5　tablespoons pesto sauce (see page 214)
½　cup freshly grated Parmesan cheese

If using fresh pasta, roll as thin as possible. Cut sheets into ¹⁄₁₆-inch-wide strips (tagliolini or tagliarini). Sprinkle with flour, cover with a towel, and set aside.

Bring to boil 4 quarts salted water. Scald tomatoes in boiling water less than a minute; keep water at a boil. Peel tomatoes, then cut into small wedges. Sprinkle salt and pepper over them and add basil.

Melt butter in sauté pan over very low flame. While butter is melting, drop pasta into the boiling water. Cook freshly made tagliolini 2 minutes, dried tagliarini 4 to 5 minutes, and dried spaghettini 6 minutes. Drain.

Raise flame under sauté pan. Sauté tomato wedges in butter 1½ minutes. Spread pesto sauce in serving platter. Arrange pasta over pesto and ladle tomato wedges and butter over pasta. Toss gently. Serve with grated Parmesan cheese.

TAGLIARINI AL SALMONE
(Pasta in Salmon Sauce)

Serve grated Parmesan cheese with this pasta, if you wish, but it is not recommended.

SERVES 6

    Fresh pasta (see page 223) or 1½ pounds imported dried tagliarini or spaghettini
1   pound smoked Scotch salmon or smoked Nova Scotia, sliced thin
4   tablespoons lightly salted butter
2   tablespoons very dry white wine
1   cup plus 2 tablespoons heavy cream
    Freshly ground white pepper

If using fresh pasta, roll as thin as possible. Cut sheets into ¹⁄₁₆-inch-wide strips (tagliolini or tagliarini). Sprinkle with flour, cover with a towel, and set aside.

Julienne the salmon. Lay strips on sheet of waxed paper, making sure strips don't stick together.

Bring to boil 4 quarts salted water for pasta.

Melt butter in a large sauté pan capable of accommodating pasta and sauce. Add wine to butter. Cook, uncovered, over low flame 5 minutes. Add cream and cook 3 minutes. Add pepper to taste.

Drop pasta into boiling water. Cook fresh tagliolini 2 minutes, dried tagliarini 4 to 5 minutes, and dried spaghettini 6 minutes. Drain.

Combine pasta with sauce. Toss well. Arrange julienne of salmon over pasta, then toss again and serve immediately.

FARFALLE BENTIVOGLIO

(Bowties Pasta Bentivoglio)

SERVES 6

6   tablespoons lightly salted butter
4   fresh tarragon leaves or 4 tarragon leaves preserved in
      vinegar
1   tablespoon chopped Italian parsley
     Salt and freshly ground black pepper to taste
1½ pounds fresh mushrooms, washed and thinly sliced
      through caps and stems
3   tablespoons dry red wine
10 pieces imported dried porcini, presoaked in warm
      water at least 1½ hours in advance, drained
1   cup brown sauce (see page 209)
½   teaspoon finely chopped garlic
2   tablespoons freshly grated Parmesan cheese
½   cup finely grated Fontina or mozzarella cheese
¼   cup fine dry unflavored bread crumbs
¼   cup olive oil
1½ pounds imported dried bowtie pasta, or any short pasta
      of your choice

Melt butter in a deep saucepan. Add tarragon, parsley, and salt
and pepper to taste. Sauté 3 minutes. Add fresh mushrooms and
sauté over a low flame for approximately 6 minutes. Add wine
and continue to cook until wine is reduced—about 3 minutes.
Add porcini to saucepan. Cook 4 minutes. Add brown sauce.
Reduce 12 minutes, still over a low flame. Remove pan from fire
and set aside. Keep warm.

In a mixing bowl, combine garlic, Parmesan cheese, and
Fontina or mozzarella. Add 2 tablespoons of the sauce, just the
liquid, blending well. Make little balls of the mixture the size of
the tip of your little finger. Roll balls in bread crumbs.

Bring to boil 4 quarts salted water.

Heat oil in skillet. Fry cheese balls very quickly to a pale golden color. Remove balls from oil to paper toweling to drain. Keep warm.

Drop pasta into boiling water and cook 9 to 10 minutes. Drain. Spread some of the sauce on a serving platter. Arrange pasta over sauce. Toss. Pour remaining sauce over pasta. Toss again. Arrange the cheese balls on top. Serve immediately.

MELANZANE IMBOTTITE DI PASTA
(Pasta-Stuffed Eggplants)

SERVES 6

6 small eggplants
2 tablespoons kosher salt or sea salt
1 cup Sauternes wine
¼ cup melted lightly salted butter
¼ cup olive oil
2 whole cloves garlic, peeled
8 slices pancetta or bacon, julienned
1½ teaspoons chopped Italian parsley
1½ teaspoons chopped fresh basil or ½ teaspoon dried
   basil
   Salt and freshly ground black pepper to taste
   Sprinkle of crushed red pepper
   Sprinkle of freshly grated nutmeg
   One can (18 to 20 ounces) imported Italian peeled
   tomatoes, drained but half the juice reserved
¾ pound imported tubettini pasta, or any small short
   pasta of your choice
½ cup freshly grated pecorino cheese

Slice off enough of the eggplant tops to allow a teaspoon in, with which you will scoop out pulp. The eggplant shells should be ⅛ inch thick. Setting tops and ¼ cup of pulp aside, sprinkle kosher salt or sea salt inside eggplant shells. Let sit for about 1 hour.

Wash away salt from inside shells with Sauternes wine. Let shells drain open side down while you preheat oven to 400°F. Coat inside of shells with melted butter, taking care not to damage shells. Coat a baking pan with a bit of the melted butter. Arrange shells in pan, open sides up. Bake about 15 minutes. Remove from oven, and reduce temperature to 300°F. Set shells aside.

Coarsely chop the ¼ cup reserved eggplant pulp. Heat oil in a saucepan. Add garlic and brown lightly, then discard garlic. Add chopped eggplant pulp and sauté 5 minutes. Add pancetta or bacon. Sauté until almost crisp. Add all the other ingredients except tomatoes, pasta, and cheese. Cook 6 to 8 minutes, stirring.

Break up tomatoes with your hands. Add to saucepan along with half the juice from can. Cook, covered, over medium flame for about 20 minutes.

Bring to boil 3 quarts salted water. Drop pasta in. Cook tubettini 10 to 12 minutes, other pasta approximately the same length of time. In any case, test it. Leave al dente. Drain. Toss pasta with sauce in a mixing bowl, then stir in cheese.

Proceed to stuff eggplant shells with pasta, being very careful not to tear shells. Place the top on each eggplant. Arrange stuffed eggplants in same baking pan in which you baked the shells. Place pan in oven. Let shells warm for 6 to 7 minutes, or less.

Serve one eggplant per person, tops removed.

VITELLO CONTADINA
(Veal Farmer's Style)

SERVES 8

5 pounds lean veal (eye of round) in one piece, trimmed
   of all sinews and flimsy skin
4 ounces imported porcini, presoaked in 1 cup lukewarm
   water at least 1½ hours in advance, drained, and
   soaking water reserved

1½   teaspoons crushed black peppercorns
 2   sprigs fresh rosemary or 1 teaspoon dried rosemary
     Generous sprinkle of freshly grated nutmeg
 3   sprigs Italian parsley
     Sprinkle of dried marjoram
     Salt
 6   bay leaves
 1   pound sliced pancetta or rashers of smoked bacon
 ½   cup lightly salted butter
 2   whole cloves garlic, peeled
 ¾   cup dry white wine mixed with ¾ cup dry vermouth
 ½   cup crushed almonds

Make a deep incision in the veal, large enough to accommodate the following ingredients: porcini, crushed peppercorns, rosemary, nutmeg, parsley, and marjoram. Sprinkle meat with salt, then seal incision with round wooden toothpicks. Place bay leaves on veal surface. Cover meat entirely with slices of pancetta or bacon. Tie up veal with butcher's twine. Set aside.

In a deep, large casserole over a medium flame, melt butter and cook garlic cloves until well browned. Do not allow to burn. Discard garlic. Place veal in casserole. Brown on all sides—about 25 minutes. Add wines and baste meat, then cover casserole. Raise flame to medium high. Cook 20 minutes, basting occasionally. Reduce flame. Add crushed almonds, mixing into butter and wine with a wooden spoon. Add porcini soaking water. Cook another 20 minutes or so covered.

Remove veal from casserole. Cut off twine and remove toothpicks. Most of the pancetta or bacon will have cooked away. Slice veal into ½-inch slices. Return veal to casserole. Simmer over very low flame 5 minutes. Spoon sauce with crushed almonds and residue of pancetta or bacon over each slice. Serve immediately.

ARISTA DI CINGHIALE
(Roast Saddle of Wild Boar)

Wild boars are plentiful in the Tuscan Maremma and on the Argentario Peninsula. Even so, they are mercilessly hunted down by everyone, by hunters, by peasants, and by the local nobility, in particular—for the sport. Its meat makes the tastiest sausages, delicious prosciutto, and excellent roasts. It is impossible to purchase wild boar in meat markets. Pork, unfortunately, cannot be a suitable substitute. In any event, if you should ever lay hands on a good fresh saddle of wild boar, here is a recipe for it. It is a delightfully succulent roast, very different from most venison roasts in taste and texture. You could make do with a saddle of young venison.

SERVES 6

1	saddle freshly killed wild boar (about 7½ pounds)
1	cup olive oil
1	tablespoon kosher salt, crushed
1	tablespoon balsamic vinegar
1	tablespoon juniper berries
1	large bunch Italian parsley
1	large onion, peeled and quartered
3	whole cloves garlic, peeled
¾	pound unrendered pork fat, cut into strips
1	teaspoon crushed black peppercorns
1	cup Cognac
2–3	tablespoons vegetable oil

Leave fat on boar but cut off fell. Let meat hang in cool place overnight. Do not refrigerate. The next morning marinate meat for about 3 hours in a mixture of the oil, salt, vinegar, juniper berries, 3 sprigs of the parsley, onion, and garlic.

Preheat oven to 450°F.

Remove wild boar from marinade. Pat dry with paper toweling. Set meat aside and strain marinade. Chop the sprigs of parsley, the onion, and the garlic fine and set aside.

Place a few strips of pork fat in a roasting pan. Set saddle of wild boar over it. Lard meat with the rest of the pork fat strips, then sprinkle with crushed pepper. Place pan in oven and roast 30 minutes, basting often.

Reduce oven to 400°F. Drain off most of the melted lard. Save for future use in other recipes. Pour liquid from marinade over roast. Add chopped parsley mixture. Replace pan in oven. Roast an additional 20 minutes. Add Cognac and roast about another 25 minutes, mixing sauce now and then with wooden spoon.

Toward end of roasting time, sauté remaining parsley lightly in a few tablespoons of vegetable oil. Drain on paper toweling.

Remove roast from pan to platter. Cut into portions between each bone. Spoon sauce over each portion. Serve on a bed of the lightly fried sprigs of parsley.

MANZO "A QUEL DIO BIONDO"
(Beef Fit for a Blond God)

"A quel Dio Biondo" is quite a common expression with Italians, used to identify excellence in the taste of food, physical appearance, films, books, music, and whatever else one likes and admires a lot.

SERVES 8

½   cup virgin olive oil
4   tablespoons lightly salted butter
5   pounds of beef (eye or rib), most of fat cut off
4   whole cloves garlic, peeled
     Salt and freshly ground black pepper to taste
     Sprinkle of ground turmeric
3   fresh sage leaves, or sprinkle of dried sage
3   whole cloves
¼   cup sultana raisins
1½   teaspoon very finely chopped lemon rind
2   cups beef consommé (see page 207)
3   cups robust red wine

3 medium bunches red wine grapes, washed under cold
    water and left whole
Braised celery (see page 139)

Heat oil and melt butter in a deep, large pot (fireproof earthenware preferable) over a low flame. Meanwhile, make 4 incisions
in beef and insert garlic cloves. Brown beef well on all sides,
about 25 minutes. Add salt and pepper to taste and all other
ingredients but beef consommé, wine, grapes, and celery.

Baste with oil and butter. Cook, uncovered, turning beef often,
30 minutes. Add consommé. Let reduce about 10 minutes. Bring
wine to boil separately. Add to beef. Add bunches of grapes.
Cover pot and cook 15 to 20 minutes more.

Remove beef and grapes from pot. Set on a warm platter.
Holding stems, shake each bunch of grapes back into the pot.
At this point the grapes will be quite well cooked and will fall
off easily. Discard grape stems. Strain sauce through fine wire
strainer. Mash remaining residue well to remove all the juices.
Replace beef in strained sauce. Cook over low flame, uncovered,
10 minutes.

Slice beef to the thickness you prefer. Make a bed of braised
julienned celery on serving platter. Arrange beef slices over it.
Spoon sauce on to cover beef completely. Serve immediately.

BRANZINO CON FINOCCHIO E PERNOD
(Striped Bass with Fennel and Pernod)

This recipe provides an unexpected dividend in leftover fish stock.
The leftover stock can be stored away in the refrigerator to cool,
then vodka can be added to it along with some lemon juice and
ice, if you so choose, to make a delightful cocktail.

SERVES 6

6 fillets (¾ pound each) fresh striped bass (from one 8-
    to 9-pound fish), head, tail, and spine reserved
Salt and freshly ground white pepper to taste

 2   fennel bulbs (best season for fennel December, January, February), green shoots cut off, or 1 bunch celery
 6   tablespoons lightly salted butter
     Sprinkle of ground ginger
1½   teaspoons chopped Italian parsley
 ¼   cup Pernod

Wash the head, tail, and spine of fish under cold running water, then boil in 1 quart of lightly salted water over medium-high flame for about 20 minutes. Strain stock through fine wire strainer lined with cheesecloth. Discard residue. Set ¾ cup fish stock aside, storing remainder away in refrigerator for other use.

Wash striped bass fillets under cold water. Pat dry with paper toweling. Sprinkle each fillet with salt and white pepper to taste, then set aside in cool place. Do not refrigerate.

Take apart bulbs of fennel. Discard tough pieces, trim bottom, cut into strips ¾ inch wide. Wash under cold water thoroughly. Let drain. If you should have to use celery, follow same process. Parboil fennel or celery in boiling water 4 minutes. Drain.

Preheat oven to 400°F.

Melt 3 tablespoons of the butter in a baking pan. Arrange fennel or celery strips in pan. Sprinkle with salt, white pepper, and ginger. Place pan in oven and bake 5 minutes. Baste with pan juices, then remove pan from oven. Arrange striped bass fillets over bed of fennel or celery. Divide remaining 3 tablespoons butter into 6 lumps, placing one on each piece of fish. Sprinkle parsley over fish. Pour fish stock into pan. Replace baking pan in oven and bake 8 minutes, or until fish begins to whiten. Douse with Pernod. Bake 3 more minutes.

Serve by scooping up each bass fillet along with fennel or celery. Spoon sauce over each serving.

SEDANO AL FORNO
(Braised Celery)

SERVES 6

1 large bunch celery, scraped and thoroughly washed
   under cold water
6 tablespoons lightly salted butter
½ cup chicken consommé (see page 207)
   Salt and freshly ground black pepper to taste
   Generous sprinkle of freshly grated nutmeg
½ cup freshly grated Parmesan cheese

Preheat oven to 400°F.

Cut each stalk of celery into 3 sections crosswise. Julienne pieces of celery. Melt butter in a baking pan; add consommé. Arrange celery in pan and spoon consommé and butter over celery. Season with salt, pepper, and nutmeg and sprinkle with Parmesan cheese. Bake for 20 minutes. Serve as a garnish.

PISELLI MANGIATUTTO CON TARTUFI
(Snow Peas with Truffles)

SERVES 6

1¼ pound snow peas or sugar snap peas, washed and
    trimmed
1 white truffle from Piemonte (if you are in an expensive mood)
3 tablespoons good dry white wine
4 tablespoons lightly salted butter
1 cup heavy cream

5   tablespoons freshly grated Parmesan cheese
    Sprinkle of freshly grated nutmeg
    Salt and freshly ground white pepper to taste

Preheat oven to 400°F.

Bring to boil 2 quarts lightly salted water. Cook peas about 2 minutes. Drain and set aside.

Wash white truffle in the wine, then set aside truffle and white wine separately.

Melt butter in an ovenproof skillet. Fold cream in with butter. Keeping pan over a medium flame, let mixture reduce 5 minutes. Mix in 2 tablespoons of the cheese. Add nutmeg and salt and pepper to taste. Add snow peas to pan, mixing well so all the peas are well coated. Add reserved wine. Shower with remaining 3 tablespoons cheese. Place in oven and bake about 5 minutes.

Remove vegetable to a warm serving platter and pour sauce over. Slice truffle into very thin slivers, and scatter on top of peas. Serve immediately.

CAVOLINI DI BRUXELLES FRITTI
(Fried Brussels Sprouts)

SERVES 6

2   pints fresh Brussels sprouts, with small, compact heads
2   eggs
    Salt and freshly ground black pepper to taste
3   tablespoons all-purpose flour
½   cup fine dry unflavored bread crumbs
¾   cup olive oil

Trim outside leaves and stem ends of Brussels sprouts. Rinse under cold running water. Bring to boil 1 quart lightly salted water. Cook Brussels sprouts about 8 minutes. Drain and let cool.

Beat eggs with wire whisk, then add salt and pepper to taste. Dust Brussels sprouts with flour. Dip sprouts in egg, coating well. Roll sprouts in bread crumbs to cover well. Heat oil in skillet and fry Brussels sprouts until golden brown all over. Drain on paper toweling. Serve hot.

CETRIOLI ALLA PANNA
(Cucumbers with Whipped Cream)

SERVES 6

4–5 fresh, firm cucumbers, peeled
      Salt
  3 hard-boiled eggs, yolks only
  8 thin slices prosciutto or ham of your choice, thinly sliced
1½ teaspoons finely chopped Italian parsley
  3 fresh mint leaves, finely chopped
      Freshly ground white pepper to taste
1½ teaspoons balsamic vinegar
  2 tablespoons virgin olive oil
  1 cup heavy cream

Cut cucumbers into very thin slices. Place on a platter in layers, showering each layer with a bit of salt. Let platter stand at inclined position to drain off water from cucumbers, about 35 minutes.

Mash egg yolks very fine, and set aside in refrigerator. Julienne slices of prosciutto or ham. Set aside.

Drain cucumbers very well. Sprinkle with parsley and mint, and shower with pepper. Arrange julienne of prosciutto or ham over cucumbers. Pour vinegar and oil over and place platter in refrigerator.

Whip cream to a medium dense consistency. Cover cucumbers with whipped cream. Dust top with mashed egg yolks and serve.

❀ ❀ ❀

DINNER WITH
PRINCIPE ALESSANDRO BORGHESE

Dinner at the exquisite home of Principe Alessandro
Borghese was served at nine punctually on the spacious terrace cut into the greenish rock of the cliff
some sixty-five meters above the, at that hour, wine-
dark sea.

The outdoor furnishing was the latest Vignelli. The
lighting a masterpiece of subtlety. The conversation
delightful, if at times a trifle too patriotic. *Ah, la bella
Italia!*

❀ ❀ ❀

FILETTI DI SALMONE CRUDO IN PINZIMONIO
(Fillets of Raw Salmon in Pinzimonio)

COSTOLETTE DI VITELLO ALLA CERTOSINA
(Veal Chops Carthusian Style)

INSALATA RUSTICA
(Salad Rustic Style)

FRAGOLINE DI BOSCO ALL'ARMAGNAC
(Wild Strawberries in Armagnac)

Wines (in order of serving): Vernaccia of San Gimignano, Aleatico of Portoferraio (from the island of
Elba), Brunello di Montalcino

FILETTI DI SALMONE CRUDO IN PINZIMONIO
(Fillets of Raw Salmon in Pinzimonio)

Pinzimonio is a Roman type of vinaigrette sauce that can be made in a multitude of ways. It is very often used with cooked fresh vegetables, raw salad greens, boiled meats. This particular type is used over poached, roasted, or raw fish.

SERVES 6

3 hard-boiled eggs, yolks only
6 anchovy fillets, drained and chopped very fine
1 teaspoon chopped garlic
1 tablespoon finely chopped Italian parsley
4 fresh leaves basil, coarsely chopped, or ½ teaspoon dried basil
  Freshly ground black pepper
½ cup virgin olive oil
  Juice of 2 lemons, strained
2 pounds very fresh salmon fillets
2½ teaspoons kosher salt or regular salt

Mash hard-boiled egg yolks through a very fine wire strainer. Add chopped anchovies, then garlic, parsley, and basil. Mix well. Shower mixture abundantly with freshly ground black pepper. Add oil and lemon juice. Amalgamate thoroughly until mixture has the texture of a liquid cream. Set aside.

Wash salmon fillets under cold water. Pat dry with paper toweling. Sprinkle salmon with kosher or regular salt. Let marinate in refrigerator 1½ hours.

Cut salmon into 18 rather thin slices. Place on a serving platter, then cover fish with *pinzimonio*. Let it marinate in refrigerator 30 minutes, then serve.

COSTOLETTE DI VITELLO ALLA CERTOSINA
(Veal Chops Carthusian Style)

The Carthusian monks or "Frati Certosini" from the Certosa (Charterhouse) of Vicenza are famous for their liqueur and elixir brewing, and for their cuisine—hence the name of this dish.

SERVES 6

  6   veal chops (each ¾ inch thick), all fat trimmed off, bones of chops scraped totally clean
  6   tablespoons melted butter, cooled
 ½   teaspoon salt
 ½   teaspoon freshly ground black pepper
 ¼   cup sweet vermouth
12   thin slices prosciutto, fat trimmed off and reserved
12   fresh basil leaves, washed
12   slices Fontina cheese, cut to fit the shape of each chop

Press down firmly and evenly on chops with heel of your hand. This is to relax the meat, sort of a massage.

Blend cool melted butter with salt, pepper, and sweet vermouth. Mix well, then taste for seasoning. Marinate chops in this mixture for 1 hour.

Drain chops, reserving marinade. Pour half the marinade into an iron skillet. Add the prosciutto fat and heat over a lively flame. Sauté chops in it on both sides, about 5 minutes per side. Remove chops to a warm platter.

Preheat oven to 400°F.

Place a slice of prosciutto on each side of chops, 1 leaf of fresh basil over each slice of prosciutto, and 1 slice of Fontina to cover basil and prosciutto on both sides. Press down with your hands, packing prosciutto and Fontina well on each side of chops. Pour remaining marinade and juices from skillet into a baking pan. Arrange chops in pan. Place in oven. Bake about 8 minutes, or until Fontina has started to melt. With a spatula carefully lift chops to serving plates. Serve hot, spooning sauce over chops.

INSALATA RUSTICA
(Salad Rustic Style)

SERVES 6

Salad:

3 firm, ripe tomatoes, trimmed and cut into small pieces

3 white stalks celery, washed and scraped, cut in half, then julienned

2 small carrots, washed and peeled, sliced into very thin rounds

1 large sweet red pepper, trimmed, cored, washed, cut into strips the width of a finger

1 bunch red radishes, trimmed and washed, sliced into rounds

1 bunch scallions, most of the green shoots trimmed off, roots cut off, washed, julienned

1 small cucumber, peeled and trimmed, thinly sliced

2 Belgian endives, trimmed, washed, and cut into lengthwise ribbons

1 small bunch arugula or field salad of your choice, very well washed and tough stems removed

Dressing:

½ cup virgin olive oil

3 tablespoons balsamic vinegar

1½ teaspoons finely chopped Italian parsley

Salt and freshly ground black pepper to taste

½ clove garlic, peeled

Combine all cut vegetables for the salad. Toss well together in a colander. Mix and blend well oil, vinegar, parsley, and salt and pepper to taste. Rub a salad bowl very well with garlic. Place all the vegetables in bowl. Pour dressing over, then toss well and thoroughly. Serve.

FRAGOLINE DI BOSCO ALL'ARMAGNAC
(Wild Strawberries in Armagnac)

Fragoline di bosco are indigenous only to the European woods, as far as I know. The type of strawberry most similar to them is the American wild strawberry. These are tiny and deliciously sweet, but unfortunately one rarely, if ever, finds them on green-grocers' counters. You can substitute strawberries available at your market. But do not be fooled by looks alone!

SERVES 6

3   pints fresh, ripe strawberries
1½   tablespoons sugar
¾   cup good Armagnac

Rinse berries gently under a spray of cold water. Drain, then hull. Sprinkle sugar evenly over strawberries and refrigerate 30 minutes. Marinate in Armagnac for 30 minutes at room temperature, then serve.

❋ ❋ ❋

LUNCHEON WITH CONTESSA GERINI

Contessa Gerini's luncheon took place in the beautiful gardens fronting her Ottocento villa, which brought to mind a Visconti film set. The guests, although illustrious, were out of Fellini's *La Dolce Vita*. The domestics looked and acted like players from the Commedia dell' Arte.

The Contessa's genius in mixing her guests proved to be superb. The manners and gentility of this lady from Connecticut were impeccable.

It was a luncheon in the rustic style, and at the end of it Contessa Gerini fetched a beautifully tooled and splendidly painted mechanical parrot, which looked terrifyingly real, and showed it to her guests. The wicked mechanism inside of it produced a raunchy voice that said, "Go home, you ———!" in English.

The Contessa seemed to get a great hoot out of it.

* * *

CAROTE RIPIENE
(Stuffed Carrots)

TAGLIOLINI AL CACIO E PEPE
(Tagliolini with Cheese and Black Pepper)

FETTINE DI MANZO CIPOLLATE
(Fillets of Beef with Sautéed Onions)

ASPARAGI FREDDI CON MAIONESE ALL'AGLIO
(Cold Asparagus with Garlic Mayonnaise)

FICHI AFFOGATI
("Drowned" Figs)

Wines: The wines served were from Campania (Naples region), which are still made the way they were made in the times of ancient Rome. In order of serving: Falerno from Campi Flegrei, Gragnano Rosso from Sorrento, Rosato from Ravello

CAROTE RIPIENE
(Stuffed Carrots)

SERVES 6

10 large carrots, the size of medium zucchini
3 tablespoons roughly grated stale bread
¼ cup milk
1 pound mortadella or ham of your choice, finely
     chopped
1 egg, beaten
     Freshly crushed black pepper to taste
2 tablespoons grated Gruyère cheese
1½ teaspoons finely chopped Italian parsley
5 tablespoons lightly salted butter
1 clove garlic, peeled
2 bay leaves
½ cup dry white wine
     Salt and freshly ground black pepper to taste
     Chicken consommé (see page 207)

Bring to boil 2 quarts salted water. Chop off tapered ends of carrots, trim tops, and peel. Cook carrots about 8 minutes. Drain and set aside.

Soak bread crumbs in milk about 5 minutes. Combine with mortadella or ham, egg, crushed pepper, cheese, and parsley. Blend well and evenly. Taste for seasoning.

Cut carrots in half lengthwise, then carefully scoop out some pulp to make room for stuffing. Discard pulp. Stuff each half carrot, using all of the mixture. Set aside.

Preheat oven to 375°F.

Melt butter in a flameproof bake-and-serve dish. Add garlic and let brown, then discard. Add bay leaves. Add wine and let evaporate about 6 minutes. Add salt and pepper to taste. Arrange stuffed carrots in dish, stuffing side up. Place dish in oven and bake 20 minutes. Baste with chicken consommé while cooking. Serve hot, first spooning butter sauce over carrots.

TAGLIOLINI AL CACIO E PEPE
(Tagliolini with Cheese and Black Pepper)

SERVES 6

Fresh pasta (see page 223) or 1½ pounds imported
    dried tagliarini, or spaghettini
4 tablespoons lightly salted butter
¾ cup freshly grated Parmesan cheese
    Freshly ground black pepper

If using fresh pasta, roll out as thin as possible. Cut sheets into
⅟₁₆-inch-wide strips (tagliolini or tagliarini). Cook pasta in the
usual way:

Bring to boil a large pot of salted water. Cooking time: 2½
minutes for fresh pasta, 4 to 5 minutes for dried tagliarini, 6
minutes for dried spaghettini.

Drain pasta, keeping ½ cup of the hot pasta water. Place
butter in pasta bowl and toss pasta in it, then add pasta water and
cheese and toss well again. Shower each serving with black pepper
from the mill. The top of the pasta should be well covered by
the black specks of pepper. Serve immediately.

FETTINE DI MANZO CIPOLLATE
(Fillets of Beef with Sautéed Onions)

SERVES 6

3½–4 pounds fillets of beef, trimmed of all fat
5 tablespoons olive oil
3 medium red onions, peeled and thinly sliced
    Salt and freshly ground black pepper to taste

Sprinkle of ground ginger
Sprinkle of paprika
2   tablespoons good red wine vinegar

Slice beef fillets into ½-inch-thick slices. Pound slices down lightly and set aside.

Heat 3½ tablespoons of the oil in a skillet. Sauté onions until translucent. Add salt and pepper, ginger, and paprika to taste. Continue to sauté onions until golden. Add vinegar. Sauté about 5 minutes longer, mixing well. Set aside and keep hot.

Coat a large iron skillet with remaining 1½ tablespoons oil. When oil begins to smoke, cook *fettine* quickly, about 2 minutes per side. Remove meat to a serving platter. Cover with sautéed onions and their juices and serve immediately.

ASPARAGI FREDDI CON MAIONESE ALL'AGLIO
(Cold Asparagus with Garlic Mayonnaise)

SERVES 6

1   lemon
1½ pounds fresh, very green, thin asparagus, trimmed and
        washed, tied in a bunch
2   cups garlic mayonnaise (see page 219)
        Freshly ground green peppercorns to taste

Bring to boil 4 quarts lightly salted water. Squeeze lemon juice into water, then add rind. Cook asparagus in boiling water about 6 minutes. Remove from water and rinse thoroughly under cold running water. Untie and arrange on serving platter. Cover tips and half of stalks of asparagus with garlic mayonnaise, evenly. Shower liberally with green pepper and serve.

FICHI AFFOGATI
("Drowned" Figs)

This recipe should be used when fresh green figs are at their peak, or very ripe, sweet, and most succulent.

SERVES 6

18–20   fresh medium green figs
   1   cup framboise, or any other fruit brandy or liqueur of
          your choice
   ¼   cup pure honey diluted in ½ cup hot water

Cut figs in half. Arrange in a deep platter, insides up. Pour fruit brandy or liqueur over figs, then pour honey over them. See that the liquids cover figs completely. Marinate 1 hour in refrigerator. Take platter out 30 minutes before serving.

Spoon marinade over to serve.

9

A Chef

Gino Ratti was a first-class chef with a marvelous sense of humor, a fastidious dresser, and a despicable miser. He was my mentor. The man who taught me all I know of the art of cooking, the quality of food and wines. The man who pulled together all the bits and pieces given and shown me by the multitude of other generous people whom you have met in the previous pages, and made me into a chef and a restaurateur.

When we met, he was in his late fifties and I in my early thirties. His entire life had been a Grand Tour of the best hotels of Europe before mass tourism; the glittering elegance of the transatlantic vessels when the tango was the rage and "Ramona" a hit song.

At age eleven he left home and took employment as a *piccolo di cucina* in St. Moritz.

At age eighteen he became the chef-saucier at the Danieli in Venice.

At age twenty-one he graduated to second in command of the *brigata di cucina* at the Ristorante Savini in Milano when Puccini was still around for rehearsals at La Scala.

At age twenty-five he sailed aboard the S.S. *Saturnia* as her first-class chef. *Primo assoluto!* Positions aboard the S.S. *Conte Biancamano*, S.S. *Conte Rosso*, S.S. *Vulcania*, and finally the S.S. *Rex*, followed.

In 1938 he decided to pack his knives and small library of culinary art and start a more stationary life in New York. He took employment at one of the then-fashionable restaurants in Little Italy. That position lasted a very short time because a mafioso *Capo di tutti i Capi* with a refined palate discovered him, and engaged him on the spot as his private chef—offering a salary he couldn't refuse.

Soon Gino Ratti became the subject of dispute between those Mafia *pezzi da novanta*, and he was vied for like the "families' territories."

Signor Gino Ratti's last employer was Salvatore Lucania, alias Lucky Luciano.

Then we met. Signor Gino Ratti became the chef of my first restaurant.

At that time I sported a bushy mustache (the beard came later), and Gino found it appropriate to nickname me "Baffi" (mustache). The nickname stuck.

Signor Gino Ratti had twelve blue serge suits all of the same cut, twenty pure cotton Countess Mara white shirts, nine gray-and ruby-striped silk ties from Sulka, one dozen pairs of black shoes (the laced kind, made by Calzaturificio di Varese), three pairs of delicately initialed gold cufflinks, one 2.5-carat diamond tiepin, two dozen fine linen handkerchiefs with hand-rolled hems, several dozen pairs of knee-length midnight-blue silk hose, also from Sulka. The several overcoats and raincoats he owned were from Burberry. He wore the same attire year in, year out, aside from his kitchen whites. He lived in a squalid little apartment on Thompson Street in Greenwich Village, of which he sublet one room to young and upcoming chefs, new arrivals to the city. He charged a monthly rental for the room that exceeded by $4 the monthly rent he paid for the whole apartment. Soap, toilet paper, towels, and bed sheets were not included. He kept his savings in ten different banks throughout the city, in ten different accounts under the same name.

Signor Gino Ratti remained a bachelor all his life.

"I came into this world alone," he would offer as a reason.

His lady friends were the lonely patrons of a bar on 14th Street that, just for the record, was New York's first singles bar.

I once asked him why he did not keep a steady relationship with one lady. The answer was: "Baffi, you are a very innocent man and a spendthrift. Christmas comes around, birthdays . . . a steady, one-lady relationship means gift giving."

But in the kitchen Signor Gino Ratti was a genius! He retired at age sixty-two to return to his little native town in Liguria and died a few years later "alone as he came into this world," to make use of his logic.

The recipes that follow are Signor Gino Ratti's, some of which I am still using to this day at Trattoria da Alfredo and Tavola Calda da Alfredo, and I have used them in other restaurants of mine in the past since his departure. In any event, what I learned in the kitchen from Gino Ratti is priceless. I have never met to this day a man who could equal his skills and his respect for the art of cooking and love for food, except for Mr. James A. Beard. But, Mr. Beard is, after all, *a fuori classe* (above classification).

Every day I would spend three to four hours in the kitchen, either assisting or watching Gino prepare and cook. He was a demanding and exacting teacher, completely oblivious of your feelings when he discovered your shortcomings. Therefore, soon I began to "cheat." I'd make up sauces of his and later go to him, passing them off as sauces prepared by him. I would ask his opinion on the taste of such a sauce, giving as a reason that I thought it had gone bad. He'd fume for a few seconds, then carefully and slowly taste the sauce. Seconds as lengthy as hours would go by before he'd pronounce his judgment: "Perfect! Absolutely perfect! How dare you question?" he'd say indignantly. Sometimes the "trick" misfired, then he'd threaten to leave my employ, and I'd have to beg and cajole him until he was pacified, the old despot. That game went on for years until he recognized me as a *mezzo-cuoco*, or "half chef." The day he left me he finally admitted, reluctantly, that I was ready to take over the kitchen.

The following recipes are some of Signor Gino Ratti's best:

❊ ❊ ❊

ANTIPASTI

NIDO D'UOVA
(Eggs in the Nest)

GAMBERI *Conte Rosso*
(Shrimp Conte Rosso*)*

PEPERONI RIPIENI *Saturnia*
(Stuffed Peppers Saturnia*)*

OSTRICHE E SALMONE DEL *Rex*
(Oysters and Salmon of the Rex*)*

ANTIPASTO DEL POVER'UOMO
(Poor Man's Antipasto)

GALANTINA DI POLLO
(Chicken Galantine)

CAVOLETTI FARCITI
(Little Rolls of Stuffed Cabbage)

NIDO D'UOVA

(Eggs in the Nest)

SERVES 6

6 extra-large eggs, hard-boiled and shelled
3 tablespoons lightly salted butter
6 fresh littleneck clams, shelled, kept cold, juice reserved if possible
Freshly ground white pepper to taste

6 tablespoons fresh or frozen crabmeat chunks; if frozen,
    defrosted, dry (using no water), at room tempera-
    ture

Salt

¾ cup Russian mayonnaise (see page 218)

½ pound imported dried cappelli d'angelo

¾ cup tomato sauce (see page 211), strained, at room
    temperature

Cut eggs in half lengthwise. Scoop out yolks carefully so as not
to damage whites. Refrigerate both, separately.

Melt 1½ tablespoons of the butter over a low flame. Sauté
clams, stirring, about 2 minutes. Sprinkle with a couple of turns of
peppermill (white pepper). Add whatever clam juice you were
able to preserve and sauté a few seconds more. Add crabmeat and
sauté 1 minute. Let cool.

Chop clams and crabmeat very coarsely; sprinkle lightly with
salt. Mash egg yolks very fine, then combine in a mixing bowl
with clams and crabmeat. Fold in Russian mayonnaise and amalgamate very well. Taste for seasoning. Proceed to stuff egg whites
with mixture, using approximately 1 tablespoon for each half.
Refrigerate.

Bring to boil 1 quart salted water. Cook cappelli d'angelo 2½
minutes. Drain and set aside to cool. Toss well in tomato sauce,
then refrigerate 30 minutes.

Melt remaining 1½ tablespoons butter in sauté pan. Sauté pasta
until crisp. Divide cappelli d'angelo among 6 salad plates, shaping
into small nests. Let cool. Place 2 stuffed-egg halves in each nest.
Serve.

GAMBERI *CONTE ROSSO*
(*Shrimp* Conte Rosso)

SERVES 6

18 large shrimp (ask for the size 15 and under; your fish
    merchant will know what to give you)

¾ pound Fontina cheese, in one piece
2 egg yolks
4 tablespoons heavy cream
  Salt and freshly ground black pepper to taste
¼ cup all-purpose flour
2 Belgian endives, trimmed and washed well under cold
  running water, cut into thin lengthwise ribbons
1½ teaspoons very finely chopped fresh coriander
1 tablespoon Cognac
¾ cup olive oil
1½ cups garlic mayonnaise (see page 219)

Shell shrimp while raw. Wash well under cold running water. Leaving tails on, cut shrimp in half lengthwise but leave them attached by tail. Refrigerate.

Remove crust from Fontina cheese and cut into 18 sticks approximately ¼ inch by ¼ inch and the length of each shrimp. Set aside.

Beat egg yolks and heavy cream together. Add salt and black pepper to taste; the mixture should be peppery. Set aside.

Proceed to stuff shrimp by placing one stick of Fontina between halves of each. Sprinkle some black pepper over cheese. Close halves and secure with two round wooden toothpicks in each shrimp. Dust lightly with flour. Soak stuffed shrimp in egg yolk–cream mixture for approximately 30 minutes.

Meanwhile, sprinkle endive ribbons with coriander and Cognac. Mix well and keep at room temperature.

Heat oil in skillet. Fry shrimp until golden brown. Keep warm.

Divide endive equally among 6 salad plates. Place 3 shrimp, toothpicks removed, on each plate and spoon mayonnaise lightly over shrimp. Offer extra mayonnaise on the side. Serve immediately.

PEPERONI RIPIENI *SATURNIA*

(Stuffed Peppers Saturnia)

SERVES 6

6   small red or yellow sweet peppers, each the size of an
      apple
6   tablespoons sweet butter
2   tablespoons dry vermouth
      Salt and freshly ground black pepper to taste
1½ pounds very lean boneless leg of lamb, in one piece
      Zest of ½ lemon, very finely chopped
1   egg yolk beaten with 3 tablespoons heavy cream
2   tablespoons freshly grated Parmesan cheese
½   packet saffron diluted in 2 tablespoons warm water
      Sprinkle of ground turmeric
1½ teaspoons Italian parsley, very finely chopped
2   tablespoons chopped pignoli (pine nuts)
½   cup chicken consommé (see page 207)

Make sure the peppers are not soft or wilted; core and clean them
of seeds. Wash under cold water, then let drain, open side down.

Melt butter in saucepan over low flame. Stir in vermouth and
cook 2 minutes. Pour mixture evenly into peppers, swirling around
to coat insides. Leave mixture in peppers for 30 minutes.

Drain butter and vermouth mixture into a skillet. Heat, then
add salt and pepper to taste. Add lamb and lemon zest. Cook,
covered, over a medium flame about 20 minutes. Remove lamb
and chop into small pieces. Let cool. In a mixing bowl combine
chopped lamb, egg yolk beaten with heavy cream, Parmesan
cheese, saffron diluted in warm water, turmeric, parsley, and
chopped pignoli. Amalgamate well with your hands. Taste for
seasoning, then set aside.

Preheat oven to 375°F.

Place peppers, open side up, in a baking pan, then pour in
chicken consommé. Bake peppers 10 minutes, then remove pan
from oven. Stuff peppers with lamb mixture, then arrange, stuffed

side up, in same baking pan. Replace in oven. Bake an additional 15 minutes. Remove and place under grill 1½ minutes. Serve immediately.

OSTRICHE E SALMONE DEL *REX*
(Oysters and Salmon of the Rex*)*

SERVES 6

3   large eggs
1   cup heavy cream
    Salt and freshly ground black pepper
    Sprinkle of freshly grated nutmeg
    Sprinkle of ground ginger
1   tablespoon minutely chopped fresh chives
2   tablespoons freshly grated Parmesan cheese
6   round slices Italian bread (each ½ inch thick), approximately the same size in diameter
½   cup olive oil
18   fresh oysters, shucked, reserved in their juice
    Juice of ½ lemon, strained
    Sprinkle of cayenne pepper
5   tablespoons all-purpose flour
4   tablespoons lightly salted butter
12   very thin slices smoked salmon, such as Nova Scotia or Scotch salmon

Beat eggs in a mixing bowl with heavy cream, then add salt and pepper to taste. Divide batter into two bowls; to one bowl, add nutmeg, ginger, chives, and Parmesan cheese. Blend well. Soak bread slices in this batter, soaking slices thoroughly without damaging them. Reserve plain batter for oysters.

Heat oil in skillet. Fry bread to a light golden brown on each side. Remove from oil to paper toweling to drain. Keep warm.

Douse oysters with the lemon juice. Sprinkle cayenne pepper over them. Dust lightly with flour, then soak in plain batter in second bowl. Melt butter in clean skillet and sauté oysters to a light golden color on all sides.

Place bread slices on serving platter. Arrange 3 oysters on each slice, drape oysters with 2 slices of salmon, pour melted butter from skillet over salmon. Serve with peppermill on the side.

ANTIPASTO DEL POVER'UOMO
(Poor Man's Antipasto)

Why "poor man's antipasto" Chef Gino Ratti never bothered explaining, since in reality it is a rather expensive dish to prepare.

SERVES 6

½   cup olive oil
1½   tablespoons balsamic vinegar
     Salt and freshly ground black pepper
1½   teaspoons finely chopped fresh basil leaves
2   pounds finely ground, very lean beef
½   cup lightly salted butter
2   whole cloves garlic, peeled
5   anchovy fillets, drained
1½   teaspoons finely chopped Italian parsley
1   teaspoon chopped fresh tarragon or the equivalent tarragon leaves preserved in vinegar
1   tablespoon Paul Corcellet mustard
1   tablespoon red wine vinegar and 1 tablespoon Cognac mixed together
1½   teaspoons medium capers, drained
2   medium cucumbers, washed, peeled, cut into small cubes

Blend ¼ cup of the olive oil, balsamic vinegar, salt and black pepper, and chopped basil together, then blend thoroughly into chopped meat. On a platter, make 6 mounds of the meat with a well in the center of each. Refrigerate.

Melt butter over low flame in a saucepan. Add remaining ¼ cup oil, then add garlic and let brown, making sure it doesn't burn. Discard garlic. Add anchovies and sauté until melted. Add parsley and tarragon; sauté 1 minute. Add mustard and blend well. Add wine vinegar and Cognac and cook 3 minutes. Add capers and cook 1½ minutes. Add cucumber cubes. Cook 1 to 2 minutes. Pour hot sauce into wells in the meat. Serve immediately.

GALANTINA DI POLLO
(Chicken Galantine)

It thrilled me whenever Chef Gino Ratti would bone a whole chicken, an operation that offers some of the magic one expects from watching a great surgeon at work. "There is nothing miraculous about boning a chicken," Gino would say. "Patience, a very sharp, short knife, and your fingers is all you need to do it," he would comment at the end of the operation, holding up the floppy, boneless chicken, now looking like a very small child's snowsuit.

Here is how it is done in order to prepare the chicken galantine.

Choose a plump, 2½- to 3-pound fresh chicken. Leave chicken out on your kitchen work table for about 1½ hours before starting boning process. Gently press down on breastbone with heels of your hands, making absolutely sure not to tear or damage skin. Repeat process over the entire chicken body.

Almost all of the chicken's carcass—backbone, ribs, and breastbone—comes out easily in one piece when properly loosened from the flesh. The thigh and drumstick bones have to be dealt with separately and must be removed first. Do not bother or attempt to bone wings. Leave them on, chopping off wing tips. Again, I *repeat*: Be very careful not to puncture or tear skin—except for the long incision you must make at the back of the chicken to get at the bones. Later you will sew up this incision.

To prevent puncturing or tearing skin, keep cutting edge of knife facing the bone you are working on.

Order of procedure:

1. Use a very sharp, short knife and a pair of poultry shears. Place chicken, breast down, resting on work table.
2. Make a straight incision from the neck all the way down to the tail. Incision must be deep enough to reach backbone.
3. Work on one side of the chicken at a time, starting from neck to tail. Separate the meat from the bones, prying it loose with your fingers, and using knife where necessary. Always keep in mind that knife edge should be angled toward bone and away from skin.
4. When you reach the midway point close to the small of the back, you will come to a small concave-shaped bone filled with meat. Pull flesh away with your fingertips or knife. A little further down you will encounter the hip joint. Loosen as much of the flesh around it as you can with your fingers. Next, with poultry shears, cut joint from carcass.
5. Hold end of chicken's leg with one hand while, with the other hand, you pull flesh away from hipbone. Whenever you come to long filaments—the tendons—cut away from bone with knife.
6. Next, you come to the joint connecting hipbone to drumstick; by holding hipbone in one hand and drumstick in the other, snap off hipbone at joint. Remove the hipbone entirely, using knife to free it from any meat still attached to it. *Repeat*: Be careful to keep skin intact.
7. At this point, the drumstick bone has to be removed. Commence from the thick, fleshy end and, with your fingers, loosen meat from bone as much as possible; use knife where necessary. Sever tendons from bones, leaving them attached to the meat. This part of the chicken can be turned inside out like a glove.
8. Now, at about ½ inch up from drumstick's knob, cut skin, meat, and tendons clean through to bone. Hold bone by knob end and push it back through the leg until it slides out.
9. You will now return to operate on the upper part of the back; using your fingers and your knife, remove flesh from rib cage of the carcass until you have reached the breast-

bone. Make sure to leave skin attached to crest of breast-bone until later.

10. Connected to the wing you will find the shoulderbone; free meat from it, still using fingers and knife. Cut bone off at joint where it meets wing; remove it.

11. Repeat same boning procedure on other side of bird until chicken is attached to carcass only at crest of breastbone.

12. Turn bird over, breast facing up, with carcass resting on work table. Carefully free skin from breastbone by using your knife. The skin is very thin at this point, so you must be extremely careful not to slit or tear it.

13. Pick up the two loose sides of bird and peel them away from carcass. Discard carcass, or use for stock. Your boned chicken is now ready to be stuffed, and you are eligible for a degree in surgery.

14. You can bone your chicken the day before, if you wish, and keep refrigerated.

Stuffing and Cooking:

6   large eggs, 3 raw, 3 hard-boiled and peeled
½   pound fresh spinach, washed well under cold running water, coarsely chopped
¾   pound chopped lean beef
¾   pound Fontina cheese, cut into 1-inch cubes
1   cup chunks of crusty bread, presoaked in ½ cup heavy cream until mushy
2   tablespoons pignoli (pine nuts)
2   tablespoons natural pistachio nuts, shelled
1   tablespoon finely chopped Italian parsley
    Salt and freshly ground black pepper to taste
    Sprinkle of freshly grated nutmeg
¾   pound boiled ham, cut into strips ¼ inch wide
½   cup olive oil
3   tablespoons lightly salted butter
½   cup dry white wine

In a large mixing bowl, beat the 3 raw eggs, then add all other ingredients but the hard-boiled eggs, ham strips, oil, butter, and wine. Amalgamate well with your hands. Taste mixture for balance.

Place boned chicken, breast side down, on work table and begin to stuff legs where bone used to be with stuffing mixture. Shape rest of stuffing into an oval ball and stuff into chicken. Bury hard-boiled eggs in stuffing in a line down the center of the bird. Place ham strips alongside the boiled eggs wherever you find space in the chicken.

Bring chicken's skin around and over; one edge of the skin should overlap the other by about 1 inch. Mold stuffed chicken, as closely as possible, into shape it used to be. Begin to sew up chicken, starting at neck and working down toward tail. Use an overcast stitch, and do as neat a job as you possibly can. Make sure you have sewn up all the openings.

Heat up oil and butter in a flameproof casserole over a medium flame. Place chicken in casserole, sewn side down. Brown it well on both sides. Add wine and let it evaporate, approximately 5 minutes. Sprinkle bird with salt and black pepper. Turn the flame to medium low. Cook chicken, covered, about 1 hour, during which time you should turn the bird at least twice.

Remove chicken to a platter and let cool to room temperature. At this point, place chicken in refrigerator for 30 minutes.

Transfer chicken to carving board and slice into ½-inch slices, starting at neck end. Each slice should show an egg medallion and squares of ham.

Serve with 1½ cups of green mayonnaise (see page 219) on the side.

This recipe should serve 10 to 12.

You will find the work involved in preparing this dish well worth the effort; it is very satisfying.

Note: This chicken can also be served hot as a main dish along with a salad or vegetable of your choice.

CAVOLETTI FARCITI
(Little Rolls of Stuffed Cabbage)

SERVES 6

1 medium head Savoy cabbage
5 tablespoons lightly salted butter
1 whole clove garlic, peeled
1 tablespoon finely chopped onion
1 pound lean veal, cleaned of all sinews
2 duck livers or ¼ pound chicken livers, cleaned
½ pound fresh sweetbreads, cleaned
1½ teaspoons finely chopped fresh basil or ½ teaspoon dried basil
Salt and freshly ground black pepper to taste
Sprinkle of freshly grated nutmeg
1½ teaspoons sultana raisins, presoaked in ½ cup Marsala or sherry wine 1 hour in advance
Beef consommé (see page 207)
Hot paprika
1 egg
1½ tablespoons freshly grated Parmesan cheese
2 tablespoons heavy cream
1½ teaspoons pignoli (pine nuts), roughly crushed

Trim cabbage of all tough leaves, and cut off hard stem. Wash under cold running water. Parboil cabbage in salted boiling water 8 minutes. Drain carefully. Shower with cold water. Place cabbage upside down to drain off water.

Melt butter in a large flameproof casserole over a medium flame. Add garlic. Brown and discard. Add onion and sauté until lightly golden. Add veal and sauté about 15 minutes, browning on all sides. Add livers and sauté 2 minutes. Add sweetbreads and sauté 3 minutes. Add basil, salt, pepper, and nutmeg. Reduce flame to low. Drain raisins and set aside. Add Marsala or sherry wine to casserole and let evaporate 6 to 7 minutes. Add some beef consommé as the meats are cooking. Remove casserole from fire.

Start to separate leaves from cabbage. You should need about

20. Place leaves on work table like sheets of pasta. Sprinkle some salt and paprika very lightly over leaves.

Remove meats from casserole, and chop rather fine by hand. Beat the egg in a mixing bowl. Add meats, cheese, and cream and blend well with hands. Add raisins and pignoli. Mix. Taste for seasoning.

Proceed to stuff cabbage leaves. Roll each leaf, overlapping each end, and keep closed by using round wooden toothpicks.

Carefully place cabbage rolls in casserole, spooning sauce over each roll. Set casserole over low flame, covered. Simmer 10 minutes. Serve immediately, spooning sauce over each portion.

❆ ❆ ❆

MINESTRE

ZUPPA *Conte Biancamano*
(Conte Biancamano Soup)

MINESTRA DI BUSECCA SAVINI
(Savini's Tripe Soup)

CELESTINA ALLA CINESE
(Celestina Chinese Style)

ZUPPA *CONTE BIANCAMANO*
(Conte Biancamano Soup)

SERVES 6–8

6   tablespoons lightly salted butter
1   small onion, peeled and coarsely chopped
2   small carrots, washed and scraped, diced
1   stalk celery, washed and scraped, diced
1   fresh ripe tomato, cut in half

½ cup dry sherry
Salt and freshly ground black pepper to taste
1 chicken (2½ pounds) or small capon
3 slices prosciutto
¼ pound Fontina cheese
1 egg
3 tablespoons freshly grated Parmesan cheese
Sprinkle of freshly grated nutmeg
12 slices white bread, crusts trimmed off
½ cup olive oil

Melt 4 tablespoons of the butter in large soup pot over a medium flame. Add onion, carrots, celery, tomato, sherry, and salt and pepper to taste. Sauté 20 minutes, stirring often so vegetables do not stick to bottom. Add some hot water, if necessary. Add chicken or capon and cook 10 minutes, turning often. Add 2 quarts hot water. Cover pot and let contents cook until chicken is done yet not overcooked, about 25 minutes. Skim off fat. Remove chicken or capon. Set aside to cool.

Strain consommé; taste for balance. Discard all residue of vegetables. Set consommé aside, off the fire.

Remove breasts from chicken; remove skin. Keep rest of chicken for other uses, such as salad or sandwiches. Chop breasts rather fine by hand. Set aside. Chop prosciutto and Fontina cheese same way.

In a mixing bowl beat the egg and combine half of the chopped chicken (reserve other half), prosciutto, Fontina, 3 tablespoons Parmesan cheese, pepper, and nutmeg. Blend well. Add a few spoons of the consommé if mixture is too dry. Set aside.

Add other half of chopped chicken breast to soup pot. Stir. Leave off fire.

Melt remaining 2 tablespoons butter. Wet each slice of bread with melted butter. Proceed to spread mixture from mixing bowl evenly over 6 of the bread slices. Place the other 6 slices of bread over them. Press gently down with palm of your hand. Cut each "sandwich" into 4 squares, or 6 if too big.

Heat olive oil in skillet over medium flame. Fry squares to golden color on both sides. Drain squares on paper toweling.

Bring consommé to boil. Place 4 or 5 squares in each soup plate and ladle hot consommé over them. Serve with freshly grated Parmesan cheese on the side, and a peppermill, if you wish.

MINESTRA DI BUSECCA SAVINI
(Savini's Tripe Soup)

In the Lombardy dialect, tripe is called *busecca,* and it is used widely in many recipes of the area's cuisine. This particular soup is truly a Milanese dish, featured both in the best of restaurants, such as Savini, and in the workingman's *osterie.*

Serves 6–10

4   pounds fresh honeycomb tripe, which you can obtain from your butcher already blanched (do not use frozen)
3   pounds spareribs, rather meaty but not too fat
1   prosciutto bone, obtainable from Italian grocer if notified in advance, or ham bone
1½ pounds cotechino sausage
5–6 cloves garlic, peeled and crushed
2–3 stalks celery, washed and scraped, diced coarsely
1   large onion, peeled and coarsely chopped
2   carrots, washed and scraped, diced
    Bouquet garni of 2 bay leaves, a few sprigs of Italian parsley, plus dried thyme, sage, marjoram, and a few leaves of tarragon, either fresh or the vinegar-preserved type, all tied in a cheesecloth bag
3   teaspoons crushed black peppercorns
    Kosher salt to taste
½   teaspoon cayenne pepper
½   cup Calvados or brandy
4   large potatoes, peeled and cooked separately in salted water
1   lemon, juice strained and zest finely chopped
1½ tablespoons tomato paste
    Freshly grated Parmesan cheese

Wash tripe thoroughly several times under lukewarm water. Remove excessive fat from tripe, then cut into large square pieces.

Place tripe, spareribs, prosciutto bone, and cotechino into a deep, large soup pot with enough water to cover all ingredients— about 4 quarts. Bring to boil and cook meats about 10 minutes. Skim off fat that comes to surface of water. Add garlic, celery, onion, carrots, bouquet garni, peppercorns, and salt to taste. Return pot to boiling point, then reduce heat and simmer for 2 to 2½ hours, continuing to skim off fat and scum from surface. After about 1½ hours check cotechino, which should be done. Remove to a platter and let cool. Check tripe, also remove when tender. Cut tripe into strips 1½ inches long by ½ inch wide; add to cotechino platter. Remove spareribs and cut all the meat from bones. Chop coarsely and add to platter containing cotechino and tripe. Slice cooled cotechino into thick rounds.

Discard all the bones and bouquet garni from broth. Let broth cool off. Skim fat from surface; repeat procedure several times.

Add cayenne pepper and Calvados to broth and bring to boil over lively flame. Let broth reduce to less than half by rapid boiling. Taste for seasoning. Lower flame. Mash boiled potatoes through a food mill, then stir into broth along with lemon juice and chopped zest. Let simmer 10 minutes. Add tomato paste diluted in a cup of the broth. Simmer a few more minutes. Add tripe and meats. Bring soup almost to a boil.

Serve very hot, with freshly grated Parmesan on the side.

CELESTINA ALLA CINESE
(Celestina Chinese Style)

Another of Chef Gino Ratti's inscrutable names for a recipe. In any event, a most tasty soup.

SERVES 6–8

Crêpes:
3   eggs
⅛   teaspoon salt

1¼   cups milk
1   cup less 1 tablespoon all-purpose flour
5   tablespoons melted lightly salted butter
2   tablespoons very finely chopped fresh chives

Broth:
2   quarts chicken consommé (see page 207)
1   pound medium shrimp, peeled, deveined, and washed
        thoroughly under cold water, each shrimp cut into
        3 pieces
3   tablespoons very dry sherry

In a food processor or blender combine all the crêpe ingredients, reserving 3 tablespoons of the melted butter, and blend or process until creamy smooth. Remove to bowl, cover, and set aside for 2 hours at room temperature (see note below).

When you are ready to make crêpes, first check consistency of batter. Beat with wire whisk, since flour will tend to settle to bottom of container. If batter seems and looks thicker than heavy cream, add some extra milk.

Heat a Teflon-lined pan with a 6-inch bottom over medium flame until very hot. Brush bottom lightly with some of the reserved melted butter. Ladle ¼ cup batter into pan. Raise pan from flame and tilt so batter runs over entire bottom of pan to cover it with a thin layer. Return pan to flame and cook crêpe until top is set. Loosen edges of crêpe with a spatula, and flip it over. Cook other side of crêpe, then turn the crêpe out onto a plate by inverting pan. Keep making crêpes until all the batter is used up, brushing pan with butter as needed. Stack crêpes on top of each other on plate and set aside at room temperature (see note below). You should have made approximately 16 crêpes with this amount of batter.

At serving time, roll crêpes, 3 at a time, and cut into ¼-inch ribbons. Separate them. Bring consommé to boil. Add cut shrimp and sherry and cook 3 minutes. Add crêpe ribbons and cook 1 minute.

Serve with a peppermill on the side, or a hot mustard of your choice.

Note: Crêpe batter can be kept refrigerated as long as 12 hours. Be sure to keep covered and mix well before using it.

If you wish to keep crêpes for later use, stack them on a dish, but insert a piece of waxed paper between each crêpe and cover. Refrigerate.

❊ ❊ ❊

PASTA

TORTELLONI DI ZUCCA
(Squash-filled Tortelloni)

TAGLIOLINI LUCULLUS

SPAGHETTINI HOTEL DANIELI

RAVIOLINI AL RIPIENO DI CERVELLA
(Little Ravioli with Brains Filling)

BUCATINI ALLA SAVINI

FETTUCCINE VIVANDIERA

TORTELLONI DI ZUCCA
(Squash-filled Tortelloni)

Tortelloni are stuffed pasta shaped like tortellini, only larger in size. They can be homemade, or bought commercially made from stores like Dean & DeLuca or Macy's Cellar in New York, or from other pasta stores that import from Fini of Modena, Italy. Tortelloni stuffing varies from region to region in Italy. The type in this recipe is one of the classics, made mostly in the fall, when the yellow squash are in season.

In making the pasta for fresh tortelloni, follow cutting instructions for tortellini (see page 229), only cut discs of pasta double the size in circumference. (Of course, if you buy the commercially made tortelloni you need not follow the filling recipe given here, for they are filled and ready to be cooked. In which case you need to buy about 2 pounds frozen or dried tortelloni; cook for about 8 minutes.)

SERVES 6–8

Fresh pasta (see recipe, page 223)

Filling:
1   ripe winter squash (about 4 pounds), such as Hubbard
6   tablespoons lightly salted butter
¾   cup freshly grated Parmesan cheese
    Freshly ground black pepper to taste
    Sprinkle of freshly grated nutmeg
1   tablespoon finely chopped Italian parsley
    Salt
1   large head escarole
¾   pound giambone (see page 259), or a ham of your
        choice
3   eggs
1   pound whole-milk ricotta cheese

Roll fresh pasta out as thin as possible, then cut into discs 3 inches in diameter. Sprinkle with flour, cover with a towel, and set aside.

Make filling for tortelloni. Cut squash into large pieces, then remove seeds and stringy portion. Boil in lightly salted water— enough to cover pieces—for 20 to 25 minutes. Drain, and when cool remove skin. Cut pulp into smaller pieces, wrap in a towel, and place a heavy object on top until all the liquid is drained out. Use a colander to drain liquid.

Melt butter in a sauté pan over medium flame. Add drained squash and sauté 5 minutes. Stir in Parmesan cheese, pepper, nutmeg, and parsley; blend well. Taste; add salt, if necessary. Sauté until mixture is dry, about 10 minutes. Remove from fire and let cool.

Remove outer leaves of escarole, then trim inner leaves and wash under cold running water. Boil leaves in a small amount of lightly salted water for 3 to 5 minutes. Drain well, squeezing all the water out. Chop coarsely. Chop giambone coarsely. Put squash mixture, escarole, giambone, eggs, and ricotta into a food processor in batches and process to a thick texture. Taste for seasoning.

Proceed to stuff discs of pasta as you would tortellini, and fold into rings in the same manner. Let tortelloni dry a little longer than tortellini.

Sauce:

1½ cups heavy cream
4   tablespoons lightly salted butter
¼   cup tomato sauce (see page 211) kept warm
3   tablespoons freshly grated pecorino cheese

Bring to boil salted water in a large pot.

At the same time, in a large sauté pan, reduce heavy cream for about 4 minutes over a medium flame. Add butter and let melt.

Cook tortelloni in boiling salted water for 3 minutes. Drain, then add to cream and butter. Mix well. Add tomato sauce and sauté tortelloni until well coated. Sprinkle pecorino cheese over and blend well. Serve immediately. A peppermill and additional grated Parmesan cheese are optional.

TAGLIOLINI LUCULLUS

SERVES 6

1   pound fresh pasta
4   tablespoons lightly salted butter
3   cloves garlic, peeled and mashed
3   cups dry white wine
4   cups imported Italian peeled tomatoes, undrained (one
        28-ounce can)
    Salt (optional)
¾   pound ready-to-eat sliced veal tongue, julienned
½   tablespoon finely chopped Italian parsley
¼   cup freshly grated Parmesan cheese
¼   teaspoon crushed black peppercorns

Roll out fresh pasta as thin as possible. Cut sheets into $\frac{1}{16}$-inch-wide strips (tagliolini or tagliarini). Sprinkle with flour, cover with a towel, and set aside.

Melt butter in a large saucepan or soup pot that can accommodate sauce and pasta, since pasta is cooked directly in the sauce. Add mashed garlic and cook until golden. Add wine and cook, uncovered, 10 minutes over a lively flame. Break up peeled tomatoes with your fingers and add to pot, including the juice from the can. Cook sauce, uncovered, 35 minutes over a medium flame. Taste; you may need to add some salt to sauce. Add julienned tongue and cook 5 minutes longer.

Blend well together the parsley, Parmesan cheese, and crushed peppercorns. Set aside.

Raise flame and bring sauce to boil—sauce should by now have reduced to about 4 cups. Add pasta and cook 3 minutes, continuously mixing with the sauce, using a long fork to prevent pasta strands from sticking together.

Arrange pasta on a serving platter. Sprinkle parsley mixture over pasta. Toss pasta once more. Serve.

SPAGHETTINI HOTEL DANIELI

SERVES 8

½   lemon
2   pounds fresh thin asparagus, trimmed and washed, tied
    in a bunch
6   tablespoons lightly salted butter
1   cup heavy cream
    Freshly ground black pepper to taste
12 thin slices prosciutto, julienned
¾   cup freshly grated Parmesan cheese
1½ pounds imported dried spaghettini

Bring to boil 4 quarts salted water. Squeeze lemon juice into water, then add rind. Cook asparagus in boiling water 3 minutes. Drain and rinse under cold running water. Cut off asparagus tips to a length of about 2½ inches each. Preserve stalks for later use, such as in soup or salad; set tips aside.

Melt butter in a large sauté pan. Add asparagus tips and sauté 2 minutes. Add cream and cook 3 minutes. Stirring gently so as not to damage asparagus tips, add pepper, prosciutto, and half the cheese, and amalgamate well. Keep warm.

Cook pasta in 4 quarts salted boiling water 6 to 7 minutes. Drain well. Add spaghettini to sauce, raise flame, and sauté until well coated—about 1½ minutes. Serve immediately, with remaining cheese.

RAVIOLINI AL RIPIENO DI CERVELLA
(Little Ravioli with Brains Filling)

To make raviolini, or little ravioli, follow directions for cutting ravioli on page 229, but cut strips of pasta smaller so that raviolini will turn out half the size of regular ravioli.

This is a most delicate and savory dish, if you are not averse to brains.

SERVES 6–8

Fresh pasta (see page 223)

Filling:
2½   pounds fresh calves' brains
    Juice of ½ lemon
10–12   leaves Swiss chard
6   tablespoons lightly salted butter
¾   cup freshly made bread crumbs
    Salt and freshly ground black pepper to taste

1½   teaspoons finely chopped Italian parsley
      Sprinkle of freshly grated nutmeg
      Sprinkle of dried marjoram
4   egg yolks
¾   cup fresh grated Parmesan cheese

     Sauce:
4   tablespoons lightly salted butter
4   slices pancetta or bacon
3   tablespoons dry white wine
1   cup brown sauce (see page 209)
      Freshly ground black pepper to taste
1   tablespoon vegetable oil

Roll out fresh pasta as thin as possible, then cut into strips 1½ inches wide with jagged-edge cutting wheel. Sprinkle with flour, cover with a towel, and set aside.

Make filling. Wash brains well and soak in ice water for 30 minutes. Carefully remove membrane covering them, and any remaining threads of blood. Place brains in a deep pan, and cover with lightly salted water laced with the lemon juice. Bring water to boil, then reduce flame and simmer for 10 to 12 minutes. Remove brains from pot, and immerse again in ice water to stop them from cooking, and to remain firm.

You can boil brains well in advance on the day you intend to make this filling, in which case you should refrigerate cooked brains until ready to use.

Trim Swiss chard leaves of tough stems. Wash well under cold running water. Put leaves in a pot with 2 cups lightly salted water. Bring water to boil. Cook chard 3 minutes. Drain, then cool under cold running water. Squeeze all water out of chard. Set aside.

Melt 3 tablespoons of the butter in a sauté pan and sauté brains 8 minutes. Add bread crumbs. Mix well. Remove pan from fire, leaving brains in pan to cool.

Melt remaining 3 tablespoons butter in another pan. Sauté Swiss chard 3 minutes. Remove from fire, leaving chard in pan to cool.

Chop cooled brains and Swiss chard by hand, leaving slightly coarse. In a mixing bowl, combine brains and chard, together with the butter from each pan. Add salt, pepper, parsley, nutmeg, marjoram, egg yolks, and ¼ cup of the cheese. Amalgamate well and smoothly. Taste for seasoning. Proceed to fill raviolini (see page 237), using, of course, less filling than you would for regular ravioli.

Make sauce for raviolini. Melt butter in a saucepan over a low flame. Add pancetta or bacon. Raise flame to medium and cook pancetta to a crisp. Remove pancetta remains and discard. Add wine to saucepan and let it evaporate 5 minutes. Add brown sauce and cook 5 minutes. Blend well. Add pepper to taste. Remove sauce from heat and keep warm.

Add vegetable oil to a large pot of salted boiling water. Cook raviolini 3 minutes. Drain carefully, so as not to damage pasta, then remove to serving platter. Pour sauce over raviolini, a little at a time, mixing until raviolini are uniformly well coated. Serve with remaining ½ cup Parmesan cheese on side.

BUCATINI ALLA SAVINI

SERVES 6–8

3	medium zucchini
½	cup olive oil
3	tablespoons lightly salted butter
¼	cup thinly sliced onion
1	clove garlic, peeled, minced
1½	pounds sweet pork sausage meat, removed from casing, or lamb sausage (preferable, if you can obtain it from your butcher)
½	cup robust red wine
	Salt and freshly ground black pepper to taste
	Sprinkle of freshly grated nutmeg
3	cups tomato sauce (see page 211)
¼	tablespoon finely chopped Italian parsley
¼	tablespoon chopped fresh basil or sprinkle of dried basil

2   fresh mint leaves, chopped
½   pound lean and fat prosciutto, thinly sliced and juli-
     enned
1½ pounds imported dried bucatini or perciatelli
½   cup freshly grated Parmesan cheese

Wash zucchini well under cold water. Trim ends, then cut into ¼-inch-thick rounds. Let rounds dry on paper toweling, sprinkling some salt over them.

Heat oil in a frying pan. Fry zucchini rounds, a few at a time until brownish golden. Set to drain on paper toweling; do not heap on top of each other.

Put oil in which you fried zucchini in a saucepan. Heat. Add 1 tablespoon of the butter, then add onion and garlic and cook until golden. Add sausage meat. Brown gently over a low flame, stirring often, about 15 minutes for pork sausage, 7 minutes for lamb sausage.

Add wine and let evaporate 8 minutes. Add salt, pepper, and nutmeg. Add tomato sauce and let simmer uncovered over low flame for 20 minutes. Stir and taste for seasoning. Remove from heat and keep warm.

Bring to boil 4 quarts salted water. At the same time, melt remaining butter in a sauté pan. Mix well parsley, basil, and mint and add to sauté pan. Add zucchini and prosciutto and warm gently over a low flame. Blend well together. Cook bucatini in the boiling water 10 to 12 minutes. Drain.

In a pasta bowl, toss bucatini and sauce. Top with zucchini and prosciutto mixture. Serve with Parmesan cheese on the side.

FETTUCCINE VIVANDIERA

The word *vivande* means "food." The word *vivandiera* means the proprietess of a country inn, and generally also the cook, hence the name of this dish.

SERVES 6–8

Fresh pasta, either green or white (see pages 223 or
    226), or 1½ pounds imported dried fettuccine
1   large or 2 small fresh squabs
5   tablespoons lightly salted butter
3   slices pancetta or bacon
½   cup thinly sliced onion
1   stalk celery, washed and scraped, diced small
1   small carrot, washed and scraped, diced small
2   leaves fresh sage or sprinkle of dried sage
    Sprinkle of dried rosemary
2   sprigs Italian parsley, chopped coarsely
    Salt and freshly ground black pepper to taste
    Chicken consommé (see page 207)
5   fresh chicken livers, cleaned
¾   cup dry white wine
1   teaspoon red wine vinegar
8   pieces imported dried porcini, presoaked at least 1½
    hours in advance, drained, and soaking water re-
    served
1½ tablespoons tomato paste
    Freshly grated Parmesan cheese (optional)

If using fresh pasta, roll as thin as possible. Cut sheets into
¼-inch-wide strips (fettuccine). Sprinkle with flour, cover with
a towel, and set aside.

Remove innards of squab(s), and retain liver or livers, which
you will add to chicken livers. Wash squab under cold water, pat
dry.

Melt butter in a large casserole over a low flame. Add pancetta
and onion and sauté a few minutes, or until onion is translucent.
Add diced celery and carrot. Sauté gently 5 to 8 minutes, stirring
frequently. Put squab in casserole and raise flame to medium,
then add sage, rosemary, parsley, and salt and pepper to taste.
Brown squab, turning it from side to side, for 15 minutes. Baste
with pan juices a few times. Add 1 or 2 tablespoons chicken
consommé, if necessary. Add chicken and squab livers and sauté
6 minutes. Add wine and vinegar and let evaporate 10 minutes.

Stir porcini into casserole. Baste squab once more and cook 5 minutes longer.

Dilute tomato paste in a few tablespoons porcini soaking water. Pour into sauce. Stir and taste for seasoning. Remove casserole from fire.

Remove squab and livers from casserole. Let cool. Mash livers with a fork and return to casserole. Pluck meat and skin off squab carcass, making sure not to leave any of the small bones attached to meat. Chop meat and skin into small chunks. Return to casserole. Replace casserole over a very low flame and let simmer, stirring with wooden spoon.

Bring to boil 3 quarts salted water. Cook fresh fettuccine 2 to 3 minutes, dried 5 to 6 minutes. Drain, then place on serving platter. Ladle sauce and meat over pasta and toss thoroughly. Serve with grated Parmesan cheese, if desired.

❅ ❅ ❅

VITELLO

SCALOPPINE OLIVATE
(Veal Scaloppine with Olives)

VITELLO PORTOVENERE
(Veal Portovenere)

UCCELLETTI DI VITELLO S.S. Rex
(Little Veal Birds S.S. Rex)

SCALOPPINE OLIVATE
(Veal Scaloppine with Olives)

SERVES 6

1 pound Gaeta or Kalamata olives or 1 jar (6⅓ ounces)
    of Olivada
3 tablespoons virgin olive oil (optional)
1 tablespoon balsamic vinegar
3 fresh basil leaves, minced
2 fresh mint leaves, minced
12 thin slices lean, tender veal, cleaned of all sinews and
    flimsy skin, pounded gently between 2 sheets of
    waxed paper or aluminum foil
¼ cup all-purpose flour
½ cup vegetable oil
5 tablespoons lightly salted butter
5 tablespoons Marsala wine or dry sherry
    Sprinkle of salt
1 teaspoon crushed black peppercorns

Gaeta and Kalamata olives have to be pitted. The best way to do so is to press down on olives with the heel of your hand, and pits will come out easily. Discard pits. Mash olive pulp in a mortar or food processor. Put mashed olive pulp in a mixing bowl. Add olive oil, vinegar, basil, and mint. Amalgamate thoroughly. Let mixture stand at room temperature 1 hour.

If you are using Olivada, add vinegar, basil, and mint, omitting the olive oil.

Dust veal scaloppine lightly with flour. Heat vegetable oil in a sauté pan. Braise veal quickly on both sides, about 2½ minutes. Place scaloppine on a platter lined with paper toweling, large enough to contain all of the slices without stacking one on top of the other. Let veal cool.

Spread olive mash evenly on top of each cooled veal slice. Melt butter in a sauté pan over a medium-low flame. Add wine and let evaporate 6 to 8 minutes. Add salt and crushed pepper. Place veal scaloppine, olive-mash side up, in hot butter, then reduce flame to low. Cook veal 6 to 8 minutes, spooning butter sauce over it while cooking.

Arrange veal on serving platter and ladle butter sauce over. Serve immediately.

VITELLO PORTOVENERE
(Veal Portovenere)

Portovenere is an enchanting little town in Liguria made famous by the British, who started to vacation there before World War I, and earlier still by Lord Byron's swimming feats and carryings-on. Portovenere is Chef Gino Ratti's birthplace.

SERVES 6–8

2	cups brandy
2	cups dry white wine
6	whole cloves
1	teaspoon crushed green peppercorns
1	teaspoon minced shallots
2	bay leaves
2	sprigs Italian parsley
5	pounds lean, tender veal, such as eye round, in one piece, cleaned of all flimsy skin and sinew
¼	cup olive oil
6	tablespoons butter
	Salt
6	tablespoons all-purpose flour
1	cup heavy cream
2	egg yolks

Combine brandy, wine, cloves, peppercorns, shallots, bay leaves, and parsley in a deep pan. Place veal in this marinade 5 hours before cooking, turning often. You could go through this preparation on the morning of the day you intend to make this dish. Leave out at room temperature.

Preheat oven to 400°F.

In a roasting pan pour olive oil and 1 tablespoon of the butter, melted. Remove veal from marinade, saving marinade, and place in roasting pan. Roll veal in the oil and butter several times. Dust lightly with salt. Place pan in oven. Roast veal 20 minutes. Pour three-fourths of marinade over veal, then reduce oven heat to 375°F and roast veal another 25 minutes, basting often.

While veal is roasting, melt remaining butter in a saucepan. Add flour and blend well with a wire whisk until mixture becomes golden yellow in color. Strain rest of marinade through fine wire strainer. Add to butter and flour mixture. Keep mixing with wire whisk. If mixture seems too liquid, add a little more flour. Cook mixture 15 to 20 minutes. Heat cream and add to mixture. Keep blending until you have a velvety smooth, creamy béchamel. Taste. You should no longer taste the flour.

Remove saucepan from heat. Let cool a few minutes. Beat egg yolks in a mixing bowl and add to béchamel. Blend well. Keep warm.

Remove roast veal from oven. Slice into rather thin slices. Arrange slices on serving platter. Ladle béchamel sauce over veal and serve with extra béchamel on the side.

UCCELLETTI DI VITELLO S.S. REX
(Little Veal Birds S.S. Rex)

SERVES 6–8

Veal rolls:
8   large, thin slices lean, tender veal, cleaned of all sinews
     and flimsy skin, pounded gently between 2 sheets
     of waxed paper or aluminum foil

   8   slices mortadella, cut the same thickness of pounded
          veal slices
  ½   teaspoon crushed black peppercorns
  ½   teaspoon dried sage
       Sprinkle of freshly grated nutmeg
 1½   teaspoons finely chopped Italian parsley
   1   tablespoon crushed pignoli (pine nuts)
  ¼   cup all-purpose flour
   1   egg yolk and 3 egg whites
   2   tablespoons heavy cream
 1½   tablespoons freshly grated Parmesan cheese mixed
          with ¼ cup fine dry bread crumbs
  ½   cup vegetable oil
 1½   pounds pork caul fat, cut into 8 pieces, each 4½ inches
          square
   8   bay leaves

       Sauce:
   5   tablespoons lightly salted butter
   1   tablespoon olive oil
   1   whole clove garlic, peeled
  ¾   cup robust red wine
       Sprinkle of salt
       Sprinkle of ground ginger
   1   cup brown sauce (see page 209)
   1   cup fresh or frozen peas; if frozen, defrosted, and dry,
          using no water, at room temperature

Place veal slices on work table. Cover each slice with a slice of
mortadella. Mix together crushed peppercorns, sage, nutmeg,
parsley, and pignoli. Spread mixture evenly over mortadella. Roll
slices of veal carefully and tightly, tucking in ends. Secure rolls
with round wooden toothpicks. Dust lightly with flour.

   Beat egg yolk, egg whites, and cream until well blended.
Immerse veal rolls in mixture. Dust veal rolls with cheese-and-
bread-crumb mixture, covering well.

   Heat vegetable oil over medium-low flame, fry veal rolls, or
uccelletti, on all sides until golden brown. Remove *uccelletti* from
oil. Set on paper toweling to drain. Let cool. Flatten caul fat
slices on work table, placing 1 bay leaf over each slice. Wrap each

uccelletto in a slice of caul fat. Hook ends of caul fat onto tooth-picks. Set aside while you make the sauce. (*Note*: Pork caul fat looks like an irregular net, snow-white in color. It is obtainable at your pork store if ordered in advance.)

For sauce, melt butter in a large casserole over a medium flame. Add olive oil, then add garlic. Brown and discard.

Place *uccelletti* in casserole. Sauté 5 minutes, turning twice. Add wine and let evaporate 10 minutes. Keep turning *uccelletti* carefully so they do not come undone. Add salt and ginger. Spoon sauce over *uccelletti* while cooking. Stir in brown sauce with a wooden spoon. Taste sauce. Add peas and cook an additional 5 minutes.

Gently remove *uccelletti* to a serving platter. Remove tooth-picks. Spoon sauce and peas around *uccelletti* and serve immediately.

❊ ❊ ❊

MANZO

CIMA DI MANZO SAVINI
(Stuffed Beef Savini)

ARROSTO DI MANZO DI COURMAYEUR
(Beef Roast Courmayeur Style)

TOMASELLE ALLA GENOVESE

CIMA DI MANZO SAVINI
(Stuffed Beef Savini)

SERVES 6–8

Stuffed beef:

4   veal kidneys
2   tablespoons red wine vinegar
    Salt
1   large beef flank steak (about 4 to 5 pounds)
    Crushed black peppercorns to taste
3–4   sprigs Italian parsley
2   cloves garlic, peeled and sliced
    Sprinkle of freshly grated nutmeg
6–7   large, thin slices of prosciutto, fat and lean
3   eggs
½   cup freshly grated Parmesan cheese mixed with ½ cup
        freshly made bread crumbs
2   tablespoons heavy cream
6   tablespoons melted lightly salted butter
¼   cup olive oil
3   bay leaves
1   sprig fresh rosemary or ½ teaspoon dried rosemary
1   cup robust red wine

Sauce:

2   tablespoons lightly salted butter
1   tablespoon all-purpose flour
¼   cup beef consommé (see page 207)
1½   teaspoons mustard of your choice
1½   teaspoons small capers, drained
2–3   fresh tarragon leaves, or the equivalent in tarragon
        leaves preserved in vinegar, finely chopped

Remove core of fat from kidneys, as well as white tubes, with knife or scissors. Wash kidneys well under cold water. Place on a deep plate and douse with vinegar and a sprinkle of salt. Let stand 1 hour at room temperature.

During this time, trim flank steak of most of its fat, then butterfly it, cutting along the grain of the meat. Pound opened-out meat
lightly between two sheets of waxed paper or aluminum foil.
Dust meat with salt and crushed peppercorns, covering the entire
surface lightly. Arrange sprigs of parsley and slices of garlic over
meat; sprinkle with nutmeg.

Wrap kidneys in slices of prosciutto. Beat eggs in a mixing
bowl. Add cheese-and-bread-crumb mixture, plus cream. Blend
well. Immerse prosciutto-wrapped kidneys in batter and coat
thoroughly. Leave to soak in batter 10 minutes, then place
kidneys lengthwise over the flank steak. Pour 3 tablespoons of the
melted butter and the remaining batter over the whole.

Make a roll of the flank steak, tucking both ends in. Tie rolled
flank steak with butcher's twine, securing the ends as well.

Preheat oven to 375°F.

Heat oil in a large casserole over medium flame. Add remaining
3 tablespoons melted butter. Add bay leaves and rosemary. Put
cima di manzo in casserole. Brown well on all sides. Add wine
and baste meat. Reduce flame and cook covered 10 minutes.

Place casserole in oven, cook meat, uncovered, about 1 hour and
10 minutes, turning it and basting it now and then.

Meanwhile, prepare sauce. Melt butter in a saucepan over a
medium flame. Add flour and blend well with butter with a wire
whisk until golden yellow in color. Add beef consommé and
blend in. Add mustard and mix well with wooden spoon. Remove
from fire.

Test meat with a fork. Remove casserole from oven when meat
is tender, and place on a serving platter. Keep warm.

Strain all the juices from casserole, discarding bay leaves and
rosemary. Return saucepan to fire, add strained juices, mix well.
Add capers and tarragon and cook 6 minutes.

Meanwhile, slice meat into ½-inch slices, removing twine as
you do so. Pour some of the sauce over bottom of serving platter.
Arrange *cima di manzo* slices on platter and pour remaining hot
sauce over. Serve immediately.

ARROSTO DI MANZO DI COURMAYEUR
(Beef Roast Courmayeur Style)

This is a simple, hearty recipe from Val d'Aosta. Gino Ratti was very fond of it and he called it: *mangiar sano*, or "healthy eating." Serve it to those of your guests who might be bored by the now out-of-mode filet mignon Rossini, the filet mignon with Béarnaise sauce, the mummified beef Wellington, or even by plain good old roast beef. There is really no substitute for the fresh fava beans.

SERVES 6

6	pounds prime beef rib roast
1	cup fine leaf lard
1	tablespoon salt
1½	teaspoons freshly ground black pepper
2	carrots, washed and scraped, cut in half
2	stalks celery, washed and scraped, cut into several pieces
1	onion, peeled and quartered
	A bouquet garni of your favorite herbs wrapped in cheesecloth and tied
1	cup dry red wine
½	cup beef consommé (see page 207)
½	lemon
1½	pounds shelled fresh fava beans (broad beans) when in season
½	pound Fonduta cheese, diced

Trim off extra fat from rib roast, and scrape away some of the fat and meat from rib bones. Melt lard over low flame. Pour half of it over beef, working it into meat with your hands as soon as you can handle it. Rub salt and pepper into meat the same way.

Preheat oven to 475°F.

Pour remaining melted lard into a roasting pan, stand rib roast in it and arrange carrots, celery, and onion around it. Place pan in oven. Soak bouquet garni in the cup of wine for 30 minutes.

Allow 9 to 10 minutes roasting time per pound. Baste meat twice, dousing with beef consommé. After the first 30 minutes of roasting, pour wine over beef and place bouquet garni in pan.

Meanwhile, bring to boil 2 quarts lightly salted water. Add juice and rind of half a lemon. Cook fava beans about 10 minutes. Drain and set aside.

At this point, the rib roast should have cooked about 50 minutes. Remove from pan, strain juices from pan, and discard all vegetables and bouquet garni. Slice rib roast between bones. Arrange slices in roasting pan, cover with juices. Add fava beans, then sprinkle all with Fonduta cheese. Return pan to oven. Roast an additional 10 minutes. Serve immediately.

TOMASELLE ALLA GENOVESE

Tomaselle, another of Chef Gino Ratti's capricious names. This tasty mélange of beef, pork, and veal, no matter what the literal meaning of the name, is certainly reflective of his culinary flair.

SERVES 6–8

1   pound lean chopped beef
1   pound sweet Italian pork sausage meat, removed from
     casing
1   pound lean chopped veal
½   pound boiled ham, chopped
     Salt and freshly ground black pepper to taste
4   eggs
¾   cup freshly grated Parmesan cheese
1½   tablespoons finely chopped Italian parsley
2   tablespoons dry vermouth
     Sprinkle of freshly grated nutmeg
2   tablespoons heavy cream
1   large red sweet bell pepper
½   cup all-purpose flour

1   cup fine dry bread crumbs
¾   cup olive oil
4   tablespoons lightly salted butter
10   pieces imported dried porcini, presoaked in lukewarm
      water at least 1½ hours before use, drained
3–4   fresh basil leaves or ½ teaspoon dried basil
¼   cup Cognac or brandy
1   cup brown sauce (see page 209)

Preheat oven to 375°F.

In a mixing bowl combine all the meat with salt and pepper to taste. Beat 2 of the eggs and add to meat. Add Parmesan cheese, parsley, vermouth, nutmeg, and the heavy cream. Amalgamate well with your hands. Taste for seasoning and set aside.

Place pepper on pan in oven. Remove as soon as flimsy skin of pepper starts to blacken. Let cool just to point where it can be handled, then peel off skin. Cut in half, core, and julienne. Set aside.

Form oval patties of the meat mixture about 5 inches across and ½ inch thick. The mixture should yield about 8 *tomaselle*. Dust *tomaselle* lightly with flour. Beat remaining 2 eggs. Dip *tomaselle* into eggs, covering thoroughly. Then coat with bread crumbs. Heat the olive oil in a sauté pan, and sauté *tomaselle* until golden brown on both sides. Set aside on paper toweling.

Melt butter in clean sauté pan over a low flame. Add porcini and sauté 5 minutes. Add basil leaves and sauté 2 minutes. Add Cognac and let evaporate a few minutes, then add brown sauce. Mix well with wooden spoon. Taste; you might find the need for some pepper and salt.

Select a pan large enough to accommodate all the *tomaselle*. Pour in the sauce, then arrange *tomaselle* over sauce and simmer over medium-low flame for 10 to 15 minutes. Remove the *tomaselle* to a serving platter, spooning the sauce over and around them, and topping them with the julienned red pepper. Serve immediately.

❉ ❉ ❉

AGNELLO

CAPRETTO DI PASQUA
(Baby Lamb for Easter)

STUFATO DI AGNELLO ALLA MAROCCHINA
(Lamb Stew Moroccan Style)

COSTOLETTE DI AGNELLO *S.S. Saturnia*
(Lamb Chops S.S. Saturnia*)*

CAPRETTO DI PASQUA
(Baby Lamb for Easter)

This is a typical springtime recipe, when you can obtain the youngest and tenderest lamb. In Italy, the observance of the Easter lamb feast is almost in the nature of a pagan rite. Italians must have that baby lamb, no matter what their financial circumstances. During the lean years of the past, the very poor would go to the extreme of pawning the most treasured linens of their dowry at the Monte di Pietà (state-owned pawnshop).

SERVES 8–10

1 baby lamb (about 15 pounds), cleaned, head and feet removed
2 cups dry white wine
Salt and freshly ground black pepper to taste
2 sprigs fresh rosemary or 1½ teaspoons dried rosemary
4 bay leaves
1 dozen very small artichokes or 6 regular artichokes
1 quart milk
Sprinkle of ground ginger

½ cup olive oil
8 slices pancetta or bacon
4 eggs
3 tablespoons all-purpose flour
1 teaspoon finely chopped Italian parsley
1–2 fresh mint leaves, chopped
½ cup olive oil
2 tablespoons lightly salted butter

In a deep platter marinate lamb in wine, adding salt and pepper to taste, rosemary, and bay leaves. Coat it well by rotating in marinade, and leave for about 1 hour at room temperature.

Meanwhile, prepare artichokes. If using small size, chop off top and stem, leaving 1 inch at bottom. Quarter artichokes. Wash under cold water thoroughly, then place in a strainer to drain. If you use large artichokes, remove all the tough outer leaves and trim stem, leaving 1 inch. Cut into wedges. Wash well under cold water. Drain. Remove sections of artichokes from strainer and immerse in milk. Add ginger. Keep in milk for 1½ hours, being certain they are completely submerged by placing heavy platter on top.

Preheat oven to 400°F.

Add olive oil, and pancetta or bacon to a roasting pan. Remove lamb from marinade, saving marinade, and place in roasting pan. Coat well with oil and place pan in oven. Roast lamb for 30 minutes, then pour marinade over lamb and return to oven. Cook an additional 30 minutes, basting often.

Meanwhile beat eggs. Add flour and amalgamate well with wire whisk. Add parsley and mint and beat to creamy consistency. Remove artichokes from milk (see note below) and soak in batter. Coat thoroughly. Heat olive oil over a lively flame. Add butter and let melt. Spoon artichoke sections into heated oil, as many at a time as the pan can contain, and brown quickly on both sides. Remove to warm platter.

By this time the lamb should be done. Remove it from pan and cut into portions. Place lamb on a serving platter. Arrange artichokes around lamb portions. Strain roasting pan juices and spoon over the lamb and artichokes. Serve immediately.

Note: Milk in which artichokes were soaked must be discarded because of the bitter taste left.

STUFATO DI AGNELLO ALLA MAROCCHINA
(Lamb Stew Moroccan Style)

SERVES 6–8

6 pounds boneless lamb (preferably from the leg)
½ cup olive oil
3 cloves garlic, peeled, crushed
½ cup minced onion
 Salt
½ teaspoon crushed green peppercorns
½ teaspoon ground ginger
1 packet saffron, diluted in 2 tablespoons warm water
¼ teaspoon ground turmeric
 Sprinkle of ground cumin
3 anchovy fillets, drained
1 tablespoon finely chopped fresh coriander
2 bunches of celery, use hearts only
1½ pounds small potatoes
1½ lemons
1 cup Gaeta or Kalamata olives

Trim excess fat from lamb and cut meat into chunks. Heat oil in a deep casserole over a medium flame. Cook garlic and onion 5 minutes, stirring frequently with wooden spoon. Add lamb chunks, salt, peppercorns, ginger, diluted saffron, turmeric, and cumin. Add lukewarm water, barely to cover. Bring to boil. Reduce flame, cover, and simmer for 45 minutes. Turn lamb pieces often. Add water, if necessary. Add anchovies and coriander and blend well. Taste for seasoning.

Wash, trim, and scrape celery hearts, then cut into pieces 2 inches long. Peel potatoes, wash, quarter. Set aside.

Test meat, and if it is almost tender, add celery and potatoes. Add water, if necessary. Mix well with wooden spoon. Keep covered and cook until lamb and vegetables are done.

Squeeze lemons and strain juice. Pit olives by pressing down on them with heel of your hand. Add lemon juice and olives to casserole. Cook an additional 10 minutes.

Arrange lamb chunks on a serving platter. Place celery and potatoes around the meat. Keep warm. Bring sauce to rapid boil, uncovered. It should have by now been reduced to a thick gravy. Pour over lamb and vegetables and serve immediately.

COSTOLETTE DI AGNELLO S.S. SATURNIA
(*Lamb Chops* S.S. Saturnia)

In order to make this dish Chef Gino Ratti convinced me that I should buy a marble-topped work table, because he wanted the smoothest and coolest surface on which to prepare the *pasta sfoglia*, a variation of puff pastry.

SERVES 6–8

8	thin slices of prosciutto, finely chopped
10	pieces imported porcini, presoaked in lukewarm water at least 1½ hours in advance, drained, and chopped rather fine
10	white truffle slivers (optional)
2	cups cream sauce (see page 216)
1¾	cups fine pastry flour
	Lukewarm water
12	tablespoons lightly salted butter
1	tablespoon Aquavit
16	thinly cut lamb chops, eye of the rib only
	Salt
	Freshly ground black pepper to taste
3	egg yolks

Amalgamate well the prosciutto, porcini, and truffle slivers with the cream sauce. Refrigerate, using a sheet of waxed paper cut to size to cover surface of sauce completely.

Make a mound of the flour with a well in the center. Add lukewarm water—about 4 tablespoons, or as much as you see fit to give you a mixture neither too sticky nor too dry; 2 tablespoons of the butter, melted; and the Aquavit. Proceed in the same way as you would to make pasta by hand (see page 224).

Work dough for at least 30 minutes, then shape into a rectangular form about 10 by 7 inches. Cover with a towel and let it rest 15 to 20 minutes.

Wet your hands with cold water and begin to work 8 tablespoons of the butter on work table. Shape it into a thin sheet the same size as the dough rectangle. Place butter sheet in a deep dish containing ice water. Be careful to keep it intact.

Roll dough with a rolling pin to double its length, so size is now approximately 20 by 7 inches. Remove sheet of butter from ice water, pat dry, and dust very lightly with extra flour. Place sheet of butter over half of the dough, and fold other half over it. Seal all sides of the dough. Press down with the palms of your hands so that no air pockets remain.

Start to roll dough on lightly floured surface. If butter should ooze out, cover with extra flour immediately. Fold dough in two and continue to roll. Repeat same process of folding over and rolling until sheet of dough is ⅛ inch thick. Let *pasta sfoglia* rest 5 minutes between rollings. If air bubbles should appear over *sfoglia*, prick with a pin and seal. Set *pasta sfoglia* aside. Cover with towel.

Remove all fat from lamb. Leave bone attached, and scrape the rest of the bone clean of all fat and other meat.

Melt remaining 2 tablespoons butter in a sauté pan over a medium flame. Sauté chops 1 minute on each side. Sprinkle chops with salt and pepper, then set aside to cool.

Cut *pasta sfoglia* into 16 equal pieces. Cover with towel.

Preheat oven to 400°F. Coat lightly with melted butter a baking pan large enough to contain all the chops.

Beat 2 of the egg yolks in a mixing bowl. Remove cream sauce from refrigerator. Mix well with yolks. Spread sauce equally over each piece of dough. Wrap a chop in each piece and seal well all around, leaving bone sticking out. Beat remaining egg yolk and brush each wrapped chop with egg yolk on all sides. Arrange in pan in a standing position, with bone resting on rim of pan. Bake 5 to 6 minutes. Reduce heat to 375°F and bake until *pasta sfoglia* puffs up and becomes deep golden in color—about 15 to 20 minutes.

Arrange chops on serving platter, placing paper frills over each bone end. Serve immediately.

✳ ✳ ✳

POLLAME

TIMBALLO DI PICCIONI
(Timbale of Squabs)

QUAGLIE CACCIATORE
(Quails Hunter Style)

ANITRA AL CALVADOS
(Duck in Calvados Sauce)

TIMBALLO DI PICCIONI
(Timbale of Squabs)

SERVES 6–8

2	tablespoons leaf lard
2	tablespoons olive oil
2	cloves garlic, peeled and crushed
½	cup grated onion
1	stalk celery, washed and scraped, minced
1	small carrot, washed and scraped, minced
	Salt and freshly ground black pepper to taste
6	fresh chicken livers, cleaned, washed, and dried
3–4	fresh basil leaves, coarsely chopped or ½ teaspoon dried basil
3	fresh medium size squabs, cleaned, ready to cook
	Sprinkle of freshly grated nutmeg
½	cup Marsala wine or sweet sherry
1	cup chicken consommé (see page 207)
1½	teaspoons crushed pignoli (pine nuts)
1½	teaspoons blanched almonds, crushed

10 pieces imported porcini, presoaked in lukewarm water
    at least 1½ hours in advance, drained, and cut in
    half
 5 tablespoons lightly salted butter
1½ tablespoons all-purpose flour
 3 tablespoons heavy cream
 5 tablespoons freshly grated Parmesan cheese
 1 egg yolk
 1 pound imported dried mostaccioli

Melt lard in a large flameproof casserole over a medium flame. Add oil. When sizzling, add garlic, onion, celery, and carrot. Reduce flame and let simmer, uncovered, 10 minutes. Stir frequently with a wooden spoon. Add salt and pepper to taste, then add livers. Continue to simmer over low flame 5 to 6 minutes. Stir. Add basil.

Arrange squabs in casserole, rolling in simmering mixture. Sprinkle with nutmeg. Raise flame to medium again. Cover casserole and let squabs cook 10 minutes, turning and basting squabs often. Uncover and add wine; let it evaporate 5 to 6 minutes. Taste for balance. Add some chicken consommé, tablespoons at a time, wetting squabs with it, and mix well into sauce. Do not use the whole cup at once; you might not need it all. Keep turning squabs.

Add pignoli and almonds to sauce, stirring and mixing well. Mix porcini into sauce. Uncover casserole and cook squabs an additional 5 minutes, then remove from casserole. Let juice drain off squabs into casserole. Lay squabs on a platter and let cool.

Reduce flame under casserole to low, adding more chicken consommé if you see fit. Work 2 tablespoons of the butter thoroughly into the flour, and make into a ball. Add to casserole, blending well. Taste. Simmer another 5 minutes. Remove from fire. Set aside.

Set a pot with 3 quarts salted water over a lively flame.

Melt 2 tablespoons of the butter in a saucepan. Add cream and cheese and blend well together. Beat egg yolk separately, and fold into mixture in saucepan. Cook 3 minutes, then remove from fire and set aside.

The squabs should have by now cooled enough for you to begin boning them. Using your fingers and a short, sharp knife, remove all the meat off squab carcasses. Do not mince meat;

keep it in chunks. Keep skin also. Do as thorough a job of boning birds as possible. Set aside.

Preheat oven to 375°F.

Bring to boil salted water. Cook mostaccioli in it 5 minutes. Drain.

Set casserole containing liver and nut sauce over medium flame. Place pasta in casserole. Mix well with sauce, and finish cooking pasta—about 5 minutes more. Remove casserole from fire. Keep warm.

Take an 8 inch round by 4 inch deep baking pan. Rub inside of it with remaining 1 tablespoon butter. Place half of the sauced pasta in pan. Smooth without pressing down. Arrange squab meat over layer of pasta. Place remaining pasta over squab meat. Spoon butter, cream, cheese, and egg sauce over the *timballo*. Place pan in oven and bake 6 minutes. Serve immediately.

QUAGLIE CACCIATORE
(Quails Hunter Style)

In the hills of Piemonte in the fall, when the sharp sounds of the hunters' guns crack the air, people say: *"Ecco, un'altro boccon d'oro"* ("There goes another golden morsel"), meaning that another quail has been bagged.

Fresh quails are not easily found in markets nowadays. Frozen quails are not the same thing, hardly even the same bird. This is a simple, deliciously tasty recipe if you can lay hands on fresh quails. I am totally opposed to the frozen variety.

SERVES 6

1   cup crustless bread chunks or 4 slices white bread, trimmed of crusts

½   cup plus 2 tablespoons virgin olive oil

1½   teaspoons finely chopped garlic

4   juniper berries, crushed
    Salt
3–4 fresh sage leaves, or the equivalent in dried sage
2   tablespoons brandy
1   dozen fresh quails, cleaned
3   tablespoons lightly salted butter
    Sprinkle of dried rosemary
8   pieces imported dried porcini, presoaked in lukewarm
         water 1½ hours in advance, and 2 tablespoons
         soaking water reserved
½   cup Barolo wine, or other robust red
1   teaspoon balsamic vinegar
    Freshly ground black pepper to taste

Soak bread in ½ cup of virgin olive oil in a mixing bowl; work oil well into bread. Add garlic, juniper berries, ¼ teaspoon salt, and sage. Knead all ingredients into bread. Add brandy and mix well. Divide mixture into 12 parts, stuff each quail with 1 part. Cover quails with a towel and leave out at room temperature 5 hours. (Actually, you can do this step on the morning of the day you intend to cook the quails.)

Take stuffing out of quails. Set quails aside. Melt butter in a saucepan over medium flame. Break up bread stuffing into butter. Cook 5 minutes. Add rosemary and porcini to saucepan. Lower flame and simmer, stirring with wooden spoon. Add porcini water and keep simmering. Add wine and let evaporate 8 minutes. Mix well. Remove from fire. Keep warm.

Split quails from breast side, leaving attached by backbone. Rub quails with a mixture of remaining 2 tablespoons olive oil, vinegar, and salt and freshly ground pepper to taste. Heat cast-iron skillet or griddle to very hot. Lay birds on griddle, open side down. Place a heavy object over them, to press them down flat. Add some extra oil if necessary and cook 10 minutes. Turn quails on their backs, replace heavy object over them, and cook another 10 minutes.

Heat sauce, stirring, and taste for seasoning. Arrange quails on serving platter, spoon sauce over birds, and serve immediately.

ANITRA AL CALVADOS
(Duck in Calvados Sauce)

SERVES 6–8

1½ cups sugar
1   cup boiling water
4   tart medium cooking apples, peeled, cored, and quartered
    Juice of 1 lemon, strained
    Sprinkle of ground cinnamon
1½ cups Calvados
3   ducks (4½ pounds each), preferably fresh; but if frozen, defrosted, dry (using no water), at room temperature
    Kosher salt
2   tablespoons unsalted butter
    Sprinkle of powdered sage
    Sprinkle of salt
    Sprinkle of freshly grated nutmeg

In a heavy skillet, melt sugar until golden, stirring frequently with wooden spoon. Add boiling water, being careful not to be splashed. Stir until caramel is dissolved. Bring to rapid boil. Cook 9 minutes, until mixture turns into a thick caramel syrup. Add apple quarters and mix well. Add lemon juice and cinnamon. Cook 5 more minutes. Remove from fire and set aside to cool. Add Calvados and let apples marinate 2½ hours.

Remove neck and giblets from ducks and save for stock. Remove excessive fat from necks and cavities. Clean livers and reserve. Rub duck cavities with kosher salt. Truss ducks.

Preheat oven to 375°F.

Place ducks in a shallow roasting pan and place in oven. Roast 40 minutes. Drain fat off thoroughly. Replace pan in oven and lower heat to 350°F. Roast 25 minutes. Drain off fat once more. Replace in oven. Roast ducks an additional 25 minutes for medium rare (2 hours total for medium). To obtain a crisper skin, raise heat to 500°F for the last 15 minutes' roasting.

While the ducks are roasting, place skillet of caramelized apples over a low flame and simmer for 30 minutes. Mash apples while cooking to make sauce into a coarse, thick mixture. Keep hot.

Melt butter in a sauté pan. Sauté livers 5 minutes, adding sage, salt, and nutmeg.

Cut ducks into halves or quarters, using poultry scissors. Arrange pieces on a warm platter. Cut livers in half and place around ducks on platter. Spoon butter sauce from pan over livers. Spoon Calvados sauce over ducks. Serve immediately.

10

A Midnight Wartime Dinner

This happened four or five weeks before partisan Colonel Valerio caught up with Benito Mussolini and Clara Petacci just outside of Salò and hanged the pair upside down, not unlike two sides of beef, in front of a suburban garage in Lombardy.

Major Thomas P. Hastings of the British F.O. Special Service and I stood outside a "friendly" farmhouse atop a hill overlooking the little town of Cadrezzate, also in Lombardy. It was afternoon. Below in the valley, death and chaos reigned. The awful mess of the blown-up bridge that, until the night before at 11:00 P.M., had been the only connection between the town and the main road to the north was the cause of it.

Major Hastings turned to me, smiling. "Terribly good show. Should be proud of yourself. How does it feel?"

"I don't know," I whispered after a bit.

"Well, you stopped Jerry for at least two or three days . . ." He looked at me seriously. "Cheer up. It's the way it works, you know."

I nodded and kept looking down at that pile of destruction that I had created the night before. The Germans were stuck in Cadrezzate with their trucks and heavy artillery—no way to move them out of there now that the bridge was gone. The American forces were nearly here from the south.

"I am hungry," Major Hastings said matter-of-factly. I nodded again. The two of us had been operating together for the past year in the Lakes region. I was twenty-three, and he exactly ten years older. It was close to the end of the war in Italy. I turned around and met the eyes of Teresa, the youngest daughter of the "friendly" farmer. Those dark eyes were so sad. How can anyone forget?

"Good God, am I hungry," Major Hastings said again. But I'm sure he was thinking of something other than food as well.

We went inside the house, not in the least hopeful of finding food. The "friendly" farmer had none to give us. He had already shared with us a few pieces of hard bread and some lard earlier that morning. We drank some water and chewed on blades of straw just to keep our mouths working.

Late that evening, food rained from the sky. The American Air Force made their periodic *lanci*, or "drops," to supply us, the members of the Resistance. The little parachutes began to float down over the hills around us, each attached to a box. Some boxes contained food, some weapons, some articles of clothing. Blessed little mushrooms.

The two of us went out after dark searching for the right box. Weapons we had—and as for clothing, at present we did not care to think about it.

We could hear Germans in the valley shouting out orders to their troops as well as to the Italians, sounding like wild dogs. They were hastily trying to throw makeshift pontoons across the torrent to move their equipment out of town. It was midnight when we found "our" box, in fact, three of them. Carefully we hauled them back to the farmhouse.

Spam, powdered eggs, powdered milk, some bars of chocolate, biscuits, some cigarettes, aspirins, quinine, packages of gauze, and a note: HOLD ON! That's what was in the boxes.

By the light of a half-burnt candle, we set about to prepare our midnight wartime dinner:

In some hot water, bring powdered eggs to liquid consistency. Do same with powdered milk. Combine the two ingredients, add some salt and pepper if you happen to have any around. Mix well. Set aside.

Open cans of Spam. Slice Spam. Let it soak in liquid.

Melt a tablespoon of fat (does not matter which kind) over a low flame. Fry slices carefully on both sides. Share with your friends while hot.

They tasted horrible, but what a meal it was!

Dessert: Chocolate and cigarettes.

Stocks, Sauces, and Salad Dressings

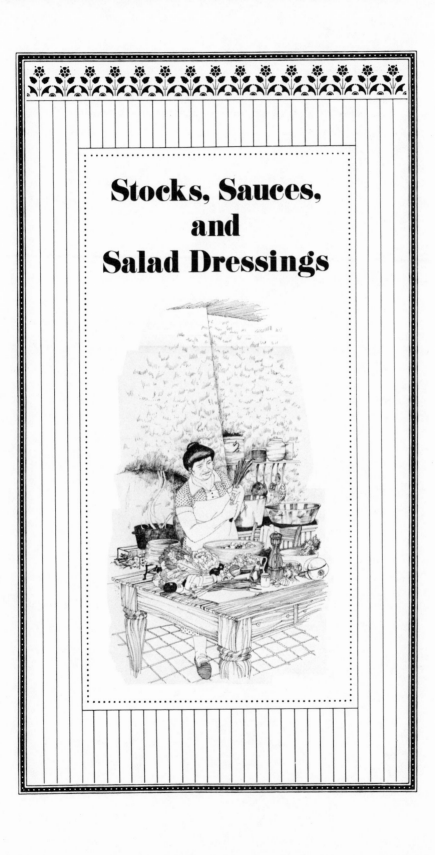

BRODO DI POLLO
(Chicken Consommé)

YIELDS 4 QUARTS

6 quarts water
1 chicken (3 pounds)
1 large fresh ripe tomato
3 carrots, washed
1 large onion, peeled and cut in half
4 stalks celery, washed
2 eggshells (to clarify consommé)
  Small bunch Italian parsley, washed
  Salt and freshly ground black pepper to taste

Pour 6 quarts of cold water into a large pot. Add remaining ingredients. Cook for 1 hour, or until vegetables are very well done, and chicken meat is almost falling off the bones. Skim fat off frequently as it rises to the surface. Pour the liquid through a fine wire strainer. It should be a clear, light, golden color. Discard vegetables and egg shells; store chicken for future use (it can be used for cannelloni stuffing or salads). Store consommé in refrigerator in a screw-top glass container. It will keep for a week.

BRODO DI CARNE
(Beef Consommé)

YIELDS 4 QUARTS

6 quarts water
2 pounds beef bones, cut into small pieces

    1½ pounds beef chuck (see note below)
     1 large fresh ripe tomato
     3 carrots, washed
     1 large onion, peeled and cut in half
     4 stalks celery, washed
     2 eggshells (to clarify consommé)
        Small bunch Italian parsley, washed
        Salt and freshly ground black pepper to taste

Pour 6 quarts of cold water into a large pot. Add remaining ingredients and cook for 1½ hours. Skim off fat frequently as it
rises to the surface. Pour the liquid through a fine wire strainer.
Discard vegetables, eggshells, and bones; store beef for future
use. Store consommé in refrigerator in a screw-top glass container.
It will keep for over a week.

Note: Beef and chicken can be cooked together to make a richer
consommé. The beef should be started cooking 30 minutes before
the chicken. The meats can be used later as a stuffing for cannelloni or can be served cold with green sauce (see page 217).

BRODO DI PESCE
(Fish Stock)

YIELDS 4 QUARTS

     8 quarts water
   4–5 pounds fish heads, tails, and bones (which you can
        obtain from your fish merchant), washed under
        cold running water
     2 carrots, washed
     3 stalks celery, washed
     1 large onion, peeled and cut in half
        Salt and freshly ground black pepper to taste

Bouquet garni (1 teaspoon dried oregano, 1 tablespoon chopped Italian parsley, 1 peeled clove garlic, ½ teaspoon dried marjoram, ½ teaspoon dried rosemary, ½ teaspoon dried basil, 3 sage leaves, coarsely chopped zest of 1 lemon, all tied in double layer of cheesecloth)

Pour 8 quarts of cold water into a large soup pot. Add all ingredients. Cook over medium flame for 35 minutes. Remove bouquet garni. Strain stock through a fine wire strainer lined with 2 layers of cheesecloth. Skim fat off top of stock. Store away in refrigerator in a screw-top glass container. It will keep for about a week.

SALSA BRUNA
(Brown Sauce)

Brown sauce can be used as a basic sauce for all types of cooking, and can be kept refrigerated for at least a month if tightly covered.

YIELDS 8 CUPS

2–3 pounds veal bones, cut into small sections
2 pounds beef ribs, or any joint bones cut into small sections
1 pound chicken wings and 1 pound necks
½ cup olive oil
1 teaspoon salt
½ teaspoon freshly ground black pepper
4 bay leaves
3 whole cloves garlic, peeled
1½ teaspoons dried rosemary
¾ cup red wine
10 tablespoons lightly salted butter

1½   teaspoons dried thyme
2   tablespoons chopped Italian parsley
4   leaves fresh basil or 1 teaspoon dried basil
4–5   leaves fresh tarragon or the equivalent in tarragon
      leaves preserved in vinegar
½   teaspoon freshly grated nutmeg
1½   tablespoons tomato paste diluted in ¼ cup hot water
1   small bunch celery, washed and coarsely chopped
5   carrots, washed and chopped in half
1   medium onion, peeled and cut in half
3   large fresh ripe tomatoes, cut in half
4   quarts warm water
2–3   tablespoons Kitchen Bouquet (optional)
4   envelopes unflavored gelatin

Preheat oven to 400°F.

Combine veal and beef bones, chicken parts, olive oil, salt and pepper, bay leaves, garlic, and rosemary in a large baking pan. Place pan in oven. Bake until bones and chicken parts are a dark brown color—about 1 hour. Watch carefully so they do not burn. Pour wine into pan and bake an additional 20 to 30 minutes. Remove from oven and set aside.

Melt butter in a 12-quart soup pot. Add thyme, parsley, basil, tarragon, and nutmeg and sauté 5 minutes. Add tomato paste and cook an additional 5 minutes. Now transfer the bones and accumulated juices into the pot, being sure to scrape in any little bits of meat from the baking pan. Add celery, carrots, onion, tomatoes, and 4 quarts warm water. Cook over high flame until water has been reduced by half, continually skimming off fat that rises to surface.

By this time, the vegetables should be cooked to a pulp. Set stock aside to cool. Skim again, and strain once to remove bones. Then, pour through a fine wire strainer lined with a layer of wet cheesecloth. Press down firmly on vegetables to make sure all the juices go into the sauce, which should now be caramel in color. For a darker brown color, add 2 to 3 tablespoons of Kitchen Bouquet at this time. Mix in gelatin and stir well with wire whisk. Refrigerate overnight. Sauce should become the consistency of jellied madrilène.

SALSA DI POMODORO
(Tomato Sauce)

YIELDS 8 CUPS

¾   cup olive oil
8   tablespoons lightly salted butter
2   medium onions, peeled and thinly sliced
½   teaspoon chopped garlic
1½ tablespoons chopped Italian parsley
½   teaspoon dried oregano
5   leaves fresh basil, chopped, or 1 teaspoon dried basil
½   teaspoon dried thyme
    Salt to taste
½   teaspoon freshly ground black pepper
1   cup dry yet robust red wine
4   tablespoons tomato paste
2   cups chicken consommé (see page 207) or beef consommé (see page 207)
2   cans (35 ounces each) imported Italian peeled tomatoes, drained

Heat oil and melt butter in a deep 4-quart saucepan. Add onions and chopped garlic and sauté for 5 minutes. Add parsley, oregano, basil, thyme, salt to taste, and pepper. Sauté until onions become golden. Add wine and let evaporate about 25 minutes.

Dissolve the tomato paste in the consommé. Add to saucepan and cook, uncovered, 10 minutes. Stir sauce frequently with a wooden spoon so it doesn't stick to bottom of pan.

Add tomatoes, and blend thoroughly with rest of ingredients in pan. Cook, uncovered, 45 minutes. The sauce should be put through a food mill as the final step. The sauce will keep in the refrigerator up to a week, tightly covered.

RAGU
(Meat Sauce)

This rich sauce can be served over any pasta. When the sauce is done, the beef—which is called *stracotto* in Italy, and which will be very well done—is often served with a fresh salad for luncheon or dinner.

YIELDS 4 CUPS

3	tablespoons olive oil
1½	pounds boneless top round of beef, in one piece
8	tablespoons lightly salted butter
½	small onion, peeled and minced
1	whole clove garlic, peeled
1	tablespoon chopped Italian parsley
	Generous sprinkle of freshly grated nutmeg
1	teaspoon salt
	Freshly ground black pepper to taste
12	pieces imported dried porcini, presoaked in lukewarm water at least 1½ hours in advance, drained and coarsely chopped
½	cup dry red wine
1	cup tomato paste
4	cups beef consommé (see page 207)

Heat oil in a deep skillet over a medium flame. Brown meat well on all sides. Set aside.

Melt butter in a heavy saucepan over a low flame. Sauté minced onion and garlic, discarding garlic when golden brown. Add parsley, nutmeg, salt, and pepper to taste and cook 5 minutes. Add porcini to saucepan and sauté 5 minutes. Add wine and let evaporate 5 to 6 minutes. Dissolve tomato paste in some of the beef consommé. Add to saucepan and cook, uncovered, 10 to 15 minutes. At this point, add meat to saucepan. Cook, uncovered, 20 minutes, turning meat often. Add remaining beef consommé, a little at a time. Cook, uncovered, an additional 50 minutes. Remove the meat.

The end result should be a rather thick sauce that should have reduced to about 4 cups.

SALSA BOLOGNESE
(Bolognese Sauce)

YIELDS 6 CUPS

2	carrots, washed and scraped
2	stalks celery, washed and scraped
½	medium onion, peeled
¾	cup olive oil
6	tablespoons lightly salted butter
8	pieces imported dried porcini, presoaked in lukewarm water at least 1½ hours in advance, drained, and coarsely chopped
½	teaspoon chopped garlic
1	tablespoon chopped Italian parsley
5	fresh basil leaves, coarsely chopped, or 1 teaspoon dried basil
	Generous sprinkle of dried thyme
	Sprinkle of dried oregano
	Sprinkle of dried rosemary
2	bay leaves
	Sprinkle of freshly grated nutmeg
1	teaspoon salt
	Freshly ground black pepper to taste
1	pound boneless beef chuck
1	pound boneless lean pork
2	cups beef consommé (see page 207)
1	cup dry red wine
2	cups tomato paste
2	cans (35 ounces each) imported Italian peeled tomatoes

Put carrots, celery, and onion through a food grinder or processor. Heat oil and melt butter in a large saucepan. Add vegetables, combined with porcini; add garlic, herbs, nutmeg, and salt and pepper. Sauté 10 minutes, stirring continually with a wooden spoon. Add beef and pork and cook, uncovered, 35 minutes, turning often. Add beef consommé as needed if mixture becomes too dry.

Add wine. Cook until it evaporates—approximately 10 minutes. Add tomato paste diluted with remaining beef consommé. Cook, uncovered, 15 minutes, testing meat from time to time to see if it is done. It should be very tender. Add tomatoes and cook, uncovered, 25 minutes. The mixture should now be quite thick. Remove beef and pork. Set aside. Strain sauce through food mill until it has a velvety consistency. Put beef and pork through grinder or processor. Combine with sauce. Blend well over a low flame for 5 to 10 minutes at most. Taste. If necessary, correct seasoning.

This sauce can be kept refrigerated for approximately a week.

PESTO
(Fresh Basil Sauce)

Pesto sauce is one of Liguria's most renowned recipes. It is used on pasta, in soups, with eggs, on meats, on fish, or whatever strikes one's fancy. It is as old as the proverbial hills, and as the natives say, *"Un felice matrimonio comincia con un buon pesto"* ("A happy marriage commences with a good pesto").

YIELDS ABOUT 4 CUPS

    10   tablespoons lightly salted butter, cut into small pieces
    1½   teaspoons finely chopped garlic
         Freshly ground black pepper to taste
     1   bunch (or about 3 cups) fresh basil, very finely
           chopped

¾ cup olive oil
½ cup crushed walnuts
¼ cup crushed pignoli (pine nuts)
¼ pound Parmesan cheese, freshly grated
¼ pound pecorino cheese, freshly grated
¼ cup heavy cream
3 tablespoons cream cheese

Blend all ingredients together, either in a food processor, by hand and with a wire whisk, or in the real Genovese style by grinding down in a mortar with a pestle. Still another way is to put basil, nuts, and garlic through a hand grinder, then combine the other ingredients. Whatever the method, the sauce must become a homogeneous paste. Leftover sauce, if tightly enclosed in a glass jar and refrigerated, can last one month.

How to Preserve Fresh Basil Leaves

I would like to share with you my way of preserving fresh basil, which is exactly the way the Ligurians have been doing it for centuries. Buy, or pluck from your garden, as much fresh basil as you can. Cut off the tough stems, leaving the more tender ones attached to the leaves. Wash carefully under a soft spray of cold water. Allow leaves to dry naturally. Take a rectangular container about 4 inches deep, preferably glass, with an airtight lid (lacking that, devise a cover with heavy-duty aluminum foil). Pour 2 cups of good olive oil into the container, add a sprinkling of salt, then a layer of basil leaves. Repeat the layers of salt and basil until all the basil has been used, making sure when you finish that all the leaves are completely covered with oil. Close the container as tightly as possible and refrigerate. Whenever you use any of the basil, be careful that the remaining leaves are still covered with oil.

With this method, you should be able to preserve your basil supply from the end of August until the middle of March. Of course, in desperation you can always use a freezer.

BALSAMELLA
(Béchamel Sauce)

YIELDS 2½ CUPS

4½   tablespoons lightly salted butter
3   tablespoons all-purpose flour
2   cups heated half-and-half
    Salt and freshly ground white pepper to taste

Melt butter over low heat in a heavy-bottomed saucepan. Mix flour into melted butter and cook slowly, stirring all the time, for about 2 to 3 minutes, or until butter and flour are well blended. Gradually stir in hot half-and-half. Raise flame to medium-high and cook, stirring all the time, until sauce is smooth, thick, and at the boiling point. Let sauce simmer, stirring, for 4 to 5 minutes. Season to taste with salt and pepper.

If the béchamel is not used right away, coat a piece of waxed paper with butter, large enough to fit inside the pan. Lay it over the surface of the béchamel, butter side down. This prevents a skin from forming.

SALSA DI CREMA
(Cream Sauce)

YIELDS ABOUT 2 CUPS

½   cup lightly salted butter
¼   cup all-purpose flour
    Salt and freshly ground white pepper to taste
    Sprinkle of freshly grated nutmeg
2   cups heavy cream
1   egg yolk, lightly beaten
1½   tablespoons freshly grated Parmesan cheese

Melt butter in a saucepan. Add flour, salt and pepper to taste, and nutmeg, stirring with wire whisk until mixture is golden in color. Heat cream in a separate pan and bring almost to a boil. Blend gradually into butter and flour mixture. Cook, uncovered, whisking often, over low flame 10 minutes, or until flour can no longer be tasted. Remove from flame and quickly blend in the egg yolk, then fold in cheese, blending thoroughly. If sauce seems too thick, add a little more heated cream.

This is a basic sauce that can be used with veal, pasta, or vegetables.

SALSA VERDE
(Green Sauce)

YIELDS ABOUT 2 CUPS

2 hard-boiled eggs, peeled
Large bunch of Italian parsley
8 anchovy fillets, drained
1 small onion, peeled
2 pieces canned red pimiento
1 tablespoon chopped garlic
1½ tablespoons medium capers
Freshly ground black pepper to taste
¾ cup olive oil
½ cup red wine vinegar

Put eggs, parsley, anchovies, onion, and pimiento through hand grinder or food processor, if you prefer. Then mix ingredients well in a deep bowl, adding garlic, capers, and pepper to taste (this recipe needs no salt). Amalgamate well, then add oil and vinegar, mixing well. Taste. Sauce must have a distinctive vinaigrette flavor; if it seems too mild, add more vinegar. Serve on the side with hot vegetables, boiled beef and other meats, fish, or with whatever food you feel the sauce would enhance.

SALSA MAIONESE
(Mayonnaise)

YIELDS 2½ CUPS

2   cups olive oil
3–4 egg yolks
½   teaspoon salt
    Generous sprinkle of freshly ground white pepper
2   tablespoons strained lemon juice or 1 tablespoon white
    wine vinegar (see note below)

Warm a mixing bowl with boiling water. Dry thoroughly. Heat oil in saucepan over low flame until lukewarm.

Place 3 egg yolks in bowl and begin to beat with a wire whisk. Add salt, pepper, and a few drops of lemon juice or vinegar, continuing to beat. Then beat in the oil in droplets. By the time you have added 4 to 5 tablespoons of oil, the sauce will have a heavy, creamy consistency. Gradually add more lemon juice or vinegar, and continue beating in oil. If mayonnaise should start to separate, beat one more egg yolk in a separate bowl, then beat mayonnaise into it a little at a time.

Of course, you can use a food processor or a blender.

Note: Lemon juice keeps sauce a lighter color.

SALSA MAIONESE ALLA RUSSA
(Russian Mayonnaise)

Follow recipe for mayonnaise (see preceding recipe), then add the following ingredients:

YIELDS 2½ CUPS

3–4   fresh tarragon leaves, finely minced, or the equivalent
        in tarragon leaves preserved in vinegar
2   small packets saffron, soaked in a small amount of
        warm water a few minutes in advance

SALSA MAIONESE ALL'AGLIO
(Garlic Mayonnaise)

Follow recipe for mayonnaise (see page 218), then add ½ teaspoon finely minced garlic. This type of mayonnaise is excellent
served with cold poached fish.

YIELDS 2½ CUPS

SALSA MAIONESE VERDE
(Green Mayonnaise)

Follow recipe for mayonnaise (see page 218), then add the following ingredients:

YIELDS 2½ CUPS

3–4   fresh tarragon leaves, finely minced, or the equivalent
        in tarragon leaves preserved in vinegar
8   fresh spinach leaves, washed and finely minced
1–2   fresh basil leaves, finely minced

SALSA PER INSALATE DELLA TRATTORIA
(Trattoria Salad Dressing)

This dressing can be refrigerated for at least a month if kept tightly covered, but should be mixed well every time it is used. It is excellent on almost any type of salad.

YIELDS ABOUT 5 CUPS

1	quart olive oil
⅔	cup red wine vinegar
1	egg yolk
2¼	teaspoons Dijon mustard
1	tablespoon chopped Italian parsley
	Generous sprinkle of dried oregano
	Sprinkle of dried thyme
4	fresh basil leaves, finely chopped, or sprinkle of dried basil
4	fresh tarragon leaves, finely chopped, or the equivalent in tarragon leaves preserved in vinegar
1–2	fresh mint leaves (if obtainable), finely chopped
	Pinch of freshly grated nutmeg
	Pinch of paprika
	Salt and freshly ground black pepper to taste
2¼	teaspoons A.1. Steak Sauce
2¼	teaspoons Worcestershire sauce
4	drops Tabasco sauce

Blend oil and vinegar in a large bowl. Using a wire whisk, mix in remaining ingredients in order listed, and beat until dressing has a smooth, velvety consistency. This sauce can also be done in a food processor or blender.

Pasta Making

The making of pasta is regarded as an art among Italian chefs. They often have contests to see who can make the thinnest sheet of pasta, the widest variety of shapes, the most subtle differences in taste. Many kinds of vegetables are used in making special pasta, either dried or fresh, such as spinach, tomatoes, beets, zucchini, and potatoes. Such ingredients create further variations in taste and texture. And, of course, a good pasta often becomes a great pasta when it is complemented by an inventive sauce.

BASIC RECIPE FOR FRESH PASTA

There are several ways in which pasta can be made, and the method you choose depends on your kitchen equipment, your work space, and your taste. There are those who feel that nothing can equal the quality of pasta kneaded, rolled, and cut entirely by hand as it has been done in Italian households for generations. But it requires technique—which can, of course, be mastered with practice—and it demands a good-sized work area.

I must admit to you that I am a great fan of the electric pasta machines now on the market that, in about 20 to 30 minutes, can produce for you enough pasta to feed 20 people, as well as great fun while you do it.

You can make the dough in a food processor, then roll and cut it with a pasta machine, and have fresh, tender pasta on your table in an amazingly short time.

YIELDS ABOUT 2 POUNDS

4   cups all-purpose flour, preferably unbleached
4   extra-large eggs
¼   cup olive oil
    Sprinkle of salt

Hand Method: Form a mound of the flour on a pastry board, approximately 18 by 30 inches, and make a well in the center. Break eggs into it, then add olive oil and salt. Break up the eggs with a fork, while with the other hand you start to mix in the flour from the top of the mound, adding it steadily so that the mixture doesn't stick to the work surface. When the flour is almost totally absorbed, begin kneading, pressing with the heels of your palms and folding the dough until it is well blended and smooth but still moist. Let pasta dry for 10 minutes, then divide into 4 pieces. To roll out the pasta, the best rolling pin to use is about 30 inches long and 4 inches round, but you can also use a long, tapered pastry rolling pin or the longest available rotating rolling pin.

First, dust the board with some sifted flour. Roll out each piece of dough to a uniform thickness of 1/16 to 1/32 of an inch—or as thin as you can get it—in the following way: First, roll it into a flattened oval. Then turn and roll the dough several times until it is completely round. Dust it with flour, and turn it over. Again, roll out and turn, dust with flour, and turn it over. Repeat this procedure about 8 times. After the second or third rolling out, it will be difficult to lift and turn the pasta by hand. Therefore, gently wrap it around the rolling pin, and roll it on the reverse side. When the dough is thin enough, roll out the edges to give uniform thickness.

Allow to dry on the board for 12 to 15 minutes before cutting.

Food Processor Method: Use same ingredients in same proportion listed on page 224. Place metal chopping blade in position in food processor workbowl. Add flour, salt, and oil to workbowl and process for 8 to 10 minutes. Add eggs and process approximately 12 seconds, or until the dough is moist but not damp or sticky. If it should be too sticky, sprinkle with 1 or 2 tablespoons of flour and process for an additional 7 to 8 seconds. If pasta feels too dry, pour a few drops of water in, and process to blend well. Place dough on floured surface. Knead with the heel of your hand for 3 to 5 minutes, or until you have a smooth, compact ball of dough. Divide the dough into 4 equal pieces and cover with a towel to keep it soft until ready to take the next step.

Pasta by Machine, Manual or Electric: Follow manufacturer's instructions for making pasta. After you flatten your dough through the kneading rollers, set on number 6. Put dough through machine at this setting. Repeat this about six times, each time folding the strip over and putting it through again, so it gets a thorough kneading. As the strip will get longer and thinner, fold it over two or three times and keep on rolling until it looks and feels velvety and supple.

Lower the gauge for each successive rolling, from 6 to 5, 4, 3, and finally 2, or 1, until you achieve the thickness desired. The final setting will give the dough an almost paper thinness. The thinner the pasta, the more tender it will be. As the pasta gets thinner and thinner, it also gets longer and longer, and you will have to cut it in half when it gets too long to put through the machine comfortably. When you have finished rolling, keep pasta strips moist on a damp towel while you change over to the cutting rollers. Use the thickness you prefer, according to the sauce and the shape of the pasta you are going to make. If you're not going to cook the pasta immediately, spread it on a board and dust with flour, or hang it on a line in the case of long, thin pasta. Let dry at least 5 minutes if you're going to use pasta immediately after making it.

PASTA ROSSA
(Beet Pasta)

Use same ingredients, in same proportions, as for Basic Pasta on page 224, but add 1 medium red beet as follows:

Trim stem of beet, leaving 1½ to 2 inches, then wash beet very well under cold water. Bring 2 quarts salted water to boil. Add beet and cook about 1 hour, or until tender. Skin under cold water. Discard stem, then mash beet very fine. Measure 1 heaping tablespoon of mashed beet and place in well formed in flour. Add eggs, oil, and salt, then follow process described on page 224. Let beet pasta dry 8 to 10 minutes longer.

PASTA VERDE
(Spinach Pasta)

Use same ingredients, in same proportions, as for Basic Pasta on page 224, but add ½ pound fresh spinach as follows:

Blanch spinach 2 minutes, then drain and squeeze dry. Chop very fine and place in well formed in flour. Add eggs, oil, and salt, then follow process described on page 224. Let spinach pasta dry 8 to 10 minutes longer.

PASTA DI POMODORO
(Tomato Pasta)

Use same ingredients, in same proportions, as for Basic Pasta on page 224, but add 2 tablespoons tomato paste to well formed in flour. Add eggs, oil, and salt, then follow process described on page 224. Let tomato pasta dry 8 to 10 minutes longer.

PASTA DI ZUCCHINE
(Zucchini Pasta)

Use same ingredients, in the same proportions, as for Basic Pasta on page 224, but add 4 medium zucchini as follows:

Trim and wash zucchini under cold running water. Cut in half
lengthwise, then scoop out and discard most of the pulp. Bring
2 quarts salted water to boil. Add zucchini and cook 10 to 15
minutes. Cool under cold running water, and either hand-mash
to pulp or put through food processor. Add to well formed in
flour. Add eggs, oil, and salt, then follow process described on
page 224. Let zucchini pasta dry 8 to 10 minutes longer.

PASTA DI PATATE
(Potato Pasta)

This type of pasta is usually made in the form of gnocchi, for
which a recipe follows.

GNOCCHI DI PATATE
(Potato Gnocchi)

An old Roman song for children goes: *"Ridi, ridi, chè la mamma
ha fatto i gnocchi"* ("Laugh, laugh, because Mama made gnocchi")—another Italian way of associating food with joy and
happiness.

SERVES 6–8

1½   pounds boiling potatoes, scrubbed
1¾   cups all-purpose flour
      Salt to taste
1½   teaspoons olive oil

Boil potatoes in their skins until tender but firm. Peel while hot
(do not run under cold water), then process through food mill or
potato ricer. Place on pasta board dusted with flour, sprinkle
with salt. Start mixing flour into potato, a little at a time, until
dough is well blended and firm. Knead gently for 6 to 8 minutes.
Sprinkle dough with sifted flour, then cut into several pieces.
Roll each piece into a long, sausage-like shape ½ inch in diameter.
Then cut into 1-inch pieces. Dust again with sifted flour. Let rest
5 minutes, covered with kitchen towel.

Using your thumb, gently roll pieces down inside a table fork so that they curl and are imprinted with the tines.

Bring to boil a large pot of salted water. Add oil, then quickly drop gnocchi into pot, stirring water with a wooden spoon so gnocchi will not stick together. In a few seconds, gnocchi will come to the surface of the water. Let them cook 1 more minute. Remove from water with strainer-skimmer to serving platter. Serve in any of the following ways:

1. Melt 6 tablespoons lightly salted butter; mix well with gnocchi and serve with freshly grated Parmesan cheese.
2. Heat 2 cups tomato sauce (see page 211); mix well with gnocchi and serve with freshly grated Parmesan cheese.
3. Heat 2½ cups Bolognese sauce (see page 213); mix well with gnocchi and serve with freshly grated Parmesan cheese.
4. Heat 2½ cups meat sauce (see page 212); mix well with gnocchi and serve with freshly grated Parmesan cheese.

PASTA CUTTING

Cannelloni and manicotti: Cut into 4-by-4-inch squares.

Lasagne: Cut into strips 20 by 4 inches.

Fettuccine: If cutting by hand, fold up each piece of pasta gently into a flattened roll, and cut into ¼-inch strips. Unfold and place on a floured board or line to dry. Or run through the ¼-inch cutting section of your pasta machine. Dry the same way.

Fettuccelle/Lasagnette: Cut by hand as for fettuccine in a slightly narrower width, or run through the appropriate cutting section of your pasta machine. Dry the same way.

Tagliolini/Tagliarini: Cut by hand as for fettuccine into ¹⁄₁₆-inch strips, or run through the ¹⁄₁₆-inch cutter of your pasta machine. Dry the same way.

Tortellini: In this case, do not let the pasta dry. Cut immediately into circles 1½ inches in diameter, with a round cookie cutter. Proceed to fill as directed on page 234.

Ravioli and pansôti: With a jagged-edged cutting wheel, cut lengthwise into strips 3 inches wide. Proceed to fill as directed on pages 236 and 238.

Agnolotti: Use same process as ravioli and pansôti above. Proceed to fill and cut to shape as directed on page 240.

RECIPES FOR FILLED PASTA

CANNELLONI

This recipe came to me via L'Osteria del Cane in Verona. The Bolognese origin is dubious, since the chef of that establishment was a large lady from Piemonte. In any case, I was one of the first to introduce this delicious dish to New York, at a time when northern Italian cooking was little known in restaurants around the city.

SERVES 8

1 small chicken (about 2 pounds)
1 pound fresh spinach or ½ package frozen leaf spinach
1 carrot, washed and scraped
1 stalk celery, washed and scraped
½ small onion, peeled
¼ cup olive oil
5 tablespoons lightly salted butter
¼ teaspoon chopped garlic
3 leaves fresh basil or ½ teaspoon dried basil
Sprinkle of dried rosemary
1 tablespoon chopped Italian parsley

1   bay leaf
      Sprinkle of dried thyme
      Sprinkle of freshly grated nutmeg
½   teaspoon salt
¼   teaspoon freshly ground black pepper
¾   pound boneless beef chuck, in one piece
¾   pound boneless pork shoulder, in one piece
⅓   cup beef consommé (see page 207)
¼   cup red wine
3½   cups tomato sauce (see page 211)
10   slices (each ⅛ inch thick) Fontina or mozzarella
          cheese
1   egg
1½   cups freshly grated Parmesan cheese
      Fresh pasta (see page 223)
1   tablespoon vegetable oil
2½   cups béchamel sauce (see page 216)

Place chicken in 3 quarts salted cold water and bring to boil, then lower flame and simmer for about 30 minutes, until tender.

If fresh spinach is used, remove stems and wash leaves thoroughly under cold water. Cook 2 minutes in 2 cups salted boiling water. If frozen is used, simply let defrost, dry (using no water), at room temperature. In either case, squeeze free of water and chop coarsely.

Put carrot, celery stalk, and onion through food processor. Heat olive oil and butter on low flame in large saucepan. Add vegetable mixture, chopped garlic, basil, rosemary, parsley, bay leaf, thyme, nutmeg, salt, and pepper. Sauté about 10 minutes. Then place beef and pork in the pan and brown on all sides, about 30 minutes, making sure meat does not stick to pan. Add a few spoonfuls of consommé, as necessary. Add wine. Let evaporate approximately 8 minutes. When meat is tender, add tomato sauce. Cook, uncovered, another 20 minutes. Remove bay leaf and discard. Remove meat from sauce and set aside. Put sauce through a food mill. Return to saucepan and simmer, uncovered, on a very low flame for another 10 minutes. Set sauce aside.

For filling, chop meat rather coarsely. Remove skin from cooked chicken and detach breast meat; chop breast meat coarsely. Reserve remaining chicken and skin for future use. Chop 2 slices of the Fontina or mozzarella. Combine meat, chicken breast, and

chopped mozzarella in mixing bowl. Add egg, spinach, and ¾ cup
of the Parmesan cheese. Blend thoroughly, preferably with your
hands. Set filling mixture aside.

Roll fresh pasta out as thin as possible. Cut sheets into 4-by-4-
inch squares (cannelloni). You should have 16 to 18 squares.

Bring to boil 4 quarts salted water, then add vegetable oil.
Carefully immerse pasta squares, one by one, into boiling water
and cook 2 minutes, stirring water with wooden spoon so squares
do not stick together. Drain gently and run under cold water.
Place squares on kitchen towels on work counter. Place 1½
tablespoons of filling mixture in line down center of each square
and form into a roll.

Preheat oven to 350°F.

Pour a layer of the sauce set aside into a baking pan. Place
cannelloni, seam side down, side by side, over sauce, then cover
with another layer of sauce. Spoon béchamel sauce over evenly.
Cut the remaining 8 slices of Fontina or mozzarella into strips;
each strip should cover 1 cannelloni.

Cook cannelloni 10 minutes in oven. Serve very hot, 2 pieces of
cannelloni per person, making sure to spoon the sauce around
each portion. Serve with remaining ¾ cup grated Parmesan
cheese and a peppermill.

MANICOTTI

SERVES 8

      1   pound whole-milk ricotta cheese
   1¼   cups freshly grated Parmesan cheese
      ¼   pound sliced prosciutto or ham of your choice, chopped
               coarsely
   1½   teaspoons chopped Italian parsley
            Salt and freshly ground black pepper to taste
            Sprinkle of freshly grated nutmeg
      3   tablespoons heavy cream

2   egg yolks
    Fresh pasta (see page 223)
1   tablespoon vegetable oil
2   tablespoons lightly salted butter
2   cups tomato sauce (see page 211)

Combine ricotta, ¼ cup of the Parmesan cheese, the prosciutto, parsley, salt and pepper to taste, nutmeg, cream, and egg yolks. Blend well and set aside as filling mixture.

Roll out fresh pasta as thin as possible. Cut sheets into 4-by-4-inch squares (manicotti). You should have 16 to 18 squares.

Bring to boil 4 quarts salted water, then add vegetable oil. Carefully immerse pasta squares, one by one, into boiling water and cook 2 minutes, stirring water with wooden spoon so squares do not stick together. Drain gently and run under cold water. Place squares on kitchen towels on work counter. Place 1½ tablespoons of filling mixture in line down center of each square and form a roll.

Preheat oven to 350°F.

Melt butter and coat a baking dish with it. Spread half the tomato sauce on bottom of dish. Place manicotti, seam side down, side by side over sauce; pour remaining sauce over. Sprinkle with remaining ¾ cup Parmesan cheese and bake for approximately 10 minutes. Serve immediately.

LASAGNE DI CARNEVALE

Stuffed lasagne for Mardi Gras! It's a meal for parties, to be consumed with a robust red wine. It's a meal of *allegria*. A waltz afterward, therefore, is in order.

SERVES 8–10

8   tablespoons lightly salted butter
⅓   cup olive oil
1   whole clove garlic, peeled

1 pound Italian sweet pork sausage, removed from casing and crumbled
½ pound finely ground loin of pork
1 pound ground lean beef
1 tablespoon chopped Italian parsley
3–4 fresh basil leaves, finely chopped, or ½ teaspoon dried basil
Sprinkle of dried thyme
Sprinkle of dried oregano
Sprinkle of freshly grated nutmeg
Salt and freshly ground black pepper to taste
1 cup imported dried porcini (about 2 ounces), pre-soaked in lukewarm water at least 1½ hours in advance, drained
½ cup dry red wine
2½ tablespoons tomato paste diluted with ½ cup warm water
3 cups tomato sauce (see page 211)
1 egg yolk
1 pound whole-milk ricotta cheese
Fresh pasta (see page 223)
1 tablespoon vegetable oil
1 cup freshly grated Parmesan cheese
1 cup freshly grated pecorino cheese
¼ pound mozzarella cheese, diced small or shredded
¼ pound Fonduta cheese, diced small or shredded

Melt 7 tablespoons of the butter and heat olive oil in a deep saucepan. Add garlic. Sauté until browned, then discard. Add sausage meat. When sausage begins to brown, add pork and cook, stirring, until well browned. Add beef and continue to cook for another 15 minutes. Add herbs, nutmeg, salt and pepper to taste, and porcini. Cook another 10 minutes, stirring. Add wine and let evaporate approximately 8 minutes. Stir diluted tomato paste into sauce. Cook, uncovered, 15 minutes, then add tomato sauce and cook 20 minutes longer. Set sauce aside.

Beat egg yolk into ricotta until smooth. Set aside.

Roll fresh pasta out as thin as possible. Cut sheets into strips 20 by 4 inches. Bring to boil large pot of salted water, then add vegetable oil. Drop sheets of pasta, a sheet at a time, carefully into boiling water and cook 2 minutes, stirring water with wooden spoon so strips do not stick together. Drain gently, then run under cold water, separating the pieces from each other. Set aside on kitchen towels.

Preheat oven to 350°F.

Coat a deep baking dish with remaining 1 tablespoon butter. Ladle some of the sauce into dish to cover bottom. Place strips of pasta on bottom of dish in such a way that they cover bottom and also drape over sides of dish. Spread some sauce over pasta. Sprinkle on a layer each of Parmesan, pecorino, mozzarella, and Fonduta, using about a third of each. Add a layer of ricotta. Cover cheeses with another layer of pasta (this time omitting the draping).

Being careful to reserve ½ cup of sauce, repeat layering procedure until rest of sauce, cheese, and pasta are used up. Then fold draped pasta over top, and smooth on remaining sauce. Bake for about 10 minutes.

Serve with additional grated Parmesan cheese, if you like.

TORTELLINI

MAKES ABOUT 125 TO 150 TORTELLINI

6	tablespoons lightly salted butter
2	medium skinned and boned chicken breasts
1	pound mortadella, cut in chunks
4	thin slices prosciutto
¼	teaspoon freshly grated nutmeg
	Salt and freshly ground black pepper to taste
1½	teaspoons chopped Italian parsley
2	eggs
¾	cup freshly grated Parmesan cheese
	Fresh pasta (see page 223)

Melt butter in skillet over a medium flame. Sauté chicken breasts on both sides until cooked through. Let cool, reserving butter in pan.

Put chicken, mortadella, and prosciutto through a food processor. Transfer to a mixing bowl and blend with nutmeg, salt and pepper, parsley, and butter from skillet. When filling is totally cool, thoroughly mix in eggs and Parmesan cheese. Blend well.

Roll fresh pasta out as thin as possible. Cut sheets into circles 1½ inches in diameter.

Place ½ teaspoon of the filling in the center of each circle. Moisten edges with water. Fold over half the dough to cover the filling but not quite meet the opposite edge of the circle. Seal the dough where it meets. Wrap these half-moons around the top of your index finger to form a ring, and seal the two ends together, first moistening the ends with water. Dust with sifted flour. Allow to dry for 10 to 15 minutes before cooking as instructed in recipe.

TORTELLINI DELLA NONNA

La nonna means "grandmother." This, therefore, is the way grandmother used to make tortellini. That's what the Romans like to call this dish. But then, all sorts of stories are told about tortellini. Some even say that their shape is a facsimile of Venus' belly button!

SERVES 6

120   tortellini (see page 234)
  6   tablespoons lightly salted butter
  1   cup heavy cream
  5   thin slices prosciutto, julienned
  ½   cup fresh or frozen peas; if fresh, cooked 3 minutes; if frozen, defrosted, dry (using no water), at room temperature
    Freshly ground black pepper to taste
  ¾   cup freshly grated Parmesan cheese

Bring to boil 3 quarts salted water. Drop in tortellini and cook 1½ to 2 minutes. Drain gently.

Melt butter in sauté pan. Add tortellini and mix together gently but thoroughly over low heat with wooden spoon. Add cream and cook 1 minute, stirring, then add prosciutto. Add peas, pepper to taste, finally ¾ cup cheese. Blend thoroughly. Tortellini must have a rich, creamy look. Serve hot, with additional ground pepper from mill and grated Parmesan cheese.

RAVIOLI

SERVES 6–8 (ABOUT 80–100 RAVIOLI)

½   cup olive oil
1   whole clove garlic, peeled
1   pound boneless lean beef, such as eye of round
8   tablespoons lightly salted butter
1   small onion, peeled and finely chopped
½   teaspoon freshly grated nutmeg
     Salt and freshly ground black pepper to taste
5   pieces imported dried porcini, presoaked in lukewarm water at least 1½ hours in advance, drained, and coarsely chopped
1½   tablespoons chopped Italian parsley
1   pound Italian sweet pork sausage, removed from casing and crumbled
½   cup red wine
2   tablespoons tomato paste, diluted with small amount of warm water
     Chicken consommé (see page 207), if necessary
8–9   tender Swiss chard leaves, or inner leaves of small head of chicory, washed under cold water and drained
2   eggs
⅔   cup freshly grated Parmesan cheese
     Fresh pasta (see page 223)

Heat oil in a skillet. Add garlic and beef. Brown beef thoroughly, then remove beef from oil and set aside. Discard garlic. Melt 6 tablespoons of the butter in skillet with oil. Add chopped onion and sauté until golden. Add nutmeg, salt and pepper to taste, porcini, and parsley and sauté 5 minutes. Add sausage and cook, stirring until quite brown. Return beef to pan, cover, and cook 5 minutes. Uncover and add wine. Cook until it evaporates, approximately 8 minutes. Pour in diluted tomato paste and cook 30 minutes, stirring continuously. If mixture becomes too dry, add small amount of chicken consommé. Let mixture cool slightly, then put through coarse setting of meat grinder. Let filling cool to room temperature.

Boil Swiss chard or chicory in salted water for 3 minutes. Drain well. Sauté in remaining 2 tablespoons butter for 2 minutes. Put through grinder, and blend well with rest of filling. Let cool. Thoroughly mix in eggs and Parmesan cheese.

Roll fresh pasta out as thin as possible. Cut sheets into strips 3 inches wide, using a jagged-edged cutting wheel.

Lay half the strips of pasta on a board or table (see note below). Place 1½-teaspoon mounds of filling 1 inch apart down the center of each strip, leaving a border of about ½ inch. Moisten edges of dough and spaces between mounds of filling with water. Place remaining strips of pasta on top, and press the moistened dough to seal filling thoroughly. Using jagged-edged cutting wheel, cut ravioli into 2- or 2½-inch squares. Be sure to cut between mounds of filling. Dust with sifted flour. Allow to dry for 10 minutes before cooking as instructed in recipe.

Note: Metal forms for assembling ravioli or agnolotti can be bought in Italian stores or kitchen equipment shops and will help you make a much more uniform and professional-looking product.

RAVIOLI AU TUCCU

"Au tuccù" is the Genovese dialect term for a meat sauce. In a moment of nostalgia any good Genovese away from home might sigh and say, "What I wouldn't do for a dish of *ravioli au tuccù!*"

SERVES 6

2½   cups meat sauce (see page 212)
1   tablespoon vegetable oil
     Fresh ravioli (see page 236)
½   cup freshly grated Parmesan cheese
     Freshly ground black pepper to taste

In a saucepan, heat meat sauce over a low flame. Set aside and keep warm.

Bring 4 quarts salted water to a boil, then add the vegetable oil. Add the ravioli and cook 2½ minutes. Drain carefully to avoid breaking. Pour ½ cup of the meat sauce into a large skillet. Add the ravioli, and mix carefully over low flame. Arrange ravioli on serving platter, then pour remaining meat sauce over. Serve with grated Parmesan and pass a peppermill.

PANSOTI

MAKES ABOUT 75–80 PANSOTI
SERVES 6–8

1   pound fresh spinach or 1 package frozen spinach
3   tablespoons lightly salted butter
1   pound whole-milk ricotta
    Sprinkle of freshly grated nutmeg
    Salt and freshly ground black pepper to taste

1½ teaspoons chopped Italian parsley
3 tablespoons heavy cream
2 egg yolks
1 cup freshly grated Parmesan cheese
Fresh pasta (see page 223)

If using fresh spinach, discard tough stems, then wash leaves well in cold water and drain thoroughly. Boil in salted water 3 minutes, then squeeze dry. If using frozen spinach, defrost, dry (using no water), at room temperature. Squeeze out all the water.

Sauté fresh or frozen spinach in butter for 3 minutes. Let cool, reserving butter in pan. Chop spinach rather fine by hand. Place in a mixing bowl, then add butter from pan, ricotta, nutmeg, salt and pepper to taste, parsley, and heavy cream. When filling is completely cool, mix in egg yolks and Parmesan cheese.

Roll fresh pasta out as thin as possible. Cut sheets into strips 3 inches wide, using jagged-edged cutting wheel. To assemble, follow directions for ravioli (see page 237).

PANSOTI ALLA SALSA DI NOCI
(Pansôti with Nut Sauce)

A typical Ligurian dish, served almost exclusively in Recco, a small town near Genoa.

SERVES 6–8

10 tablespoons lightly salted butter
½ clove garlic, chopped very fine
1½ teaspoons chopped Italian parsley
4 fresh basil leaves, finely chopped, or ½ teaspoon dried basil
1 tablespoon finely chopped pignoli (pine nuts)
6 ounces walnuts, finely chopped
Freshly ground black pepper to taste

2   cups heavy cream
1   cup freshly grated Parmesan cheese
1   tablespoon vegetable oil
    Fresh pansôti (about 80) (see page 238)

Melt 8 tablespoons of the butter over a low flame in a deep, quart-size pan. Add garlic, parsley, and basil and sauté for a few minutes. Add pignoli and walnuts and stir with a wooden spoon, being careful not to let nuts burn or stick to bottom of pot. Add black pepper to taste. Add heavy cream and stir until mixture comes to a boil and thickens. Add ½ cup of the Parmesan cheese, continuing to stir and cook for another 15 minutes. Remove from flame.

Bring to boil 4 quarts salted water, then add the vegetable oil. Add pansôti, making sure they don't stick together. Cook 2½ minutes. Drain carefully to avoid breaking.

Melt remaining 2 tablespoons butter in a large sauté pan. Add pansôti and turn with wooden spoon until well coated. Gradually add sauce to pan. Heat thoroughly over low flame until pansôti are completely covered with sauce. Serve immediately, adding remaining ½ cup cheese and additional freshly ground black pepper, if desired.

AGNOLOTTI

MAKES ABOUT 80 AGNOLOTTI

½   cup olive oil
1   whole clove garlic, peeled
½   pound boneless lean beef, such as eye of round
1   chicken breast, skinned and boned
½   cup lightly salted butter
    Sprinkle of freshly grated nutmeg
1½ teaspoons chopped Italian parsley
    Salt and freshly ground black pepper to taste

½ cup red wine
½ pound prosciutto, sliced
2 eggs
½ cup freshly grated Parmesan cheese
   Fresh pasta (see page 223)

Heat oil in a skillet. Add garlic and beef. Brown beef thoroughly, then remove beef from oil and set aside. Brown the chicken breast on both sides, then remove and set aside. Discard garlic. Melt butter in skillet with oil, then return to it the beef and chicken. Add nutmeg, parsley, and salt and pepper to taste and sauté for 10 minutes. Add wine and let it evaporate, about 8 minutes. Add prosciutto and cook 3 minutes. Taste for seasoning, then remove from heat and let cool.

Put cooled mixture through coarse setting of a meat grinder. Fold in eggs and Parmesan cheese. Amalgamate thoroughly and set aside.

Roll fresh pasta out as thin as possible. Cut sheets into strips 3 inches wide, using jagged-edged cutting wheel. Lay strips of pasta on a board or table (see note, page 237). Place 1-teaspoon mounds of filling at 1½-inch intervals down the center of each strip. Moisten edges of dough and spaces between filling with water. Carefully fold the strips in half to cover the filling. Press along moistened dough to seal mounds thoroughly. Then cut into half-moons by using a half-moon cookie cutter (available in almost any specialty cookware shop). Press cut edges to seal. Dust with sifted flour. Allow agnolotti to dry for at least 15 minutes before cooking as instructed in recipe.

AGNOLOTTI AL RAGU E FUNGHI
(Agnolotti with Ragù and Wild Mushrooms)

This richly filled pasta, shaped like a half-moon, is typical of the region of Emilia, which is also the source of Italy's best dried porcini.

SERVES 6

2½   cups meat sauce (see page 212)
½   cup imported dried porcini, presoaked in lukewarm
        water at least 1½ hours in advance, drained, and
        coarsely chopped
1½   teaspoons chopped Italian parsley
        Fresh agnolotti (see page 240)
1   tablespoon lightly salted butter
⅓   cup freshly grated Parmesan cheese
        Freshly ground black pepper to taste

Pour meat sauce into a saucepan, add the porcini and parsley, and heat over a low flame for about 20 minutes. Set aside and keep warm.

Bring to boil 4 quarts salted water. Cook agnolotti 2½ minutes. Drain carefully. Melt butter in sauté pan. Add 5 tablespoons of meat sauce, then add agnolotti; mix well. Turn agnolotti onto serving platter, then pour remaining sauce over. Serve immediately with grated Parmesan and pass a peppermill.

At the Marketplace

The cooking of good food begins with the selection of top-rate ingredients. Shortcuts and substitutions can only be excused when one must make do with whatever one can find in one's larder in an "emergency," or with the available supply in the markets where one lives. And there appears to be less and less reason for such excuses, since it seems to me that in the last year or so, every time I take a stroll, a new food market has just opened. Good! America has entered an exciting new era in culinary history.

Enough with frozen and antiseptic, cellophane-sealed foods. "Ladies and gentlemen," I feel like addressing anyone willing to listen to me, "stop buying packaged food, frozen food, canned food. Let's have a large rally to abolish the frozen goods. Come with me to the fresh food markets, and let's fill our baskets with real food, fresh produce, fresh meat and fish." Alas, it doesn't always work, entirely.

On practically every block in New York one comes face to face with neatly built pyramids of brilliantly colored fruits and vegetables—"the Oriental greengrocers." They have become like a rash, spreading, spreading, spreading. They have mastered the art of "looking good." A leaf amputated here, a stalk removed there, shined-up apples, a little surgery on that bunch of grapes. But, above all, the water sprinkler at the ready, to douse those symmetrical mounds of fruits and vegetables. Shoppers, look out! A wet head of lettuce weighs more than a dry one! In any event, these markets are making it a lot easier for you to bring quasi-fresh goods to your table, and in a larger variety. Items that once you had to travel far and wide to obtain. So it's not so bad.

Then you have the "gourmet" shops, usually well stocked with interesting, exotic specialties, even though the prices compete with that of gold. For those who can afford it, these shops are a great plus. However, most of the items on their well-polished shelves are often enough only cosmetics for making a dinner look good and, like cosmetics, one has to know how to apply them for the best results.

Next you come across the super-super-special food markets the like of New York City's Dean & DeLuca, Balducci's, and Zabar's. Here you are playing a different game, in a major league. *Rule 1:* Stuff your pockets with money. *Rule 2:* Unleash your fantasies and run amok along the aisles, for everything your palate desires *is here*. Beware! You might have to mortgage the house after the first visit. On the other hand, what is money for? And what's more, what these stores have to offer is truly extraordinary. They are authentic shrines for the curious, the hungry, the discriminating, the fastidious cook. They are the no-nonsense stores. They are the hard core of the real food fantasies. Like galleons of centuries past, ploughing the treasured spice routes, these markets have their holds filled to the gunnels with the most delectable condiments, spices, herbs, meats, fish, produce, pasta, sweets, breads, butters and oils, along with implements to reduce your toiling in the kitchen to a trick of legerdemain.

Further up the street you may encounter one of the burgeoning "pasta" stores, which run in quality from excellent to poor. While your preparation work can be trimmed down even more, you must be careful, because the money involved is, again, not inconsiderable. So, return to your little greengrocer, your special butcher shop, your fish store. Learn how to bake bread. Mr. James Beard's book *Beard on Bread* can teach you all you need to know and how to do it. Grow some of the herbs in window boxes, or on a patch of land or a terrace. It's fun!

AMARETTI

Amaretti di Saronno are the elite of the Italian almond macaroons obtainable on the American markets. There are domestic brands made by local pastry shops, but they cannot compete in quality or taste with Amaretti di Saronno. They are delicious soaked in Asti Spumante or Moscato wine, or crushed over zabaglione, or simply eaten the way they come, in their handsome tin can, along with a good cup of cappuccino.

ANCHOVIES

I use anchovies in many recipes. I prefer Masso anchovies, a Portuguese brand packed in olive oil that can be purchased at most Italian grocers. Unfortunately, it is only obtainable in 14- and 28-ounce cans. Therefore, almost any of the smaller cans of imported anchovies packed in olive oil will suffice. However, avoid using the so-called cocktail anchovies, which are generally preserved in a strongly aromatic liquid.

Keep any leftover anchovies refrigerated in their own oil. But do not keep more than a week after opening the can. They will get very salty and the taste will change radically. Whenever you make a recipe that calls for anchovies, avoid the use of salt until the very end of the cooking, when you will taste the food to see if any additional salt is needed.

Actually, the best anchovies are those packed in salt (Italian, Portuguese, or Spanish). You have to wash off the salt and bone this type of anchovy, and marinate them in olive oil. However, they are well worth the trouble.

BUTTER

I use more butter (lightly salted) than oil in my recipes, since butter gives delicacy and a more subtle flavor to food. A great many of my sauces are also made with cream, with which butter blends nicely.

CAPERS

Capers are usually obtainable in jars, preserved in brine. Like olives, they are a very versatile vegetable/fruit, rather strong but marvelously flavorful and distinct in the taste they give to sauces, and especially to fish dishes.

CHEESES

Italian cheeses are as innumerable as the types and shapes of pasta. Every Italian region is known for its special cheeses.

PARMIGIANO/PARMESAN

The most widely known among the Italian cheeses is Parmigiano. There are two distinct types of Parmesan cheese. One, called *grana*, is a fairly young cheese, usually light yellow in color. It is flakier than the Parmesan cheese used for cooking and is often eaten with fruit or served as a table cheese. The other type of Parmesan cheese, specified in most of my recipes, is a more aged cheese. It is drier, harder, and a very light yellow, or almost white, in color. The best Parmesan cheese comes from Emilia-Parma, although excellent Parmesan is now made in Wisconsin and Argentina. I am totally opposed to grated cheese sold in containers.

PECORINO

Derived from the Italian word for sheep, *pecora*, pecorino is made from sheep's milk. In this country it is often called "Romano cheese." It is sharper than Parmesan and is used only with certain dishes, such as pesto and *spaghetti amatriciana*. It is also mixed with Parmesan to garnish soups and for stuffing. Fresh pecorino, when obtainable, can be used as a fine table cheese. Pecorino is mostly used in the South Italian kitchen.

The finest pecorino cheese comes from the island of Sardinia. Very hard in texture and strong in flavor, it is called *Sardo*.

RICOTTA

Fresh ricotta is a soft cheese with a delicate flavor. It does not keep for more than a few days. It generally comes in two different grades—whole-milk ricotta or skim-milk ricotta. It is used mostly for filling, but can also be eaten by itself with olive oil, salt, and pepper added to it. Served with fresh fruit, it is an excellent diet dessert cheese. It is also used in many desserts, such as cheesecake and pastry.

MOZZARELLA

Mozzarella comes in three different forms: a hard type, used for filling, pizza, topping, and baked dishes; a fresh, softer type, used in many recipes or served as a table cheese; and smoked, which is excellent as an appetizer and piquant in flavor. Fresh mozzarella should not be kept for more than a few days.

FONTINA AND FONDUTA

Fontina is a mild cheese, generally used as a table cheese or as a topping on baked dishes. I prefer Fontina to mozzarella because it's more delicate and more flavorful. Fontina should not be too dark a yellow in color. A slightly oily surface indicates that it is past its prime and no longer a good eating cheese. The best Fontina comes from Val d'Aosta, where it is widely used in that region's cooking.

Fonduta is a type of softer Fontina, and coarser in texture. It is used almost exclusively in stuffing. Both Fontina and Fonduta are an integral part of North Italian cooking.

GORGONZOLA

Gorgonzola cheese originates from Lombardy in North Italy. It is rich and very creamy, with a strong flavor and lasting aroma, and though it has a finer texture, is somewhat similar to the French Roquefort. Gorgonzola should be served at the proper degree of ripeness, when the white part of the cheese is soft, almost runny. There is no domestic Gorgonzola; the imported brand that I recommend is Colombo. When buying Gorgonzola, watch for excessive dryness, which indicates that the wheel of cheese has been in storage for too long and is therefore past its prime.

There are many uses for Gorgonzola, including one of my favorite sandwiches. This consists of fresh Italian bread, split in half, buttered, then filled with a goodly amount of Gorgonzola and baked in a preheated oven of 350° F for about 5 minutes. Gorgonzola should always be served at room temperature when served as a table cheese.

CACIOCAVALLO

Caciocavallo is a semihard type cheese, milder than provolone, often used in stuffing, grated over pasta, or for baking. It is indigenous to southern Italy. It is a wonderful cheese in both taste and texture.

CACCIOTTA

Cacciotta is a Tuscan cheese. You can find as many types of cacciotta in Tuscany as there are villages. Cacciotta is a semi-hard cheese with a slightly smoky taste. It is a delightful cheese to be eaten with crunchy fruit, such as pears and apples.

TALEGGIO

Taleggio is another great cheese from Lombardy. Very creamy, white in color, it is Italy's challenge to the superb French Brie. It is a delicious table cheese, most suited to be eaten with fruit such as figs, peaches, and very ripe plums. It is an excellent cheese to be used with polenta and in fine cream sauces.

FORMAGGIO INCANESTRATO

This is a soft goat cheese most popular in Sicily. Its consistency and taste is very similar to the French chèvres. It is pressed into wicker baskets (canestri), hence the name. It's mostly used for stuffing, or eaten with soft fruit. It is a delectable table cheese that unfortunately is not easily found in American markets.

STRACCHINO

A creamy, mild cheese from Lombardy—used most often as a table cheese with fresh fruits or with gnocchi (baked).

CORN MEAL

Polenta is a versatile food that is delicious in its many uses. A staple food of the Venetians, it is also widely used in other northern regions of Italy. It is served mainly in the fall and winter. I prefer loose *farina di polenta* bought by the pound rather than the packaged type. It is usually found in Italian grocery stores, many of which advertise whenever there is a fresh shipment. If you buy an American packaged brand of corn meal, such as Quaker, you should put it through a flour sifter before using it.

There is also on the market a packaged instant polenta, mostly imported from Italy, which requires exactly 5 minutes to cook, simplifying the process. The results are satisfying enough.

CREAM

I use a great deal of heavy cream in my cooking, in preference to milk and butter or half-and-half. The butterfat content of heavy cream varies from one area to another. I have a supplier from New Jersey who services my restaurants and who supplies me with a cream product of great consistency, and also fresh sweet whipped butter, which I serve as an accompaniment to bread.

EGGS

Eggs come in all sizes, but are usually marketed as small, medium, large, extra-large, and jumbo. In grading, they are AA, A to B and C. The usual grade is A. I don't believe there is any difference in flavor or nutrition between white eggs and brown eggs. Where eggs are part of a recipe, it's usually understood that you should use the large size. You can store eggs in the refrigerator, but do not let them lie around too long. Buy eggs in small quantities, and keep them in the box in which they are purchased so they will stay fresh longer. Remove eggs from refrigerator 30 minutes in advance of using them in any recipe. In making mayonnaise, there is the possibility that the sauce may curdle unless the egg yolks and the oil are the same temperature.

FISH

The continental United States enjoys a bountiful supply of fish and in great variety, fished from its fresh and salt waters. Unfortunately, the handling process from fishing boat to fish merchant is such a long and time-consuming one that the customer very seldom sees the real fresh fish, unless he or she lives where the boats come in with their daily catch. Or if you do your own fishing.

Fresh fish should look and smell fresh, have bright eyes and shiny scales, and, under the pressure of your fingertip, the flesh should spring back instantly. After purchasing fresh fish, refrigerate immediately, either wrapped in waxed paper or on a covered platter. Do not keep fish too long. Cook as soon after purchasing as possible. It is understood that certain varieties of fish do not come from local waters—you might, therefore, be forced to accept the frozen. That is certainly true for places in the interior rather than on the coast. Try, whenever possible, to buy fish that is in season and that comes from nearby waters. One of my favorite fish is striped bass, which is one of the most delicious of eating fish, and very adaptable to many ways of cooking. My other choices are swordfish, red snapper, and salmon, in that order.

Have your fish merchant clean the fish for you, leaving the head and tail on it if you buy a whole fish, because the presentation of it at table will be far more impressive. If you buy a fish that you intend to use as fillets, insist on having the head and tail because it will make a marvelous fish stock for you.

Short of getting up at three in the morning—if you live in New York City—and going to the Fulton Fish Market to purchase your fish as soon as it comes off the boat, search for a fish merchant who deals with good restaurants, a store that does a lively business so that the chances of "old fish" are minimized. I use the

Greenwich Village Fish Market, which is a reliable distributor and a busy one. However, wherever you live, make inquiries at your favorite restaurant and ask the food buyer where he purchases his fish. It's a pretty safe bet.

FLOUR

Try to use the flour specified in a recipe, if it is a type other than all-purpose. The all-purpose flour is the most commonly used for cooking, from sauces to cakes and cookies. It is a blend of hard- and soft-wheat flours, and it comes both bleached and unbleached. I prefer the unbleached. Hard-wheat flour is a high-gluten flour used for certain breads, making the loaves firmer and providing a tougher texture, especially Italian or French breads. It is sold in health-food stores or by mail from mills. Since I do practically no baking at all, I use all-purpose flour almost exclusively.

FRUITS

APPLES

McIntosh and Golden Delicious are the most common and all-year-round eating apples. On the East Coast we have the deliciously tart and firm Granny Smith and Greenings, which are also excellent for cooking and baking. In the spring you find wonderful Pippins and in the fall Gravensteins. In any case, look for other varieties, especially if you should visit a farmers' market in the fall. Apples should have bouquet, crispness, and texture. A mealy apple is a disaster. Apples, like pears, are perfect with cheese. I fell in love with apples a long time ago, but when I came to the United States, I fell *madly* in love with apple pie—my favorite dessert.

LEMONS

Lemons are, perhaps, one of the most important ingredients in any cuisine. Under any circumstances, I would advise you not to use concentrated lemon juice that comes in bottles, cans, or plastic containers *shaped* like lemons. Since lemons are available in markets all year round, everywhere, the use of ersatz lemon juice is a crime. When you buy lemons, make sure that the skin is shiny and brilliantly yellow. Roll them between your palms to make sure that they are not too hard, that the smell is a pungent, fresh one, and also that the skin is not too thick.

MELONS

Cantaloupes, casabas, Crenshaws, honeydews, Persians, Spanish melons, watermelons. These are just a few members of that large society. Some are seasonal, while others—like cantaloupes—are obtainable all year round. Since it is next to impossible to choose the "right" melon, let your trusty greengrocer, if you have one, pick one out for you, and hope for the best.

A perfectly ripe honeydew or casaba is wonderful served with thinly sliced prosciutto. A small ice-cold slice of ripe watermelon makes an almost perfect "intermezzo" between dinner courses. And melons offer all kinds of possibilities as desserts.

PEARS

Unfortunately, virtually all types of pears are artificially ripened. However, it is one of the most delectable fruits, along with peaches and good apples. We have the Bartlett pear, the Seckel, the Bosc, the Anjou, and my favorite, the Comice. There are other types as well. If you should be lucky enough to find ripe and soft-to-the-touch pears, snatch them up. Buy some very good cheese, smuggle the whole thing home, and have yourself a feast. In Tuscany there is an old saying that goes something like this (as a matter of fact, it goes exactly like this): "Don't let the farmer know that pears are excellent companions of cacciotta cheese, for you'll never see another single pear at the market."

RASPBERRIES

One of the most elegant and sinfully tasting fruits is the raspberry. They have a very short season, and are usually very high priced. There are no other berries that equal them in taste. Raspberry jam is perhaps the most popular of all preserves. But I say to eat them fresh with sugar and cream, or laced with a liqueur of your choice. Raspberries are a very delicate fruit, and it's difficult to find a whole pint of perfect ones.

STRAWBERRIES

Another fruit now available all year round, either from California, Mexico, or New Zealand—the latter, terribly expensive. The buying of strawberries is tricky; often they put up a beautiful appearance but are a delusion to the palate. Try as well as you can to inspect the boxes before buying, smell them for their fragrance and their ripeness. The very large ones, sold usually with a long stem attached, are incredibly tasty dipped in powdered sugar, or, as I learned from Mr. James Beard and Ms. Barbara Kafka, doused with lemon juice, sugar, and showered with freshly ground black pepper.

HERBS

The growing of fresh herbs can be relatively simple, either in a small plot of ground or in a window box in your kitchen. And what pleasure to be able to snip off what you want when you need it! Whenever possible, I use fresh herbs, especially basil, tarragon, rosemary, sage, mint, marjoram, and particularly Italian parsley. Italian parsley leaves are flat and resemble vine leaves in shape. I use it exclusively because the flavor is far superior to the American curly variety, which is better used as a garnish.

Dried herbs are chancier to use because frequently they have gone beyond their shelf life, so they lose flavor. Furthermore, they are much stronger than the fresh and they should be used sparingly, in smaller amounts than the fresh.

Not to be overlooked is fresh coriander. It looks very much like Italian parsley, but has a distinct flavor of its own, somewhat like anise. Coriander is widely used in Oriental cuisines. I use it occasionally when I need that extra, distinctive taste, and only fresh—never dried. It's obtainable in most Oriental markets.

Then we have the most flavorful of herbs, tarragon, which I suggest you purchase fresh. Or, the type preserved in vinegar with the leaves still attached to the stem. Avoid using *dried* tarragon whenever possible. The aroma and taste that these slender little

leaves impart to food is priceless. However, like coriander, it has
to be used judiciously because it could very easily overpower all
other bouquets in your sauces, meat or fish dishes, or omelets.

LARD

Good lard, especially if you buy the pure and delicate leaf lard
from pork kidney fat, has no equal for roasting, frying, pastry
making, and sautéing. The flavor of good rendered leaf lard is
much superior to that of commercial shortenings. I generally use
prosciutto fat in my roasting. Since I use prosciutto, the fat is at
hand, and of course in flavor it's even superior to lard. Italian
groceries can supply you with prosciutto fat if you let them know
in advance of your needs.

To render leaf lard: Cut a large chunk of leaf lard (according to
your need) and melt slowly in a 300°F oven, pouring off fat as it
melts and placing in a sterilized jar. Continue to do this until all
fat is rendered, leaving only crisp bits remaining. Place jar in
refrigerator until fat is firm and set. Use as needed.

MEATS

BEEF

The amount of beef consumed in America surpasses all other
meats. The cuts and ways beef is used are far more varied than
that of other animals. Beef is sold in this country under the
different grades of Prime, which is the finest; Choice, next best
and the most commonly used; and Good. Prime beef is grain-fed
steer; its meat is well marbled with flecks of fat that melt down
in cooking, therefore lubricating the meat. Most of the Prime beef
is used in good restaurants. A smaller amount of it can be found
available to the public in specialty meat markets.

Choice beef contains less marbling of fat; therefore, it should
be cooked longer to become tender, and more condiments should
be used with it to compensate for its lack of fat. Generally, its
texture is chewier, but not necessarily less flavorful. Good-graded

beef is definitely less tender and contains the least fat. It is almost always used for sausage-making or adding to other products, and is very good for flavoring soups and stocks.

Beef tongue is excellent when boiled and served with a *salsa verde*, or as part of the *bollito misto* (a classic Italian dish of mixed meats such as beef, cotechino, chicken, tongue, etc., served with *salsa verde*). Shoulder or chuck is good for stews, braising, pot roasts, and ground for hamburger. The rib section, when it comes from the right cut, is exquisite, and usually sells for a high price. Short ribs are good for braising or to marinate or barbecue. Round of beef is divided into top round, bottom round, and eye round, which is the choicest section.

The so-called flank steak makes good London broil, or can be stuffed and made into a *cima di manzo*. The brisket is definitely the most favored part for boiled beef, or for corning. Beef kidneys are a negligible part of the beef, in my opinion. Beef liver can be quite tasty, even though it has a much stronger flavor than calves' liver, and has high nutritious value. Then, of course, there is tripe, which, if cooked properly, makes some of the most savory dishes. Beef testicles are considered a very special delicacy in the Roman cuisine. I wouldn't know what to do with them because I've never cooked them in my life.

LAMB

Yearling lamb—about one year old—is, for the most part, what you will find in butcher shops. Smaller and younger lamb, or "spring" lamb, is obtainable only at certain times of the year, generally for a period of 3 to 4 weeks, at butcher shops that deal with a European clientele. This type of lamb weighs about 15 pounds when trimmed and cleaned. It is usually so tiny that the whole lamb may scarcely feed 8 to 10 people. Of course, it is a delicacy!

As I have mentioned in recipes in previous pages, overcooked lamb constitutes a *crime* on the part of the cook. Naturally, in the case of stews or potted lamb dishes, lamb must be cooked a longer length of time.

Neck and shoulder cuts of lamb are excellent for stews or braising. The cut most in demand is the leg, weighing between 4½ to 10 pounds.

The loin is the choicest cut. This part of the lamb is often offered as a double loin, and it then becomes a saddle of lamb.

Rib chops can be cut thick or thin, or made into a roast known as a "crown roast." Lamb kidneys are a delicacy.

PANCETTA

I use pancetta in most of my recipes; however, bacon can be used as a substitute. Pancetta is a type of Italian bacon that is cured in salt and black pepper and made up in a casing like salami. It has a more delicate flavor and it is less greasy than bacon. Pancetta is also called *guanciale*, which is processed the same way but is kept in slabs. The best Italian pancetta or *guanciale* comes from Norcia in Umbria and from Amatrice (Latium), hence the name of the dish *spaghetti amatriciana*. Pancetta is obtainable in most Italian grocery stores.

PORK

Pork is king among the meat-yielding animals. There is absolutely no waste in a pig, starting from ears to tail. Good pork meat and products should always be purchased at pork stores rather than at a general butcher market. In New York, one of the top pork stores is Faicco on Bleecker Street. Pork is widely used in most cuisines around the world. It plays a very large role in the Italian cuisine.

The loin is the choicest cut. It includes the rib and the tenderloin. However, rib chops are smaller and less flavorful than loin chops. The loin is most commonly used for roasts, and the best is the center cut, which is also the most expensive.

The fatback is sold for larding. There is bacon, the spareribs, pork kidneys, pork liver (generally ground for pâtés and terrines for a succulent flavor), pigs' feet, hocks, and shoulder, with which the Italians make *zampone*, and still other bits and pieces of the pig that are used in various kinds of sausage. The pigs' blood is used in the making of blood sausage.

There is a vast variety of hams available, and almost every country in the world has its own specialty. The choicest, in my opinion, are prosciutto (see below), Westphalian, Black Forest, Kentucky, Vermont, and Virginia hams. I consider the least flavorful hams the canned hams, or the so-called ready-to-eat hams. However, they are very practical to keep in your larder for an emergency.

Prosciutto: Among the several types and brands of prosciutto available in this country, I prefer Volpi. It is a domestic brand that I use in cooking. If you can obtain imported prosciutto, you might wish to try Danieli for a treat, to serve with melon or figs, though it is very expensive.

When buying prosciutto, look to see that it does not have too much fat. The color should be pinkish-red, not dark red, and it should be cut in paper-thin slices. If it has any iridescent traces in it, do not buy it. This indicates that it is about to go "bad," which is also true of ham. A good substitute for prosciutto is Westphalian ham.

Prosciutto Cotto (Giambone): *Giambone* is an Italian boiled ham quite similar to our boiled ham, but ½ inch of fat is left around the outside; the fat should be milk-white, to ensure the freshness of the giambone. Giambone is not easily obtainable on the American market. American Black Forest ham can be substituted for it, however.

RABBIT

It is amazing how few people consider rabbit a meat they would consume regularly, as most people do beef, lamb, or pork. In my opinion, the main reason is that in this country the rabbit is associated with Walt Disney, pets, and the Easter Bunny; therefore, eating rabbit is taboo, because you don't eat your *best friend*. Rabbit is a fine, delicate, and flavorful meat, and as useful as chicken. A properly roasted rabbit, either whole or in pieces, or a stew of rabbit are among the finest dishes to offer at special dinner parties. In my experience as a restaurateur, I was successful in selling rabbit to American clientele perhaps only three times. It's the same with tripe. A sad story.

SALAMI

In Italy there are almost as many varieties of salami as there are dialects. Some well-known types are Genoa, Citterio Milanese, the wonderfully flavorful Finocchiona from Tuscany, the salami of

Varsi from the Piemonte region, *salame cotto* and the mortadella from Bologna. From Modena we have the best coppa, pancetta, culatello (cured rump of pork). From Venice comes the most delicious sopressata, and from Valtellina, that wonderful *bresaola*, which actually is not a salami, but an air-dried beef that is served sliced paper-thin, with a few drops of virgin olive oil, some lemon juice, and freshly ground black pepper. And of course there are innumerable types of *salami nostrani* that you will find in small inns throughout the countryside.

An American-made salami that I use and recommend is available under the brand name Oldani, from St. Louis, Missouri. It is a Genoa-type salami that, when served to Italian Italians, got rave reviews.

SAUSAGES

Sausages are an integral part of the Italian kitchen. We have the sweet and hot sausage, mostly from the southern regions of Italy; lamb and cheese sausage typical of Bari (Puglia); luganega, a very thin pork sausage from the Veneto region. Also common in the northern region is cured fresh sausage that must be boiled before eating or adding to recipes. One of the best known is the Milanese cotechino; the *zampino di maiale* and the zampone from Modena, which are sausages stuffed into the skin of a pig's trotter, must also be boiled before eating. They are usually served in the winter, and almost always with lentils, beans, and cabbage. Served with other boiled meats, this becomes a dish called *gran bollito misto*, which is one of the classic Italian recipes.

For stuffing and sauces I use sweet sausage exclusively.

VEAL

In this country, people have been brainwashed by the misconception that the best veal is ivory-colored, or the so-called "milk fed." This type of veal is, in reality, anemic and comes from anemic animals that are fed a special formula, or Provimi Dutch process, and are herded into pens of a certain size, which will ultimately determine when the animal has reached its slaughter time. This "process" is very expensive and requires a great deal of attention, since the calf is weaned very early and fed this "scientifically" prepared formula designed not to color the meat—

therefore, your ivory-colored veal. Another fallacy about veal heard only in the United States is "it is so tender it can be cut with a fork." What is wrong with using a knife as well as a fork? There is not much quality veal on the market, and most of the veal sold in supermarkets is reddish in color and is, in fact, very young beef. Veal is an expensive meat, but buying the best— which is, in my opinion, nature veal—is well worth the expense. Nature veal is produced by allowing the animals to be unpenned and to eat some fresh grass and grains. That makes for much happier and tastier veal. In texture and taste, nature veal is far superior to "milkfed" and not so characterless.

The loin and saddle of veal are definitely the tenderest parts of the animal. The scaloppine and cutlets are generally cut from the leg, then pounded thin before cooking. A rolled saddle of veal, with or without bone, can make a delicious roast, or can be cut thick into chops.

The breast of veal is at its best when stuffed and made into a *cima*. The rump of veal can make a worthwhile roast also. Veal kidneys are truly a delicacy. Nothing can compare with the flavor of good calves' liver and sweetbreads.

Then we have the most succulent part of the veal, the shank, from which we get *ossi buchi*.

Not to be forgotten are the deliciously tender veal tongue and brains, which are, without a doubt, the best animal brains. Veal bones are extremely adaptable for making stock, to which they impart a very special flavor.

VENISON

Since deer are a game animal, venison is not marketable. However, you can obtain imported venison, which is usually sold frozen.

Deer liver is perhaps the best part of the animal if cooked properly. Other cuts include the tenderloin, the rack, steaks, and finally the saddle, which is regarded as a dish for memorable dinners. Except for very young deer, venison should be marinated before cooking. Incidentally, my butcher, Ottomanelli, imports wild boar from New Zealand and makes it into link sausage at Christmas time. They are truly one of the most delicate and superlatively savory among sausages.

MUSHROOMS

The numerous and most flavorful variety of wild mushrooms are not available aside from imported dried porcini from Italy, cèpes in cans from France, and fresh Black Forest mushrooms, not always worth the high price asked for them. On one or two occasions I have bought fresh porcini from Italy. What a disappointment it was, because they had been frozen for the trip over and defrosted later. Result—no taste whatsoever.

The cultivated variety is at our disposal all year round. This type of mushroom is flavorful enough, and the texture is very satisfactory. They often need only a wiping with a wet cloth to clean them, or wash them under a soft spray of cold water. Choose those with the whitest caps and firmest stems. When caps are spotted with brown or discolored, they usually are sold at a cheaper price and can be used in a variety of ways: in sauces, stuffings, or made into a paste that can be spread on toast and served as appetizers; they can be mixed with other vegetables, or added to eggs and omelets. Do not keep mushrooms more than a few days. I never use canned or frozen mushrooms.

PORCINI (DRIED WILD MUSHROOMS)

Most dried wild mushrooms come from Europe and China. I prefer the Italian variety from Emilia called Borgotaro-Bruschi. The name for this type of mushroom is *porcini*. They are expensive because of their seasonal nature and the long process involved in drying them. A great number of my recipes call for imported dried porcini. They have a wonderful flavor and add a great deal of distinction to food. Porcini can be found in most Italian markets. They should be carefully selected because a rather large amount of dirt is often still on them. The pieces should be rather large, since small fragments are practically unusable. They should be of a creamy brown color, not black. Store them in a cool place.

To prepare, first place porcini in a strainer and wash under cold water until thoroughly clean. Soak the exact number of pieces you plan to use in ½ cup lukewarm water at least 1½ hours before using. If you have cleaned the mushrooms properly beforehand, you can safely use the water after it has been strained in some of your sauces. Do not keep mushrooms soaking for more than a day.

NUTS

Nuts most commonly used in Italian cooking are walnuts, pignoli, almonds, pistachios. Pignoli, or pine nuts, are pale yellow in color, slender, and delicately flavored. Walnuts can be obtained in their shells or shelled. I prefer the latter. All four nuts are used in stuffing and sauces, and almonds and pistachios are widely used in desserts.

OLIVES

GAETA OLIVES

Gaeta olives are a variety of black olives indigenous to the Campania region of Italy. They are actually reddish-purple in color and, along with Greek Kalamata olives, are the most succulent and flavorful of olives.

Gaeta olives are used mainly in cooking. When they are fresh they are called *olive amare* (before being cured and bottled). They are quite bitter in taste but are delicious with fresh bread and hard cheese. Gaeta olives are rather expensive and can be obtained in better Italian grocery stores.

SICILIAN OLIVES

Black, shriveled, rather bitter type of olives that are preserved in a small amount of olive oil and red crushed pepper. They are very flavorful and tasty.

GREEN OLIVES

Rather large green olives, usually imported from Spain, used often in salad or as a garnish and in fish sauces. They are flavorful and a bit salty.

OLIVADA SAN REMO

This is an excellent black olive "mash" preserved in virgin olive oil, wonderful as a spread or to be used in the preparation of sauces, or even as a pasta sauce. A truly fine product from Liguria, made by Crespi e Figli from San Remo. Obtainable at Dean & DeLuca and at some other specialty stores.

OLIVE OIL

Since olive oil does not burn as easily as butter, it is preferable for sauces that require a longer cooking time. In general, olive oil rather than vegetable oil should be used whenever the oil is going to become part of a sauce. The oil I most often use is Re di Puglia olive oil. This oil can be purchased only through a restaurant supplier, but brands that I would recommend are Sasso, Bertolli, and Berio, which are among the more easily obtainable. Of exceedingly high quality are Olivieri; the Tuscan extra virgin olive oils such as Poggio al Sole, Fonterutoli, Cacchiano, Antinori; Ligurian virgin olive oils such as Crespi e Figli. A new oil I find excellent is L'Olio del Cooperatore. The high-quality oils mentioned above can be purchased at Balducci's, Dean & DeLuca, Zabar's, and some of the better stores in Italian sections. Note that in some of my recipes I refer very generally to "olive oil" and in others "virgin olive oil." The reason is that the virgin olive oil is the first cold pressing of the olives, and it is heavier in density, greener in color—in other words, the "crème de la crème" of olive oil. In most cases I use it for salad dressings, or when it is not cooked.

PASTA

Pasta has become so popular in America that it now ranks as number four of all foods appearing on menus in terms of frequency. It is one of the most satisfying of staples, and one of the most versatile. Pasta can be sauced with almost "anything."

The variety of pasta made in Italy is vast. Nowadays, with food processors and electric pasta machines, pasta has become a very easy food to prepare. Of course, there are many pasta shops in most major cities in America now, but I advocate making your own. However, the very best of imported dried pasta often surpasses in taste and in texture even the homemade kind, which can turn out gooey and limp.

Fresh Pasta

Fresh pasta should be dried briefly and cooked immediately after for best results. For pasta making, and types of fresh pasta, see pages 221–242.

Dried Pasta

In dried, commercially made pasta, I always use products imported from Italy. My favorite brands are De Cecco, Agnesi, Martelli, and Cirio. These pastas retain their texture and freshness longer than domestic pastas. These pastas are generally of a slightly darker color because they are made with hard wheat, and because of the process used to make them. Packaged dried pasta should be stored in a cool, dry spot in the kitchen, and never be refrigerated.

Fusilli: Short pasta in the shape of a corkscrew.

Orecchiette ("little ears"): Round pasta about the size of a nickel.

Penne: Tubular pasta cut on the diagonal in short lengths.

Mostaccioli: Grooved, tubular pasta cut on the diagonal in short lengths similar to penne.

Perciatelli or Bucatini: Long, hollow macaroni, thicker than spaghetti.

Rigatoni: Grooved, tubular pasta about 3 inches long.

Occhi di Lupo ("wolf eyes"—why I do not know): A short tubular pasta, twice the size of rigatoni in circumference.

Farfalle (bowties): A ridged, bowtie-shaped pasta.

Spaghettini: Thinner form of spaghetti.

Capelli d'angelo ("angel's hair"): Very fine spaghettini.

Mafalde: Strips of pasta with curled edges, 9 inches long and 1 inch wide.

Tubettini: Tubular-shaped pasta, about ½ inch long, often used in soups, or in the form of *pastasciutta*.

POULTRY AND GAME BIRDS

Chicken

As I have stated often enough in my recipes, I prefer fresh chicken to frozen. My first restaurant was located across the street from a live poultry market; at that time I was using only fresh-killed chickens. They are infinitely superior. Do not use fresh chicken later than 3 days after time of purchase.

Broiling chickens are usually small birds weighing 1½ to 2½ pounds. Split in two lengthwise; be sure to cut out the backbone.

Frying chickens usually weigh 3 to 3½ pounds, and their flavor varies depending on the way they are raised and fed. Cooking time is a little bit longer than for broilers.

Boiling chickens are usually fairly good-sized hens, weighing 4 to 5 pounds. Just remember that this type of chicken requires slower and longer cooking to reach tenderness; yet, per pound, there is relatively a greater proportion of meat to bone.

Roasting chickens, weighing 4 to 5 pounds, should be plump and tender birds with a goodly amount of fat. If you can find good capons, which are usually larger in size, by all means buy them for your roast. They are generally more expensive.

Baby chickens, weighing about 1 pound or so, are no longer easily found in the market. The last time I had the most delicious so-called squab chicken was in November 1981, in Sag Harbor, New York, when I was a guest of Mr. Jason Epstein. He took me to Salvatore Iacono's chicken farm in East Hampton, where we made our selection of the fowl we wanted for that night's dinner. That's the way to do it!

In my restaurants I often use Cornish hens. I recommend buying fresh Cornish hens rather than any frozen variety.

There is a delightful story included in the Toulouse-Lautrec/ Maurice Joyant book *The Art of Cuisine*, on "How to Make

Chicken Tender." Even though it's a nineteenth-century tale, I suppose it could still be applicable today.

In order to make chickens immediately edible, take them out of the hen-run, pursue them into open country, and when you have made them run, kill them with a gun loaded with very small shot.

The meat of the chicken, gripped with fright, will become tender. This method used in the country of the Fangs (Gabon) seems infallible even for the oldest and toughest hens.

Ducks

To find a fresh duck, you have to live either in New York, San Francisco, Los Angeles, or—preferably—near a Long Island duck farm. Otherwise, you'll have to put up with frozen ducks. Frozen ducks, when defrosted, are generally very wet, and they need to be left out at room temperature for 4 to 5 hours in order to dry out; or, dry duck inside and out by wrapping it in paper toweling, stuffing paper toweling in the cavity as well. Or use an electric fan to blow on the duck for a couple of hours, as this will help the drying process. The weight of ducks varies from 4½ to 8 pounds. Always reserve duck livers for another use, if the recipe doesn't call for them, because they are truly a delicacy.

The best wild duck I've ever eaten was in Maremma in Tuscany. It's quite a different bird from the domesticated. It has practically no fat, but the breast is well fleshed. However, the legs and thighs are less tender. The size of a wild duck is rather small, usually weighing from 1 to 2 pounds.

Quails

Quails are expensive little game birds; therefore, they've become a luxury unless you do your own shooting. However, nowadays quails are raised on farms, and they can be purchased fresh or frozen—although they are far more plentiful in the market frozen rather than fresh. I would like to recommend that whenever you roast, braise, or pan-sauté quails, you use fresh birds. I never use frozen quails. Two birds per person is usually an adequate amount per serving.

Squabs, or Pigeons

Another delicious bird, also rather expensive, weighing from 1 pound to 1½ pounds. Squabs are obtainable at your butcher's, cleaned and ready to be cooked. Squabs, too, are more plentiful frozen rather than fresh. I recommend the fresh squabs. Roast squab should not be cooked more than 20 to 25 minutes. An overcooked squab becomes stringy and dry, and loses flavor.

RAISINS

In some of my stuffings and sauces I use sultana (golden) raisins, which are the closest to the golden zibibbo from Sicily. I generally presoak raisins for these uses in either Marsala or sherry wine.

RICE

I always use imported Arborio rice, which comes from the Lombardy region in Italy, because it maintains its texture and taste longer, when cooked properly. I use rice primarily for risotto, but I also recommend Arborio rice for fillings, soups, and salads. Arborio can be found in most Italian markets. Although not as desirable, other types of rice can be substituted.

SPICES

In the Europe of the Middle Ages, pepper was chiefly used as a preservative for meats, and was only affordable by the wealthy; indeed, it was very often used in lieu of money. English landlords charged a rent tax of one pound of pepper a year. It was called the spice "fit for a king." Later, the more exotic spices of the Orient were introduced to the Europeans. These new spices were, of course, completely alien to their palates. Again, it was mainly the rich who had their cooks learn how to make use of the new ingredients—which at times were even considered aphrodisiac.

At first the spice trade was in the hands of the Arabs, then the Venetians. Then it was returned to the Arabs, and ultimately the British, the Dutch, and the Americans—amassing enormous fortunes for each group. Spices have remained to this day very expensive. Whatever the history, God bless the first "user" of such spices as mace and nutmeg, saffron, cinnamon, mustard, paprika, et cetera, et cetera.

One of the best stores in New York that carry the largest variety, the freshest, and the best display of spices is Aphrodisia at 28 Carmine Street.

PEPPER

I prefer grinding black peppercorns using a peppermill. You will discover that the taste is far more fragrant then the usual ground pepper in containers.

Green peppercorns are more easily obtainable in brine, but I prefer the dry variety, and, like the black pepper, to grind it fresh. I do the same with white peppercorns, which I use in sauces for the appearance as well as the taste.

BAY LEAVES OR LAUREL

The bay tree is one of the oldest and most celebrated of trees. Its leaves were fashioned into crowns to adorn the noble heads of gods, poets, triumphant warriors, kings, and doctors—hence the title of laureate. In the kitchen bay leaves are generally used in dried form for both flavor and fragrance. Bay leaves, because of their aromatic quality, are an essential ingredient in the roasting of meats and the making of sauces, and are a must for marinades.

MACE AND NUTMEG

Mace is the outside covering of the nutmeg seed or nut. The mace and nuts (nutmeg) are both dried first over a fire and later in the sun. The period required is usually a month. Mace is finely ground on the spot after this process, and is an excellent spice to use for desserts, and chicken and turkey stuffing, because of its mild, sweet taste. The nuts or nutmeg are exported whole to retain their aroma and flavor. I suggest grating the whole nutmeg rather than using the powdered form.

SAFFRON

Many people believe that saffron is used only for coloring, whereas it is a spice with a most definite taste. Saffron is one of the most expensive spices in the world, and the reason is that to obtain a pound of saffron 75,000 blossoms of the flower (*Crocus sativus*) must be gathered. Saffron is widely used in the kitchens of northern Italy. It is a very interesting spice when used judiciously. The color of saffron represented the sun to Queen Nefertiti, and it is said to have been one of Cleopatra's favorite cosmetics.

CINNAMON

Cinnamon is the dried ground bark of the cassia tree. It can be used in stick form as well as ground, in the preparation of varieties of food, and it is a perfect companion to poached fruits and a multitude of desserts.

MUSTARD

Mustard has been known to man and used since prehistoric times. It comes in the form of seeds, powder, or as an already prepared condiment. Prepared mustard, as we know it, is a rather recent product. It goes back to a few hundred years ago, the "inventor" a woman from Durham, England. I use, almost always, the prepared kind, and my favorite brands are Paul Corcellet from France and the various mustards from Dijon. The use of an excellent mustard is as pivotal as the selection of the main ingredients in any recipe worth doing.

PAPRIKA

Paprika can be a mild to sweet spice, such as that which comes from Spain, or the very hot Hungarian and Yugoslavian variety. I use paprika whenever I want to give that extra "zing" to a dish, and often to add color. There are many recipes where paprika is the major spice; however, paprika plays a minor role in Italian cooking. It has been claimed that the use of paprika maintains good eyesight.

SALT

One of the oldest roads in Rome is called Via Salaria ("salt road").
It was a major salt transportation route. Salt has played an
enormous role in the history of civilization. Salt has been used as
a seasoning and preservative for food since time began. Caravans
of thousands of camels used to cross the Sahara desert to reach
the salt mines of Taoudenni, where it was quarried in blocks and
brought to Timbuktu and Goundam to supply central Africa. The
United States is the largest salt producer in the world.

I prefer using kosher salt, which comes in small nuggets. I
grind them to a coarse consistency. The reason is that this type of
salt brings an extra dimension to the taste of food, especially to
vegetables. However, commercial iodized salt is an excellent
substitute.

TOMATO PASTE

I use a tomato paste from California sold by my wholesale supplier. Since it is not available in retail shops, other brands I
recommend are Contadina, Pastene, and Progresso. However, for
the home use I strongly recommend buying tomato paste that
comes packaged in tubes, like toothpaste, in which case you can
use only what you need and store the rest away, eliminating
waste. This type of tomato paste is imported from Europe.

TRUFFLES

Truffles are as ugly as they are delicious. They are a fungus that
grows from 3 inches to a foot underground, usually in stony,
porous soil near the roots of shrub oak or beech trees. As far as
I know, no one has been able to cultivate truffles. For centuries,
Europeans have trained pigs and, more recently, hounds, to find
truffles. The aroma of truffles permeates any food.

There are two types: the black variety that grows mostly in
two districts of France, and the white "summer" Italian truffles
from Piemonte and Umbria. Among connoisseurs there are two
camps: those who prefer the black and those who swear by the

white. I am among those who think that the whites are superior. Their price—black or white—is extremely high and competes with Russian caviar. In spite of the price, I use them because they are "slivers of Paradise." The fragrance and flavor they bring to the table are absolutely incomparable.

Of course, some people wrinkle their noses when you expose them to the smell of truffles—Philistines! The best way to keep truffles is to bury them in uncooked rice, and when you're done with the truffles you should cook the rice, because it will be the best rice you have ever tasted.

TUNA

In canned tuna I prefer those brands packed in olive oil. The taste and texture of the meat is far superior to the types of tuna packed in water, brine, or soybean oil. I highly recommend the Parodi brand, especially their packaging of *ventresca*, tuna belly. Parodi is not easy to locate, so I would also recommend the Pastene and Genova brands. Whenever I use an oil-packed tuna, I use the oil as well as the meat; however, in the case of the other types, I suggest that you drain off the water, brine, or other packing oil.

VEGETABLES

ARTICHOKES

Artichokes are reputed to have been among the bounty of gifts Cleopatra brought to Rome—baskets and baskets of beautiful artichokes from Judea. The Romans immediately invented a way to cook them, and artichokes have remained one of the most delectable vegetables in the Roman cuisine to this day.

Round artichokes come in different sizes, from the very small ones (less than the size of a lemon) to the large ones, 5 to 6 inches across at the fattest point. These can be trimmed down of all the tough outer leaves, if necessary. You can cook them or eat them raw, dipped in an oil and vinegar or vinaigrette dressing.

Take care that the leaves on the artichokes you are about to buy are not spotted with brown, or woody to the touch. I prefer the smaller kind whenever obtainable. The artichoke is an extremely interesting vegetable that offers all kinds of challenges in its various uses.

ASPARAGUS

Today we can enjoy fresh asparagus for almost the entire twelve months of the year. Its sizes vary; usually, the larger stalks are woody and rather tough, as opposed to the medium stalks, or the deliciously tender grass-asparagus. When the large stalks are at their prime, I find it necessary to peel the lower part of the stalk so that more of the asparagus is edible. A short paring knife will accomplish the job quickly. I find that it's not necessary to peel the thinner asparagus. Try to choose the greenest and the firmest of the bunches. Make sure that the spears are intact.

BEANS

Cranberry beans: Spotted white and dark pink. They can be obtained fresh (in season) or dried.

Cannellini: Creamy in color. Commonly found either dried or in cans.

Red kidney beans: So-named for their reddish-brown color and their shape. Commonly found dried or in cans.

Roman beans: Creamy in color but much larger and flatter than cannellini, resembling lima beans. They are seldom found fresh in America, but can be obtained in cans.

Fava beans (broad beans): One of the most flavorful and delicious of all the beans; can be found fresh or dried, are a bottle-green color, and larger than the usual lima bean. The pod has a fuzzy texture, almost like that of a peach. This type of bean is widely served in the springtime, and it is eaten raw. A delicious combination is a thin slice of salami wrapped around two or three fava beans.

Chick-peas or Ceci beans: Usually found dried or in cans. In the Ligurian region, a very tasty pizza is made with chick-pea flour mixed with water and salt. It is rolled very thin and baked in olive oil in wood-burning ovens. Chick-peas are also used in salads, soups, and pasta sauces.

Green beans: The snap bean is the most common variety of green bean. In the past, it was known as a "string bean" because it needed stringing. Fortunately, this is no longer true, unless the beans are past their prime. Choose the tiniest, greenest, and crispiest you can find. They should break with a snap. In specialty vegetable markets you might find the very tiny beans called *haricots verts*. They are expensive, but worth buying. In preparing your beans for cooking, make sure to snap off the one end that attaches to the stalk.

BROCCOLI

Broccoli is generally sold in bunches of approximately 2 pounds. Pick bunches with slender stems. Make sure that the tops of the florets haven't turned a brownish-yellow color. In cooking broccoli, I generally chop off the stems and cook them separately from the florets. The cooked stems, julienned, can make delicious salads in the company of other greens, or can be used in soups.

BRUSSELS SPROUTS

Buy only those with small, compact heads. Do not overcook, because limp, soggy sprouts is the reason they got a bad name. In special markets they are sometimes available as they grow in the fields—still clinging to their stalks like little buds.

CABBAGE

When choosing white, green, or Savoy cabbage heads, make certain they are firm and compact, that the leaves are not limp or discolored. Cabbage, too, is one of the most popular of vegetables. I myself prefer using the Savoy type because it has a gentler, sweeter flavor than the others. It is an excellent source of vitamins and minerals and offers much-needed roughage in the diet.

CARROTS

When buying carrots, try to avoid those huge, woody roots that are good only for a soup stock. Try to choose what are called "finger" carrots. I prefer buying loose carrots as opposed to the cellophane-wrapped bunches sold in supermarkets.

CAULIFLOWER

We are now able to enjoy cauliflower all year round. Buy firm, snow-white heads, and make sure that the leaves at the base are green and not discolored. Cauliflower can be cooked either cut into florets or whole. Do not overcook, because nothing is as sad as a mushy cauliflower.

CELERY

With this vegetable, too, you will have to be careful to select crisp green, or Pascal, celery. Celery is a very versatile vegetable whose flavor enhances stews, stuffings, vegetable combinations, and sauces. It is delicious eaten raw, or in salads. Be certain to wash thoroughly.

CUCUMBER

We have two types of cucumbers—the fat, seeded kind that is rather watery and very often waxed, and a slender, practically seedless and drier one called "Chinese cucumber," which is more expensive but of better quality. This is another versatile vegetable, and I like it especially as a garnish for fish.

EGGPLANT

Eggplant is one of the best-looking, pleasing to both eye and touch, of all vegetables. In buying eggplants, pick the firmest, smoothest, and shiniest ones, with unwrinkled skin. Eggplant has a most distinctive flavor as well as texture, and is used extensively in the cuisines of the Orient, the Middle East, Greece, Italy, Spain, and France's Provence. Among the different types of egg-plant, we have the commonly available rather large, bell-shaped purple eggplant that is usually full of seeds and of a coarse texture and bitter flavor (which can be alleviated by salting). The slender, elongated, light-purple eggplants sold in Italian markets and the round, white Oriental eggplants occasionally obtainable in specialty vegetable stores are of a superior texture and have a more delicate flavor.

FENNEL/FINOCCHIO

This is a cultivated vegetable that has the crisp texture of celery but a strong flavor of anise. It can be served and eaten raw, as a crudité, or cooked like celery. Like celery, fennel should be washed thoroughly, and you should select the firmest and whitest head. Fennel is particularly good during the winter months, when it is found in abundance in vegetable markets.

LEAF GREENS

The number of different types of greens is staggering. To mention a few, we have collards, kale, mustard, spinach (see also page 278), Swiss chard, beet, and broccoli di rape, or broccoli rabe, which is usually found in Italian greengrocers. Select the greenest and crispiest, and cook a very short time to preserve flavor and vitamins.

LEEKS

The noblest of onions. Italians have always been particularly fond of leeks, and we cook them in numerous ways. Leeks are a rather expensive vegetable, and a most difficult one to clean. You should first trim the root end, and most of the green tops, and rinse well under cold water. Or you might find it necessary to slit them in half in order to clean them thoroughly. Leeks are equally good whether small or large.

ONIONS

Onions are part of a very large family: the round, large sweet variety; the red Italian—often called "Sicilian" onion—which is excellent for salads; oval, slim bulb onions (big and small), used mainly for cooking; the ordinary yellow onions; the green onions, also called "scallions." Choose ones most solid to the touch; avoid buying those that have sprouted.

PEAS

I think fresh peas are marvelous! Unfortunately, too few people remember them since the institution of frozen peas. Of course, the season for fresh peas is rather short. When buying fresh peas, open a pod and taste one or two peas for their juiciness and sweetness before you purchase. Try to avoid pods that seem to be empty, or those that have yellowed in color.

Piselli mangiatutto, or snow peas, are a delicacy, green in color, flat as two sheets of ordinary paper and resembling wider fresh pea pods. *Mangiatutto* means "eat all." They are crunchy and delightfully flavorful—excellent when sautéed in butter with a sprinkle of ginger and freshly ground black pepper. Sugar snap peas, similar, but not as flat, are also an edible pod-type, full of flavor, and with a distinctive taste. Remove the stem and short strings, and eat the whole thing. Be certain they are crisp when purchasing.

PEPPERS

Green bell peppers are usually more plentiful in the markets than the red and yellow peppers. The red and yellow varieties, from a decorative point of view in presentation of a dish, are more attractive than the green, and they definitely are more flavorful and sweeter.

In selecting peppers, whether red, yellow, or green, be certain that they are firm and meaty, bright in color, with no blemishes on the skin.

There are also hot peppers, usually long and thin in shape, green or red, if your palate can take the heat. This variety is most popular in the cuisines of Mexico, India, and Hungary, and also in Southeast Asian cuisines. In Sicily there is a special show of *machismo* that takes place in front of wine shops, where you will observe groups of men eating sandwiches of this type of hot pepper doused with olive oil and garlic, attentively watching one another's faces for the eyes that tear the most. The most tearful one is the sissy in the crowd.

POTATOES

When buying potatoes, choose the variety according to the use you will be making of them. The California long whites and the red-skinned new potatoes are the best for boiling and slicing for salads. Idaho potatoes are superior for baking and stuffing. The Long Island potato is an all-purpose potato. Avoid potatoes that are soft and have wrinkled skins; and definitely avoid those with sprouts. The potato is one of the greatest and most satisfying foods known to man. Like pasta, it is one of the more nutritious and wholesome staples—economical and easily available.

SALAD GREENS

Boston, bibb, romaine, dandelion, endive, escarole, field salad, arugula, leaf lettuce, watercress, ruby red, radicchio.

A good salad is poetry! Salads are often my "dinners," along with some cheese and crisp bread scented with a rubbing of garlic. Salad dressing should be clean tasting and uncomplicated, for salad is spring in a bowl.

All of the above salad greens are mostly obtainable all year round, aside from the delicate field salads and the incomparable arugula, which are not always on the market. The now very fashionable radicchio is an old-fashioned salad to me. I first ate radicchio fifty-two years ago in Italy, and I haven't changed my mind about it yet. Its taste is not worth the money you are asked for it. Pretty it is, with its creamy-white leaves and the ruby-red abstract design painted on it. However, it stops there.

The buying of salad greens needs some scrutiny: crisp, fresh, no blemishes—and no ice bruises on the leaves—and, above all, not waterlogged by the menacing water sprinkler ever present at the Oriental vegetable markets. Salad greens should be well washed under cold water, and equally well dried before tossing them with your favorite dressing. Salads are wonderful!

SPINACH

One of the most delicious greens, and definitely one of the most versatile. It can be eaten raw, steamed, sautéed, puréed. It combines marvelously with most foods, especially fish and eggs. I avoid frozen spinach because the fresh is a totally different vegetable in taste and texture, and very available in the markets.

TOMATOES

From my point of view, there is nothing more beautiful among all the vegetable-fruits than a perfect, ripe, deep-red tomato. Unfortunately, it's not an easy task to find them in urban areas. Some of the best tomatoes that we get in New York markets are from Mexico and California. But none equals either the home-grown or the commercially grown in the northeastern section of the country, in season. Selecting tomatoes is, for the most part, a grab-bag game, because most often looks and feel disguise what lies underneath.

I prefer to use fresh, well-ripened tomatoes for sauces, cooking, or salads; however, since one can rarely obtain a vine-ripened tomato nowadays, I most often use canned, peeled plum tomatoes imported from Italy for cooking. My favorite brand is Vitelli, from San Marzano. I like this particular brand best because of its consistency in the degree of ripeness of the tomatoes, the juice content, and the well-balanced seasoning of basil leaves added to each can. There are also some excellent brands from California, Spain, and Morocco. I would not recommend any brand that has sugar added to it, as I am definitely against adding sugar when cooking tomato sauces.

Pumate: *Pumate* are tomatoes dried in the open air in the sun. The dried tomatoes are then preserved in olive oil and spices. *Pumate* are excellent served over slices of smoked mozzarella or used on a pasta of your choice in this manner:

Place a large dollop of butter in a bowl, add 2 tablespoons of concentrated Italian tomato paste (the kind that comes in tubes). Place a colander over the pot of boiling water in which you are cooking your pasta. Place the bowl with butter and tomato paste in colander. When the butter is melted, mix it with the tomato paste using a wooden spoon. When the pasta is cooked, remove the bowl from the colander. Use colander to drain pasta. Toss the pasta in the bowl and add to it some chopped *pumate.* Mix well.

Serve hot and sprinkle each plate of pasta with freshly grated Parmesan cheese.

Pumate is another product of Crespi e Figli from San Remo, and is obtainable at Dean & DeLuca, and certain other specialty food stores.

ZUCCHINI

The favorite Italian squash, and one of the most delicious vegetables. Available all year round, it is adaptable to many different uses, imparting its own special flavor to salads, pasta sauces, and eggs, or, hollowed out and stuffed, then baked. The best zucchini are slender, about 5 to 6 inches long, dark green in color, firm to the touch, with a fuzzy stem. Try to choose zucchini that still carry traces of the earth; avoid the artificially waxed type.

The flowers of the zucchini are, to me, a rare delicacy when dusted with flour, dipped in egg yolk, and deep-fried or sautéed. Zucchini blossoms can be obtained in Italian markets in the summer, and they are usually sold in bunches.

There are many other squashes available, such as summer squash, winter squash (which the Italians use as stuffing for some pasta), acorn, butternut, banana, and spaghetti, to name a few.

VEGETABLE OILS

Vegetable oils should be used for cooking purposes, for example, in frying or in preparation of food when the oil is either discarded or is not incorporated into the final sauce. Vegetable oil can be discarded after use or strained through a fine wire strainer, refrigerated, and used again. I like to use a tablespoon of vegetable oil in the pot of salted boiling water in which pasta is cooked in order to avoid the pasta sticking together. Or, for instance, I sauté scaloppine first in vegetable oil, discard it, and use butter in the final cooking. There are also many exotic vegetable oils on the market, such as walnut oil, almond, hazelnut, and sesame oil—which are easily obtainable at specialty shops or health-food stores.

VINEGAR

I almost always use red wine vinegar in my recipes. I recommend the Regina brand if you can find it, otherwise, Sasso or Paul Corcellet. Of course there are many other types of vinegars, such as tarragon, shallot, champagne, black currant, nutmeg, garlic, clove, green pepper. These types of vinegar are obtainable in New York City in special food stores such as Balducci's, Dean & DeLuca, Zabar's, and some of the better Italian stores in Italian sections.

BALSAMIC VINEGAR

This is a vinegar that is aged over a very long period. It is excellent in the preparation of salad dressings, sauces, and gravies. Sprinkled sparingly on meats already cooked, it lends aroma and flavor. It is a centuries-old specialty of the city of Modena, and during the time of the Este rulers (1288–1796) it was believed to contain medicinal properties, which is the origin of the word *balsamico*. It is precious because, in order to obtain a small amount, a very large quantity of cooked wine mash produced from special grapes of high sugar content is needed. It is then aged for many years in vats made of juniper, mulberry, and chestnut woods. Its color is a warm brown tone and it is slightly viscous. Its flavor is both sour and sweet. My favorite brands are Fini and Monari-Federzoni. They can be purchased at Balducci's, Dean & DeLuca, Zabar's, and better-quality Italian stores.

WINES FOR COOKING

In my cooking I generally use dry white or red California wines. I prefer robust wines. For some recipes I often use wines of more definite aroma and bouquet, such as Barolo or Marsala, dry Cinzano vermouth and Martini & Rossi sweet vermouth, Cognac or brandy, Calvados and Armagnac.

It is my belief that the wine used for cooking should be suitable for drinking as a table wine. One learns how to use wine in cooking by smelling or tasting, or both. It is important to know when the wine has evaporated enough and will not leave a harsh taste on the palate. The flavor of a dish can easily be ruined if the wine is not used judiciously or reduced to the proper degree.

In peasant Italian cooking, especially in the north, you often see people putting a few tablespoons of red wine directly into a piping hot bowl of soup. There goes my theory about letting wine evaporate!

Wine List

The wines included in this list are not ordinarily found in American wine merchants' shops. Some of these wines are often not exported because of the limited quantity of production and their sensitivity to traveling. Or, in some cases, they have not caught the eye of the importer. But this list might assist and intrigue you during your travels through Italy. The list is compiled region by region.

PIEMONTE

The region of Piemonte is one of the largest producers of wines in Italy. The wine industry is represented chiefly by their "reds." Among these, the very best derive from the Nebbiolo grapes.

Barolo, Barbaresco, Carema, Gattinara, Barbera, Freisa, Dolcetto, Moscato d'Asti (from which derives Asti Spumante, known the world over), Grignolino, Fara, Sizzano, Ghemme, Boca, Cortese

VAL D'AOSTA

Most of this region's production is consumed locally. Only a small amount is exported to other countries.

Moscato di Chambave, Enfer di Arvier, Donnaz

LIGURIA

The vineyards of major importance in this region are between Cinque Terre and Albenga. Here the better wines are produced, although in a very small quantity; therefore, it is rather difficult to come by a truly excellent bottle of any of them.

Vermentino, Cinque Terre, Rossesse

LOMBARDIA

Most of this region's wine comes from the provinces of Brescia, Sondrio, Pavia, Mantua, and Angera on the Lago Maggiore.

Franciacorta, Cellatica, Lugana, Rosso dell'Oltrepò, Riesling, Valtellina, Inferno, Sassella, Grumello, Sfursat

VENETO

The Veneto region has developed a large wine reputation for quality and the expert cutting and blending of the variety of their grapes. The most prolific provinces are Padua, Verona, Treviso, Venice, Vicenza, Rovigo, and Belluno.

Soave, Valpolicella, Prosecco, Breganze, Gambellara, Lison di Portogruaro, Tocai, Merlot, Cabernet, Rosso dei Colli Euganei, Sauvignon

TRENTINO–ALTO ADIGE

This region, situated in the heart of the Alps, has plateaus at high altitudes, where the vineyards produce some excellent wines.

Pinot Bianco Trentino, Riesling dell'Alto Adige, Traminer, Teroldego, Lago di Caldaro

FRIULI–VENEZIA GIULIA

The major vineyards of this region are located between Cividale del Friuli and Gorizia.

Tocai, Refosco, Malvasia del Collio, Verduzzo, Picolit, Pinot Grigio, Pinot Nero, Pinot Bianco

EMILIA–ROMAGNA

The wine-producing provinces of this region of great food are Ravenna, Reggio nell' Emilia, Modena, Forlì, Parma, Bologna, Piacenza, and Ferrara.

Gutturnio, Albana, Sangiovese, Lambrusco

TOSCANA

The entire wine production of Tuscany is principally based on the famous "Chianti," which is known all over the world. Chianti comes from many of the provinces of this region: Florence, Siena, Greve, Castellina, Gaiole, Poggibonsi, San Casciano, Val di Pesa, Montalbano, Pontassieve, San Gimignano.

Chianti, Chianti Classico, Vernaccia di San Gimignano, Brunello di Montalcino, Vino Nobile di Montepulciano

The "mystery" is how such a small region can produce so much Chianti to be distributed everywhere in the world in such abundance!

UMBRIA

This is one of the smallest regions of Italy, but the winemaking industry, along with its olive orchards, plays a very important part in Umbria's economy.

Colli del Lago Trasimeno, Orvieto, Torgiano, Rosso, Trebbiano, Verdello, Grechetto

MARCHE

The wine production of this region is not very large, but some of its wines, such as the following, are among the best known.

Verdicchio di Matelica, Verdicchio di Jesi, Rosso Conero, Rosso Piceno, Bianchello del Metauro

LAZIO

The wine production of this region is not one of the highest on the national scale. The most well-known zones for wine making are Castelli Romani, Colli Albani, and the Colli Lanuvini.

Velletri Bianco, Velletri Rosso, Est-Est-Est di Montefiascone, Maccarese, Cesanese del Piglio, Merlot, and Sangiovese di Aprilia

ABRUZZI E MOLISE

The only wine worthy of mention from this region is Cerasuolo di'Abruzzo, which is made with the grapes of Montepulciano.

CAMPANIA

Even though this region is low on the national scale of wine production, its wines are widely known in Italy as well as internationally. The zones most typical for these wines are Capri, Sorrento, Ischia, Procida, Monti Lattari.

Ischia Bianco Superiore, Ischia Rosso, Taurasi, Gragnano, Vesuvio, Capri Bianco, Lacryma Christi

PUGLIA

This region is one of the most prolific in wine making. So much so that its wines are used for blending and cutting with many of the wines produced in the northern part of Italy. Most of its wines are sweetish in taste; some are used in the making of vermouths.

Primitivo di Manduria, Rosso di Cerignola, Castel del Monte Bianco, Castel del Monte Rosso, Castel del Monte Rosato, Martina Franca (this is the most important wine for the production of vermouth), San Severo Bianco, Rosso di Matino

CALABRIA

The wines of this region are still made in the ancient tradition of the past. They are rather specialized. The most famous among the Calabrese wines are

Cirò Rosso, Cirò Bianco, Cirò Rosato

SICILIA

Wine is made everywhere on this island, but the most well-known provinces are those of Messina, Catania, Siracusa, Trapani, and

Palermo. The wines of this region are also used for blending and cutting with the wines of the north. The most typical and well-known wines are

Faro Rosso, Faro Bianco, Capo Bianco, Rosso dell'Etna, Rosato dell'Etna, Cerasuolo di Vittoria, Alcamo, Val di Lupo, Grecanico (one of the best whites from the island), Corvo Rosso, Corvo Bianco, Rapilata

SARDEGNA

The wine industry on this island is rather modest. Most of its wine is very good as table wine; only a few outstanding wines are produced.

Vernaccia di Oristano (good as an apéritif or a dessert wine), Oliena, Vermentino di Gallura, Moscato di Sorso (this is a superior wine for desserts)

CALIFORNIA WINES

Years after the strange phenomenon in the history of the United States called Prohibition, wine making became an industry.

The one person most responsible for development of the wine industry in California is Agoston Haraszthy de Mokcsa, a learned, cultivated man of Hungarian origin and a member of the minor nobility of that country. He was an energetic enough personality to point out to the California growers the necessity for higher standards and quality, and the importance of better grapes and the need to plant them in the right places.

Today, wine grapes are the largest agricultural crop in the state of California. At present, a few of the wines produced in California are on a par with, if not superior to, some of the European. Granted, the very "fine" wines are not that many, and furthermore, not all are ready to be consumed.

The most renowned wine districts of the state are the Central Valley, which—for the most part—produces cheap dessert wine, and the North Coast. The North Coast with, at its head, the two counties of Napa and Sonoma, north of San Francisco Bay, is wine country at its best. Essentially, Napa and Sonoma are red-wine, rather than white-wine country, with Napa producing twice as much red as white, and Sonoma perhaps as much as four times more red than white. Of course, all the wines produced here are not "excellent." But, as opposed to the Central Valley and other districts, Napa and Sonoma wines are consistently superior and some are a revelation. Along with these two districts are Santa Clara, Alameda, and the Livermore Valley, famous for their white wines. The Concannon's Cabernet of Livermore is still outstanding.

In the Napa Valley we have such wine makers as Joseph Phelps, Beaulieu, Louis Martini, Sebastiani, Beringer, Charles Krug, Robert Mondavi, Heitz, Sterling, Souverain, Chappelet.

In the Sonoma Valley, the wine makers are Nervo, Cambiasco, Simi, Martini, Pedroncelli, Rege, Foppiano, Gallo, Weibel, Cresta Blanca. This district is booming as production of wine goes. However, it will take Sonoma a long time before it will catch up with the Napa's wines.

Among California's most outstanding types of wine are

Sauvignon Blanc, Sauvignon Red, Chardonnay, Cabernet, Gamay Beaujolais, Gamay, Merlot, Pinot Noir, Zinfandel, Barbera, Sauterne, Carneros Creek Rosé, Petite Sirah

At present, the better brands of the above-listed wines are next to impossible to obtain at your neighborhood wine merchant. Only a handful of shops will have them.

My Favorite Eating Places in Europe, Morocco, New York, and California

It is true that an excellent dinner has a great deal to do with the company one keeps at the table. The unspoken promises in your guest's eyes are as much part of the dinner as the food itself. Or Signor Gino Ratti would have assured you that to taste and enjoy good food one has to be happy, and come to the table with a healthy appetite.

These are my favorite places where I have felt happy and hungry, and where often I read all kinds of unspoken promises in my companion's eyes.

So, let's go forth:

ITALY

PIEMONTE

Asti

Gener Neuv, Lungo Tanaro 4. Located on the shady riverside of the Tanaro. Moderately priced. Specialties: Sliced raw veal with cheese and truffles, peppers *astigiana* style, *agnolotti, spiedini di maiale alla brace,* stuffed roulade of rabbit. Wines: Grignolino, Barbera d'Asti, Barolo.

CARTOSIO*

Cacciatore, Via Moreno 22. A panoramic view of the hills. Moderately priced. Specialties: Homemade ravioli, risotto with porcini, lasagne, venison, roast baby lamb. Wines: Bianco Cortese, Dolcetto d'Acqui, Brachetto, Moscato.

TORINO

Al Gatto Nero, Corso Filippo Turati 14. Chic, catering to business people. Moderately high priced. Specialties: Grilled meat and fish, fish salads, beefsteak Florentine style. Wines: Montecarlo Bianco, Buonamico Rosso (proprietor's reserve).

Tastevin, Corso Siccardi 15-bis. Chic, catering to business people. Moderately high priced. Specialties: *Antipasto ducale, risotto al Tastevin, tagliarini al brucio,* codfish à la Monterossina. Wines: Barberone del Monferrato, Cinque Terre di Manarola.

VAL D'AOSTA

COGNE

Lou Ressignon, Via Borgeois 81. Romantic setting with a panoramic view of the Mont Blanc. Moderately priced. Specialties: *Antipasti valdostani, carbonada con polenta, fonduta alla valdostana.* Wines: La Salle white, Donnaz, Petit Rouge, Chambave Rouge.

LIGURIA

BORGIO VEREZZI

Antica Trattoria Bergallo, Via Roma 9. Telephone (019) 68087. Reservations advisable. Service on the terrace, view of the bay. Prices moderate. Specialties: Snails, ravioli, rabbit, *capretto, budino.* Wines: Rosato di Bergallo, Sassella, Vermentino.

* My father's birthplace.

Bussana di San Remo

Ai Torchi, Via al Mare 6. Romantic ambience, by the sea. Prices moderate. Specialties: *Antipasti di pesce, sardinara,* stuffed vegetables, *risotti (alla marinara, ai funghi, e ai carciofi).* Wines: Rossese and Vermentino.

Genova

Antica Osteria Pacetti, Via Borgo degli Incrociati 22R. Telephone (010) 892848. Reservations necessary. Rustic, but elegant and comfortable ambience. Prices moderately high. Specialties: *Antipasti Liguri, cappon magro, condiggion, minestra di bianchetti,* and a large variety of authentic dishes from the original Ligurian cuisine. Wines: A vast selection of wines from Liguria and France.

Gran Gotto, Via Fiume 11R. Business people and stockbrokers. Prices moderately high. Specialties: *Antipasti vari di verdure, gnocchi alla fonduta, pasta al pesto, scampi in busara, crêpes al salmone, portafoglio alla Cavour, scaloppine monferrine.* Wines: A large selection of wine from Tuscany and France.

Italia, Via Cinque Maggio 30R. Telephone (010) 388498. Service on terrace overlooking the sea. Prices moderately high. Specialties: *Risotto mantecato alle vongole, spaghetti alla pescatora, trancia di pesce Luigi II, gamberoni in salsa rosa.* Wines: Cortese di Gavi, Coronata, Cinque Terre, Veronesi, Friulani.

Imperia

Salvo-Cacciatori, Via Vieusseux 12. Rustic and elegant. Moderate prices. Specialties: *Risotto primavera, zuppa di fagioli, tortino di carciofi, triglie all' imperatrice, orate al forno, condiglione di aragoste, stoccafisso alla Genovese, cima alla Riviera di Ponente.* Wines: Bianco Vermentino, Rosso di San Biagio.

Lanterna Blu, Via Scarincio 32. Rustic, elegant. View of the waterfront. Moderately priced. Specialties: *Risotti, zuppa di datteri, tartufi di mare, ostriche, moscardini alla Lucia, orata al Mabruk, crema di gamberi, capone di mare all'acqua pazza.* Wines: Pigato, Rossese, Vermentino di Artallo.

SAN REMO

Osteria del Marinaio, Via Gudio 38. Romantic ambience, elegant. Moderately priced. Specialties: *Zuppa di seppie, calamarettini in tutti i modi, branzino imborrato al forno.* Wines: Vermentino di San Remo and French wines.

SAVONA

San Marco, Via Leoncavallo 4. Rustic. Moderately priced. Specialties: *Antipasti, corzetti alla savonese, lasagnette verdi con pesto vecchia maniera, zuppa di frutti di mare, fritto misto.* Wines: Rossese, Sassella, Vermentino.

RECCO

Manuelina, Via Roma 300. Telephone 74128. The best restaurant in Liguria. Service in the garden. Elegant. Prices high. Specialties: *Trofie al pesto, pansoti alle noci, focaccia di formaggio, vegetali ripieni, pesce e vitella.* Wines: Barolo, Barbera, Vermentino, Sassella. Superb wine cellar, with unparalleled selections.

SANTA MARGHERITA LIGURE

La Brace, Via Montebello 43. Elegant and romantic. Service on terrace, view of the bay. Moderately priced. Specialties: *Antipasti, profiette al pesto, pappardelle ai funghi, focaccia alla salvia.* Local wines.

LOMBARDIA

CERNOBBIO (COMO)

Sporting Club "Villa d'Este," operated by the Grand Hotel Villa d'Este, located in their park with view of Lake Como. Moderately priced. Specialties: *risotto al salmone, crespelle Bell'Otéro, pollastrella alla Crapoudine.* Wines: Lambrusco, Barbera, Berbaresco.

COMO

Cervetta, Via Cardona 26. Moderately priced. Specialties: Risotto with spinach, *paglia e fieno*, minestrone, *polenta uncia*, oxtails *in umido*, stuffed veal. Wines: Inferno, Grumello, Valpolicella, Tocai.

MILANO

Da Alfio, Via Senato 31. Telephone 700-633. Reservations only. Elegant, artists, actors, and business people. Moderately high priced. Specialties: Fish, *bollito misto, cassoeula*, tripe, cotechini. Wines: Barbera, Valpolicella, Oltrepò Pavese.

Giannino (perhaps the best restaurant in Italy), Via Amatore Sciesa 8. Telephone 542-948. Reservations only. Very elegant, beautifully appointed and frequented by Milanese society, actors, singers. Moderately high priced. Specialties: *Cappelloni alla Giannino, agnolotti di ricotta*, risotto Caruso, *crespelle*, a great variety of grilled meat, fish, excellent and inventive antipasti. Wines: vast selection of national and international wines.

Savini (where Signor Gino Ratti was second in command of the kitchen), Galleria Vittorio Emanuele II. Telephone 898-343. Reservations only. Sidewalk café in the Galleria. One of the oldest and most prestigious places in Milano, frequented by La Scala singers. Fairly high priced. Specialties: *Risotto alla Milanese*, filets of beef Woronoff, *ossobuco in gremolata*, breast of turkey Savini. Wines: Sassella, Inferno, Castel Chiuro, Crù Melini, and a vast selection of the best Italian wines.

VENETO

ASOLO

Villa Cipriani, Via A. Canova 298. Telephone 0423-52166. Reservations necessary. Elegant, excellent, chic. View of the hills of Asolo and Monte Grappa. Fairly high priced. Specialties: Tagliatelle with cream and prosciutto, *risotto primavera, risotto alla marinara*, braised beef *all'asolana*, grilled fish and meat, fillet of beef *alla Duse, frittata di porcini,* and a variety of specialties that only Cipriani can prepare. Wines: Prosecco, Pinot, Traminer, Merlot, Cabernet, Venegazzù, and a large selection of the best.

CORTINA D'AMPEZZO

El Toulà, Via Ronco 123. Telephone 0436-3339. Reservations necessary. Elegant, dining on the terrace, view of the valley of Cortina. Fairly high priced. Specialties: blini with salmon, *porcini pasticciati, frittata* of artichokes, *blanc et noir El Toulà,* veal alla Bassanese. Wines: Sfursat, Pinot Noir, Barbera, Beaujolais Nouveau, Blauburgunder.

PADOVA

Da Giovanni, Via Maroncelli 22. Regional, rustic, catering to business people. Service in garden. Moderately priced. Specialties: tagliatelle, gnocchi, agnolotti, pasta e fagioli, risotti, boiled meat, roast lamb. Wines: Merlot, Cabernet, Amarone, white wines from Verona and Treviso.

VENEZIA

Trattoria alla Colomba, San Marco, Piscina di Frezzeria 1655. One of the truly wonderful Venetian *trattorie.* Moderately priced. Specialties: *prosciutto di Montagnana, riso e luganega, pasta e fagioli,* grilled meat and fish, *seppie alla Veneziana con polenta, pesce al cartoccio.* Wines: Pinot Grigio, Soave, Refosco, Pinot Nero, Recioto.

La Fenice, San Marco 1938. Telephone 30124/23856. Reservations necessary. Near the Teatro La Fenice. Elegant. Moderately high priced. Specialties: *spaghetti all'isolana, risotto nero La Fenice, cartoccio di pesce, rombo di casa,* and various other Venetian specialties. Wines: Pinot Grigio, Soave, Cabernet, Merlot, Refosco, Pinot Nero, Recioto.

Harry's Bar, San Marco, Calle Vallaresso 1323. Telephone (041) 85331. Reservations necessary. Elegant and very well appointed. Panorama of the Canal Grande and San Marco. Prices high. Specialties: *Risotto primavera, carpaccio, baccalà mantecato* or *alla Vicentina con polenta abbrustolita,* fettuccine Harry's Bar. Wines: Merlot Angoris di Attimis, Venegazzù, Montello Bianco e Rosso.

Locanda Montin, Accademia, Fondamenta Eremite 1147. An artists' hangout with covered garden, very gay and boisterous atmosphere. Food is fine "casalinga" style, typical Venetian, portions are huge. A good place to meet interesting people. Fried polenta is used in lieu of bread. The wines are an assortment of locals. Very moderate prices.

VERONA

Dodici Apostoli, Vicolo Corticella, San Marco 3. Telephone (045) 246680. Reservations advisable. Elegant and appointed in sophisticated rustic, like a country inn. High priced. Specialties: *Pasta e fagioli, salmone cotto nel pane, costata all'Amarone, costoletta Dodici Apostoli.* Wines: Sfursat, Valpolicella, and the typical Veronese wines.

Marconi, Vicolo Crocioni 6. Elegant, romantic. Moderate prices. Specialties: *Antipasti, tuffoloni alla Marconi, tagliatelline al salmone, stinco di maiale al forno.* Wines: typical Veronese.

Re Teodorico, Piazzale Castel San Pietro 1. Chic and romantic. Service on the terrace. View of the city and the river Adige. Moderate prices. Specialties: *Pasta ai quattro formaggi, riso con scampi flambé al whiskey, scaloppine Re Teodorico, filetto di manzo alla rustica.* Wines: Typical Veronese.

EMILIA–ROMAGNA

BOLOGNA

Don Chisciotte e Sancio Panza, Via degli Albari 2. Elegant. Prices moderately high. Specialties: *Gocce d'oro Don Chisciotte, tortino, raviolini primavera, petto di tacchino vecchia Bologna.* Wines: Albana di Monte San Pietro, Sangiovese del Rubicone.

Nerina, Piazza Galileo 6. Elegant, romantic. Service in garden. Moderately high. Specialties: *Balanzoni alla Petroniana, gramigna della casa, buongustaia Nerina, fritto misto fantasia.* Wines: Lambrusco, Sangiovese, Albana, Sparvo.

Al Pappagallo, Piazza Mercanzia 3. Regional rustic, elegant. Moderately high prices. Specialties: *Tortellini alla Pappagallo o in pasta sfogliata, filetti di manzo allo Champagne, filetto di tacchino alla cardinale, suprema di pollo con tartufi, faraona all'uva, costoletta di vitello alla Pappagallo.* Wines: Albana, Sangiovese, Lambrusco.

Rosteria Luciano, Via Nazario Sauro 19. Rustic, elegant. Prices moderately high. Specialties: *Armonie dell' Appennino, manicaretto Garisenda, rifreddo di cappone con gelatina, scaloppine al cartoccio.* Wines: Sparvo, Albana, and local regional wines.

CESENA

Rugantino, Via Comunale San Mauro 1110. Rustic, elegant. Service in garden. Prices moderate. Specialties: *Antipasti, "monfrigul" con spinaci, puntarine coi fagioli, tagliatelle con sugo di coniglio, strozzapreti, gramigna con salsiccia, piadina romagnola, spianata all'aglio, coniglio in porchetta.* Wines: Trebbiano, Albana, Venetian, Piemontesi, Friulani, Trentini.

FERRARA

Italia O Da Giovanni, Largo Castello 32. Elegant. Service on terrace. Moderately priced. Specialties: *Tortellini alla panna, pasticcio di maccheroni, bolliti misti.* Wines: Lambrusco, Sangiovese, Albana, Trebbiano.

Vecchia Chitarra, Via Ravenna 11. Rustic, elegant. Service on terrace. Moderately priced. Specialties: *Risotto allo Champagne, anguille con polenta, coniglio al vino rosso.* Local wines.

MODENA

Cervetta, Via Cervetta. Elegant, rustic. Located in the historic part of the city. Moderately priced. Specialties: Cannelloni, *mac-*

cheroni al pettine, tagliatelle al prosciutto, arista alla panna, piccioni in salmì. Wines: Lambrusco and a variety of local wines.

Fini, Rua dei Frati Minori 54. Business people, elegant, located in historic center of the city. Moderately priced. Specialties: *Tortellini alla panna, salumi della casa, zampone, bolliti e arrosti misti, tortelloni al sugo.* Wines: Lambrusco di Sorbara and many local wines.

Zelmira, Via San Giacomo 27. Rustic. Moderately priced. Specialties: *Nidi di S. Vincenzo, bocconcini al prosciutto, cosce di maiale, stracotto al Barolo, stracchino della duchessa.* Wines: A great variety of local wines.

PARMA

Angiol d'Or, Vicolo Scutellari 1. Elegant. View of the Duomo and the Battistero. Moderately priced. Specialties: *Spaghetti all'aragosta, pasta alla vodka, cedanino alla Romito, risotto del signore, scaloppine delizia del mare, filetto alla bresciana, filetti di trota alla Caruso.* Wines: Italian and French varieties.

Da Marino, Via Affò 2. Rustic, elegant. Moderately priced. Specialties: *Pasta Marino, risotto al limone o ai frutti di mare, penne alla cipolla, chicche Maria Stuarda, crespelle ai funghi, scampi all' avaiana.* Wines: Piacentini Nostrani, and a variety of French wines.

RAVENNA

Alla Torre, Via Costa 3. Regional rustic. Moderately priced. Specialties: *Lasagne al forno, cappelletti Torre, lingua salmistrata al Madeira, misto di carni fredde.* Wines: Lambrusco, Albana, Sangiovese.

REGGIO NELL' EMILIA

Amarcord, Via Martiri di Cervarolo 76. Amusing place, frequented by young writers and students. Service on terrace. Moderately priced. Specialties: *Antipasti, minestre locali.* Wines: A good variety of local.

RIMINI

Nello, Via Flavio Gioia 7. Elegant. Moderately priced. Specialties: *Spaghetti alle seppie, risotto alla marinara, grigliata di pesce dell'Adriatico, calamaretti alla tarantina.* Wines: Verdicchio, Trebbiano.

TOSCANA

FLORENCE

Sabatini, Via de' Panzani 41/43 r. Elegant. Moderately high priced. Specialties: *Zuppa alla paesana, manicotti ai quattro formaggi, bistecca alla fiorentina, noce di vitello tartufato al brandy, petti di pollo alla San Vincenzo, soufflé all'arancia.* Wines: Best assortment of Tuscan wines.

Oliviero, Via delle Terme 51. Trattoria-type ambience. Very "in" place. Moderate prices. Specialties: *Spaghetti della casa, panzerotti gratinati, portafoglio all'Onassis, filetto di manzo al pepe verde.* Large variety of regional specialties. Wines: the best of Chianti, Brunello di Montalcino.

Otello, Via Orti Oricellari 28. Caters to business people. Moderately high prices. Specialties: *Tagliarini Otello, arrosti allo spiedo, costola di vitella alla zingara, trippa alla fiorentina.* Wines: the best of Chianti and large assortment of French wines.

FORTE DEI MARMI

Cervo Bianco, Via Risorgimento 9. Trattoria-type ambience. Moderate prices. Specialties: *Pesce arrosto, bollito, pollame, cacciagione allo spiedo, fritture miste.* Wines: A good assortment of wines from the hills of Pisa.

GROSSETO

Ombrone, Viale Matteotti 71. Elegant. Rustic. Service on terrace. Moderate prices. Specialties: *Spaghetti alla buttera, zuppa alla maremmana, grigliate di mare.* Excellent selection of Roman and Tuscan wines.

PISA

Antonio, Piazza della Repubblica 6. Rustic. Moderate prices. Specialties: *Gnocchi al gorgonzola, tortelloni ai funghi, portafoglio all'Antonio, faraona con polenta, spiedino primavera.* Wines: The best from the hills of Pisa and a large variety of Chianti classici.

Da Nando, Via Contessa Matilde 68. Rustic, elegant. Service on veranda. Prices moderate. Specialties: *Antipasto mare, crostini della casa, marinata di pesce, zuppa toscana, pappardelle alla lepre, fusilli alla norcina, ossobuco, trippa, spiedini misti mare.* Wines: Chianti, Trebbiano, Brunello di Montalcino.

Sergio, Lungarno Pacinotti 1. Chic, rustic. Prices moderately high. Specialties: *Zuppa pisana, zuppa di funghi, risotto con tartufi, pesce del Tirreno, tagliata di manzo.* Wines: Chianti classici, Tegolato, and an excellent variety of French wines.

SAN GIMIGNANO

Le Terrazze, Piazza della Cisterna 23. Elegant. View of the San Gimignano valley. Moderately priced. Specialties: *Risotto alla Cisterna, zuppa alla paisana, pollo alla massaia, arrostino senese.* Wines: Chianti, Vernaccia, and a large variety of regional wines.

SIENA

Al Mangia, Piazza del Campo 42. Regional rustic. Service in the open on the square. View of the square where the Palio takes place in July and August. Moderate prices. Specialties: The best of the Sienese kitchen. Wines: A large variety of Chianti.

REPUBBLICA DI SAN MARINO

La Taverna, Piazza della Libertà. Elegant, romantic. Service on the terrace. Moderately priced. Specialties: *Maltagliati con ceci, strozzapreti, arrosti misti.* Wines: Sangiovese, Trebbiano, Moscato.

UMBRIA

Assisi

Pozzo della Mensa, Via del Pozzo della Mensa. Elegant, romantic. Moderately priced. Specialties: *Canoletti alla Pozzo, gnocchetti di ricotta, riso al curry, anitra in porchetta, coniglio all'agro.* A large assortment of regional wines.

Perugia

Falchetto, Via Bartolo 2. Rustic. Moderately priced. Specialties: *Falchetti verdi, zuppa di cipolle, polenta con salsiccia, torello alla perugina, scampi e lumache di mare, capretto e agnello scottadito, trecciole alla brace, trippa al sugo.* Wines: Torgiano, Trasimeno, Orvieto, and a good selection of Chianti.

La Rosetta, Piazza Italia 19. Caters to business people. Service on terrace. Moderately priced. Specialties: *Crostini di tartufi, spaghetti alla norcina, bruschetta, porchetta al finocchio, palombaccia ghiotta, agnello brodettato.* Wines: Some of the best Orvieto, Vernaccia, and a good assortment of local wines.

LAZIO

Frascati

Cacciani, Via A. Diaz 13. Rustic. Moderate prices. Specialties: *Agnolotti, pollo alla diavola, abbacchio alla cacciatore, quaglie arrosto.* Wines: Frascati, Velletri, Orvieto.

Roma

Passetto, Via Zanardelli 14. Chic, elegant, frequented by actors and artists. Service on the terrace. Moderately high prices. Specialties: The best of the Roman cuisine. Excellent service. Wines: Frascati, and a large assortment of regional and national wines.

Mastro Stefano, Piazza Navona. Elegant, frequented by actors and artists. Service on the terrace. Moderately high prices. Specialties: *Ravioli di ricotta, tonnarelli alla Rigorè, salsicce di Amatrice con fagioli, rognoncino trifolato coi funghi.* Wines: Frascati, Orvieto and a large selection of national and local wines.

Del Bolognese, Piazza del Popolo. Elegant, frequented by television celebrities and newspaper people. Moderately high prices. Service in the open. Specialties: *Risotto Coriolano, zuppa di fagioli, pesce, abbacchio al forno, capretto alla cacciatora.* Wines: Frascati, Orvieto, Velletri, and a large assortment of local wines.

La Campana, Vicolo della Campana 18. Elegant, rustic. Prices moderate. Specialties: *Carciofi alla Romana, abbacchio al vino bianco, petto di vitello alla fornara.* Wines: Frascati, Velletri, Chianti.

Hostaria Romana Giggi Fazi, Via Lucullo 22. Very Roman. Prices moderately high. Specialties: *Bucatini all'amatriciana, pasta e ceci, abbacchio allo spiedo, involtini al prosciutto.* Wines: A large variety of local wines.

El Toulà, Via della Lupa 29-B. Elegant. Prices moderately high. Specialties: *Pasta e fagioli, risotti, carpaccio, gigot di abbacchio, coniglio con peverada e polenta.* Wines: Frascati, Orvieto, Velletri, and a large selection of national and local wines.

ABRUZZI

PESCARA

La Barcaccia, Piazza 1 Maggio 33. Rustic, elegant. Moderately priced. Specialties: *Antipasti di pesce, pasta munuta in brodo di pesce, spaghetti con pesto di alici, linguine con sugo di pesce, brodetto.* Wines: Trebbiano di Abruzzo, Cerasuolo.

CAMPANIA

AMALFI

La Marinella, Lungomare dei Cavalleri. Rustic. Service on terrace. Panorama of the coast of Amalfi. Moderate prices. Specialties: *Cannelloni di frutti di mare, zuppa di pesce, cozze al tegame, aragoste.* Wines: Gragnano, Farnese, Lacryma Christi.

CAPRI

La Canzone del Mare, Marina Piccola. Excellent ambience. Swimming pool, cabanas for reposing after dining, panorama of the Faraglioni and the sea. Prices high. Specialties: *Denti di elefante ai frutti di mare, risotto di pesce, aragoste variate, tagliatelle allo Champagne.* Wines: Gragnano, Faraglioni, Falerno.

Da Gemma, Via Madre Serafina 6. Rustic. Service on terrace. View of the valley of Capri. Prices moderate. Specialties: *Pizze, frittata di maccheroni, pesce.* Wines: Local and national varieties.

ISCHIA

La Romantica, Forio, Via Monte Verde 35. Romantic and chic ambience. Service on the beach. Moderately high. Specialties: *Pizze, pesci al forno, ai ferri e a zuppa, coniglio a la cacciatora.* Wines: From the island and nationals.

NAPLES

Le Arcate, Via Aniello Falcone 249. Romantic and chic. Service on terrace and in garden. Panorama of the entire Bay of Naples. Prices moderately high. Specialties: *Risotto ai frutti di mare, maccheroni alla Sophia Loren, aragosta alla Fra Diavolo, filetti di sogliole, involtini alla De Sica.* Wines: Gragnano, Falerno, Lacryma Christi, Ischia.

Ciro a'Mergellina, Via Mergellina 21. Chic, frequented by artists and actors. Prices high. Specialties: pesce: *a zuppa, arosto, fritto; frutti di mare; pizze,* and other regional dishes. Wines: Gragnano, Ischia, Vesuvio, and a variety of national wines.

Giuseppone a Mare, Via Ferdinando Russo 13. Romantic and chic. Panorama of the Bay of Naples. Prices high. Specialties: *Zuppa di frutti di mare, pignatiello di polipi, risotto di pesce, spigola alla Rivafiorita.* Wines: Ischia, Vesuvio, Gragnano, Falerno.

POSITANO

Covo dei Saraceni, Via Marina. Chic. Panorama of rocky harbor. Prices moderate. Specialties: *Pizze, spaghetti alle vongole, risotto di pesce,* and a variety of regional dishes. Wines: Monte di Procida, Vesuvio, Gragnano.

RAVELLO

Caruso-Belvedere, Via Toro 52. Chic. Elegant. Service on terrace. Panorama of the bay and the mountains. Moderately high prices. Specialties: *Cannelloni, pollo ai funghi, pesce.* Wines: Gran Caruso, Ravello, Vesuvio, Gragnano.

SORRENTO

La Favorita—o' Parrucchiano, Corso Italia 67. Rustic. Service on terrace and in garden. Moderate prices. Specialties: *Antipasti, gnocchi alla sorrentina, sartu di riso, risotto di vongole, latticini sorrentini, parmigiana di melanzane, treccia di scamorza.* Wines: Cerasuolo, Gragnano, and other local wines.

SICILIA

AGRIGENTO

Akrabello, Parco Angeli. Rustic and elegant. Moderate prices. Specialties: *rigatoni alla francescana, fettuccine all'Akrabello, involtini di pesce spada, medaglione alla castellana.* Wines: Corvo, Rapilatà, Val di Lupo.

CANICATTI

Al Faro, Via Lamarmora. Rustic. View of the hills. Specialties: *Pasta casareccia, cavati al cartoccio, stigliole alla brace, cacciagione.* Wines: Local and regional

CATANIA

Turi Finocchiaro, Via Cestai 8. Rustic. Moderate prices. Specialties: *spaghetti finocchiaro, farsu magru, pesce, mussi alla catanese.* Wines: Corvo, Rapilatà, Val di Lupo.

ENNA

Centrale, Via 6 Dicembre 9. Rustic. Moderate rices. Specialties: *Sformato di maccheroni, farsu magru, pasta con le sarde.* Wines: Regionals.

ERICE

Taverna di Re Aceste, Viale Conte Pepoli. Rustic. Service on terrace. Moderate prices. Specialties: *Cuscusu, rigatoni all'ericina, triglie al cartoccio, cuscinetto di Re Aceste.* Wines: Corvo, Rapilatà, Val di Lupo.

MESSINA

Alberto, Via Ghibellina 95. Chic and elegant. Moderately high prices. Specialties: *Pasta incaciata, ventrette e stocco a ghiotta, riso e pasteddi alla eoliana, farsu magru.* Wines: Faro, Val di Lupo, Corvo.

PALERMO

Charleston Le Terrazze, Viale Regina Elena. Chic, elegant. Service on the terrace over the sea. Moderately high prices. Specialties: *Pasta con le sarde, maccheroni Paolina, al buso, involtini alla siciliana, pesce.* Wines: A large assortment of Sicilian wines.

Harry's Bar, Via Ruggero Settimo. Chic, elegant. Prices moderately high. Specialties: *Antipasti, mini vastedde, mini focacce con mitza, mevusa, piatti montanari delle Madonie, sfoglio petralese al formaggio dolce.* Wines: Large variety of Sicilian, Italian, and French wines.

SIRACUSA

Jonico "A Rutta e Ciauli," Riviera Dionisio il Grande 194. Rustic. Elegant. Service on the terrace. Moderate prices. Specialties: *Antipasti rustici, risotto alla pescatora, tonnina alla siciliana, pesce spada, polpettone siciliana.* Wines: White and red from Santa Vittoria.

TAORMINA

San Domenico Palace Hotel, a fourteenth-century Dominican monastery converted into a very elegant, exceedingly comfortable hotel. Beautiful gardens, excellently appointed. Their restaurant is one of the best in Taormina. Prices high. Specialties: Sicilian and Northern Italian. Wines: A selected variety of Sicilian, national, and French.

CASTELMOLA

Quattro Stagioni. Rustic. Frequented by the aristocracy of Taormina. Overlooking the coastline and the sea. Perched on top of the mountain. Prices high. Specialties: Rustic, truly Sicilian fare. Wide selection of Sicilian wines. Worth a drive from Taormina (30 minutes by car).

FRANCE

PARIS

Taillevent, 15 Rue Lamennais, 8th Arrondissement. Telephone 563-39-94. Reservations necessary. Ambience elegant, aristocratic, also one of the most consistent restaurants in Paris for the quality of its food and its inspired cuisine. Prices very high. Nouvelle cuisine: salad of warm sweetbreads; salmon with fresh mint; lobster with tarragon; lemon duck. Wines: prodigiously rich wine cellar.

Brasserie Lipp, 151 Boulevard St.-Germain, 6th. Turn-of-the-century décor, one of the most comfortable, relaxed restaurants in

Paris. Moderate prices. The clientele is a potpourri of notables from every field. The fare served is adequate, and there is a good wine cellar. It is definitely worth a visit.

L'Archestrate, 84 Rue de Varenne, 7th. Telephone 551-4733. Very elegant, but lacks warmth, and the service is often rather rude. The cuisine is nouvelle. Prices high. Specialties: Leeks stuffed with lobster, lobster in vanilla sauce, honey duck, roast pigeon with ginger. Wines: some of the best Bordeaux and Burgundy.

La Ciboulette, 141 Rue St.-Martin, 4th. Telephone 271-7234. Elegant ambience. Prices high. The fare is innovative and nouvelle. Wonderful wine list. Fairly priced for the quality offered.

Chez l'Ami Louis, 32 Rue du Vertbois, 3rd. Telephone 887-7748. Reservations necessary. Rustic. The owner is an eighty-year-old man who has handed down his recipes of sumptuous grilled farm chickens, lamb and beef, thin, crisp *frites*, and a garlicky potato cake, wonderful foie gras to start, moderate to high priced. An adequate wine cellar.

Pierre Traiteur, 10 Rue de Richelieu, 1st. Telephone 296-0917. Not one of the loveliest restaurants of Paris; however, the food is almost always satisfying, especially such home-cooked dishes as stuffed cabbage and stuffed breast of lamb. Reasonably priced. A good wine list.

Brasserie Flo, 7 Cour des Petites-Ecuries, 10th. Telephone 770-1359. One of the city's best brasseries. Charm, and hearty food. Very reasonable. Adequate wine list.

Les Bouchons, 19 Rue des Halles, 1st. Telephone 233-2873. One of the newest and prettiest places that have opened in Les Halles, offering pretty people and a very attractive menu. Wine served by the glass and bottle. Very reasonably priced.

Robert Vattier, 14 Rue Coquillière, 1st. Telephone 236-5160. One of the last old-style Les Halles bistros. Open night and day, serving the "famous" onion soup—a cure for all sorts of hangovers. Very reasonably priced. Adequate wine list.

La Coupole, 102 Boulevard du Montparnasse, 14th. A Parisian landmark and the best people-watching place in town. Serves acceptable brasserie fare. Very reasonable prices. Passable wine list.

Allard, 41 Rue St.-André-des-Arts, 6th. A wonderful bistro, with a classic zinc counter, sawdust on the floor, and waiters in long cotton smocks. Allard is an institution. The cuisine is bourgeois from Burgundy: game terrine, scallops in beurre blanc, beef braised in red wine, coq au vin, cassoulets, and sometimes the best duck with turnips. A superb wine list. Moderately high prices.

Les Deux Magots, 170 Boulevard St.-Germain, 6th. A wonderful spot for drinking and people-watching. Reasonably priced. The menu is the usual café fare.

Café Flore, 172 Boulevard St.-Germain, 6th. Again, another place to watch and to be watched. The whole world passes and stops at least once at this café.

Gaston Lenôtre's Pré Catalan, Route de Suresnes, Bois de Boulogne. Telephone 524-5558. Reservations necessary. Sumptuous garden, attracting an extravagant clientele. Superb food: Haddock stuffed with potatoes, tagliatelle with salmon, lobster and turbot, fresh salmon with scrambled eggs and truffles, soufflé of sea urchin, and calves' feet stuffed with mushrooms. The desserts have no equal in this world. The dining room is spectacular Belle Epoque. Prices high. A serious wine list.

La Tour d'Argent, 15 Quai de la Tournelle, 5th. Telephone 354-2331. This restaurant is a French monument. It goes back 400 years. It's extremely luxurious and elegant, offering eighteen different ways to prepare a duck; each one a small masterpiece. The wines will not disappoint you. High prices.

Maxim's, 3 Rue Royale, 8th. Telephone 265-2794. The ambience is made up of dreams and fantasies. Maxim's is magic! Turn-of-the-century décor, and a swarm of famous faces every night. The cuisine is surpassed by dozens of other restaurants in Paris, but you don't go there to dine—but to be dazzled. The best food to order at Maxim's is smoked salmon and caviar. Wine: Champagne! Be prepared for an astronomical bill.

ENGLAND

LONDON

The English House, 3 Milner Street, London SW3. Telephone 01-584 3002. Reservations necessary. Extremely elegant. Very expensive. Specialties: Chicken stuffed with saffron rice, chicken and tripe ragoo, veal olive pie with green pea purée, roast grouse with wild raspberries, double-crusted pigeon pie. The fare offered by The English House comes from the recipes used in the wealthy houses of England in the seventeenth and eighteenth centuries. The host, Malcolm Livingston, is charming and knowledgeable. A large assortment of very selective wines from France, and some terrible English wines stocked only for laughs.

Keats Restaurant, Downshire Hill, Hampstead, London NW3. Telephone 01-435 3544/1499. Reservations necessary. Provincial English. Frequented by writers and artists. Prices high. Cuisine is French, and in my estimation it is on a par with some of the good places in which I have dined in France. A very selective wine cellar.

Cecconi's, 5A, Burlington Gardens, London W1. Telephone 01-434 1500/1509. Reservations necessary. Ambience elegant. Prices high. Frequented by the crème de la crème. Northern Italian cuisine at its best. A wonderful selection of wines.

The Connaught Grill, Carlos Place, London W1. Telephone 499-7070. Splendid late Victorian. Prices high. The best in Continental fare. Excellent service. A must!

WEST SUSSEX

Gravetye Manor. Near East Grinstead. Telephone (STD 0342) 810567. Reservations essential. Located thirty miles from London. Gravetye Manor is an Elizabethan stone mansion built in 1598 for Richard Infield and his wife, Katherine. Its beauty and elegance is still preserved today. Prices high. It offers a most imaginative à la carte menu, embracing both French cuisine and classic British dishes. The wine list offers a choice equal to that of any country inn in France.

HUNGARY

BUDAPEST

Vadrozsa, 1025 Budapest 2. ker., Pentelei Molnar ut 15. Telephone 351-118. Reservations necessary. Elegant and romantic. Prices high. Some of the best Hungarian food in Budapest. Selection of national wines.

Matyas Pince. Close to the Hotel Inter-Continental. Excellent peasant Hungarian food (do not miss the stuffed cabbage Transylvania style). They have one of the best Gypsy music groups in Hungary. Ambience is rustic, prices moderate. Selection of national wines.

Aranyszarvas, B.p. - 1 - Szarvaster. A must for native game dishes. Rustic, elegant. Moderately priced. Selection of national wines.

The Ruszwurm Pastry Shop, in the Var. It is two hundred years old—a must. Marvelous pastries and espresso. To be visited after lunch on Sunday, or any other day.

The Vorosmarthy or Gerbaud Pâtisserie is the meeting place for Budapest's old and new "society." A great pastry shop. Old World ambience. Moderately priced.

AUSTRIA

VIENNA

Zu den Drei Husaren, 1010 Wien, Weihburgg Gasse 4. Telephone 0222/521192. Reservations necessary. Very elegant. Prices moderately high. One of the best, if not the best, restaurant in Vienna. A large cellar of Austrian, German, and French wines.

Demel Café Pastry Shop, in the Kohlmarkt Section. Opened in 1888 and distinguished for having been the official pâtissier of the House of Habsburg. A superb, most elegant pâtisserie, as important to be visited as any of the museums in Vienna. You owe it to your taste buds. Prices moderate.

MOROCCO

CASABLANCA

Al-Mounia, 95 Rue du Prince, Moulay Abdallah. Telephone 22-26-69. Reservations necessary. Ambience is Moroccan at its most authentic best. It is probably the finest of its kind in Moroccan food. Very expensive, but worth it. If you're going for your first Moroccan meal, make it at Al-Mounia. Wines typical Moroccan, and a small selection of French.

Restaurant Imilchil, 27 Rue Vizir Tazi. Telephone 22-09-99. Reservations necessary. Here is where you should have your second Moroccan meal. Stunning décor. First-rate service. Here, too, the food is superlative Moroccan cuisine. Moderately high priced. Wines are Moroccan, with some French.

FEZ

Palais Jamai, located in the hotel of the same name, Bab el Guissa. Telephone 343-31. This is a super-sumptuous restaurant, which offers the splendid specialties of Moroccan food at a fancy price, but it's a "fun" place to splurge. Service is a fulfillment of all the fantasies you might have formulated in your head when you embarked on your trip to Morocco.

All-Anmbra, Boutouil 16. Deep in the medina—you'll never find it without a guide. The food is the best in Fez. The décor is authentic opulent Moroccan. The small collection of genuine artifacts displayed on its walls are as valuable as you would be likely to see in a museum. Its owner, a handsome old gentleman, presides over his establishment seated on a miniature throne in the main salon, dressed in a simple white Berber jellaba, wearing around his neck a camel-skin money purse, which serves him as a cash register for his business. The *harira* soup and the *bisteeya* served in this restaurant are worth the "pangs of fear you experience in order to get there." It deserves several visits to taste it all and see it all. Expensive.

MARRAKESH

Some of the best food in Marrakesh is found in little native restaurants around the "fantastic" enormous Djemaa-el-Fna Square, where everything happens; if you are adventurous and "open" enough, and have a touch of Sidney Greenstreet and Peter Lorre in you, you'll venture there.

Riad. Rue Arset el Maach. Telephone 254-30. Reservations necessary. This is a splendid restaurant located in a former harem of a wealthy merchant, where birds fly freely around you while you dine. The food is excellent; staff is very attentive and friendly. The entertainment is of the non-tourist nature. Frequented by the well-to-do upper class of Marrakesh. Here, too, is a place to unleash your dreams. Expensive.

La Maison Arabe, 5 Rue Derb Ferran. Telephone 226-5 (on order only). A superbly run place, owned by a French lady. It caters to the crème de la crème of Moroccan and European society. Elegantly appointed. Food exceptional. Service faultless. Very expensive. Excellent wine list.

ASNI

If you should find yourself traveling through Asni, a small town 3,770 feet high in the Grand Atlas Mountains, make a detour to Ourigane, a few miles away. Ourigane is a mountain village where Le Sanglier Qui Fume, a delightful inn, will welcome you and offer you Berber food with no comparison anywhere in Morocco.

The owner, an ex-Foreign Legionnaire who remained in Morocco after its independence, will charm you with stories of his past, each one good enough to turn into a Hollywood film, and just as questionable for its authenticity. Peacocks, pigs, turtles, and scrawny storks will come to beg at your table. His homemade wine is another reason to stop by. Prices moderate.

NEW YORK

The Four Seasons, 99 East 52nd Street. Telephone 212/754-9494. Reservations necessary. One of the most beautiful restaurants in the world. Owned by two elegant, charming, and very knowledgeable gentlemen, Paul Kovi and Tom Margittai. Architecturally the place is a masterpiece of both grandeur and drama. It was created for Restaurant Associates by Joseph Baum, and for a while it was the flagship of that restaurant chain. The place was designed on such a scale as to accommodate and justify the marble staircase, floor, and pool in the middle of the main dining room; the dark, rich wood walls; the immense Picasso tapestry; the thousands of bottles of wine; the three-story-high windows; the giant pots holding luxuriant trees that reach to the ceiling (and these lucky trees are sent on a winter vacation to Florida every year). The Four Seasons kitchen turns out, for the most part, very inventive and highly commendable food. Some of their specialties are superlative. The wine list of the establishment is extraordinary, including one of the best assortment of American wines available in New York. Prices are high. A meal at The Four Seasons is a must for any visitor to New York from anywhere in the world. For the New Yorker it is what New York is all about.

Lutèce. 249 East 50th Street. Telephone 212/752-2225. Reservations essential. I would like to introduce this restaurant by saying that its chef/owner André Soltner is, in my estimation, one of the great contemporary chefs of the French cuisine here and abroad. Lutèce is located in a three-story townhouse. The décor is unpretentiously elegant, tastefully appointed. The service is impeccable. Among the remarkable dishes this establishment offers are the famous snails styled as *timbales d'escargots à la chablisienne, pèlerins à la méridionale, truite fraîche à l'oseille,* or other specialties such as *cassoulet de crabe "Vieille France," poussin basquaise,* the delicious seafood sausage, and incomparable pâtés. Prices high. Wines: An ambitious and intelligent assortment of some of the best wines of France. A visit to Lutèce is equal to dining at one of the best four-star restaurants of France.

The Coach House, 110 Waverly Place. Telephone 212/777-0303. Reservations essential. Physically an elegant, charming room characterized by Colonial décor, the restaurant is an institution among the food establishment of New York. Frequented by monied clientele. Mr. Leon Lianides, the proprietor, strives for perfection in both the service and the food. He is a very knowledgeable restaurateur and a chef of renown. The food is mainly American in style; the restaurant is famous for its black bean soup, the rack of lamb, roasted to a crisp, and the tripe soup, which is a masterpiece. Wonderful desserts are offered, and an equally comparable wine list, especially the selection of American wines. Expensive, but a must.

La Caravelle, 33 West 55th Street. Telephone 212/586-4252. Reservations essential. Monsieur Robert Meyzen, the proprietor, is perfection itself, and most often, so is the food served in this establishment. Elegant. The walls are decorated with wonderfully airy scenes of Paris. The service is impeccable. Frequented by a wealthy clientele. Try the *pâté toulousain* (splendid!), *caneton rôti au poivre, escalope de veau au citron, homard Washington.* La Caravelle squabs and fish are usually superlative dishes. At the end of the meal you are brought a plate of glazed fruits to nibble on. The grapes and berries and orange sections are delightful. The wine list rates among the best. Expensive, but a trip to New York is not complete without a meal at La Caravelle and the pleasure of meeting Robert Meyzen.

La Tulipe, 104 West 13th Street. Telephone 212/691-8860. This is a little jewel of a restaurant. The simplicity of the appointments is almost perfect. It was created and, you can tell, with great love by its owner, Sally Darr. The food is first class. Ms. Darr herself is in the kitchen, and her cooking standards are very high. The wine list is very good. Prices high. It is an experience.

Parioli Romanissimo, 1466 First Avenue. Telephone 212/288-2391. Reservations essential. This restaurant serves some of the best Italian food in the city. It is elegantly appointed, offers fastidious service. The pasta dishes, along with the veal dishes, are superlative. Highly priced. A very ambitious and good Italian wine list.

Odeon, 145 West Broadway. Telephone 212/233-0507. A large New York cafeteria transformed into one of the most pleasant, elegant, and excellent restaurants in the city. The food is American-French and nouvelle, and it rates among the best of its kind. It is well worth a trip all the way to Tribeca for the food and for the fun of people-watching, which can turn out to be an experience. A good wine list, prices moderately high.

CALIFORNIA

BERKELEY

Chez Panisse, 1517 Shattuck Avenue. Telephone 415/452-5605. Reservations necessary. This is truly one of the most unusual eating places in the United States. Chef/owner Alice Waters is a remarkable person and an exceptionally inventive and brilliant cook whose impeccable taste and solid knowledge of the culinary arts is reflected in her daily menus. She made of this three-story house, surrounded by a beautiful garden, a mecca for connoisseurs of good food, with the latest addition on the top floor of a café and pizzeria. If you should find yourself anywhere in the vicinity, make a detour to Berkeley for an unforgettable dinner. Prices moderately high. The cuisine is essentially French, with the distinctive imprint of Alice Waters. There is a superlative wine list, especially in California wines. I highly recommend *The Chez Panisse Menu Cookbook* (Random House, 1982) for everyone's collection.

SAN FRANCISCO

The Mandarin, on Ghirardelli Square.
The first time I dined at Ms. Cecilia Chiang's Mandarin I felt I had never before eaten Chinese food. The style of her food and preparation is completely unique. Even though the names of the dishes on the menu might be familiar to you, your palate would tell you the difference, and you will come to the same conclusion that I did. The setting is elegant, and it is located in one of the

old buildings of the Ghirardelli Chocolate Factory overlooking the Bay. The service is impeccable. The gentility of the staff is truly in the old Oriental tradition. Prices are moderately high. A good wine list.

Index

ABOUT THE AUTHOR

Born in Savona, Italy, ALFREDO VIAZZI
is the author of the very well-received cookbook
Alfredo Viazzi's Italian Cooking. He owns and supervises
three successful restaurants in Greenwich Village:
Trattoria da Alfredo, Tavola Calda da
Alfredo, and Café Domel.
The author says: "After all, the most
interesting demand in the kitchen is to unlearn
what you learned and know well, and to cook better.
I love the whole process."